Mastering

C Programming

MACMILLAN MASTER SERIES

Accounting
Advanced English Language
Advanced Pure Mathematics
Arabic
Banking
Basic Management
Biology
British Politics
Business Communication
Business Law
Business Microcomputing
C Programming
Chemistry
COBOL Programming
Commerce
Communication
Computer Programming
Computers
Databases
Economic and Social History
Economics
Electrical Engineering
Electronic and Electrical Calculations
Electronics
English as a Foreign Language
English Grammar
English Language
English Literature
English Spelling
French
French 2

German
German 2
Human Biology
Italian
Italian 2
Japanese
Manufacturing
Marketing
Mathematics
Mathematics for Electrical and
    Electronic Engineering
Modern British History
Modern European History
Modern World History
Pascal Programming
Philosophy
Photography
Physics
Psychology
Science
Secretarial Procedures
Social Welfare
Sociology
Spanish
Spanish 2
Spreadsheets
Statistics
Study Skills
Word Processing

Mastering

C Programming

W. Arthur Chapman

MACMILLAN

First published 1991 by
THE MACMILLAN PRESS LTD
Houndmills, Basingstoke, Hampshire RG21 2XS
and London
Companies and representatives
throughout the world

ISBN 0–333–49842–9

A catalogue record for this book is
available from the British Library.

Printed in Malaysia

10   9   8   7   6   5
00   99   98   97   96

Contents

List of Figures and Tables

FIGURES

TABLES

Preface

This book is intended as a first course in C programming. It is suitable for those new to programming as well as for those already familiar with another programming language. Access to a computer running C is assumed. With this condition the text is suitable for use in self-study, directed study through open or distance learning as well as via a more traditional approach as a class text. All the example programs and functions have been tested using Turbo C version 2.0. However, with very few exceptions, no changes should be necessary if other C compilers are used.

The main aim of the book is to introduce C and to provide the essentials of the language. The standard used throughout is the draft ANSI standard, and its counterpart the draft British Standard Specification (ISO/IEC DIS 9899), which is summarised in the second edition of the classic text for C *The C Programming Language* by Brian W. Kernighan and Dennis M. Ritchie, Englewood Cliffs, NJ: Prentice Hall 1988.

The text begins by looking at problem solving in fairly general terms before moving on to a first C program in Chapter 2. These first two chapters form an important introduction to the main text and are especially intended for anyone new to programming. Subsequent chapters develop the C language, its syntax and semantics. The material is designed to take the reader step by step from the basics (Ch. 3) through control structures (Chs. 4–6) and data structures (Chs. 8 and 10) to the more advanced topics of lists and list processing (Ch. 11). New elements of the C language are illustrated by numerous examples of program fragments, functions and complete programs.

Throughout the book a number of rather more substantial programs are developed to provide a context for the use of C in rather larger projects. As and when appropriate, these programs, their design and implementation are discussed and functions developed. Three main programs are dealt with in detail; they are a calculator, a line editor and a simple bridge tutor. The calculator is discussed in detail, and the program is developed, in Chapter 7. We introduce the line editor in Chapter 1 and develop various parts of it throughout the book. The bridge tutor is introduced in Chapter 2 and provides a simple program to simulate shuffling, dealing, counting points and suggesting opening bids. For the most part no knowledge of bridge is necessary but a familiarity with cards and card games such as whist would be helpful. These latter two programs are listed in full, and their functions are discussed in detail, in Appendices B and C respectively.

Most chapters conclude with a summary which highlights the main points covered in the chapter and which serves to act as a revision aid to the reader. In addition, most chapters contain exercises which are designed to reinforce the topics covered and to develop the readers understanding of C. Some of these exercises refer to the larger programs and as such the answers can be found in the relevant program listings.

As you work through the material presented here you should develop a good understanding of C and C programming. If by the time you have completed your study of this text you have a desire to continue programming in C, wish to move on to more advanced aspects of the language, and have even more importantly found that C programming is both challenging and also fun, then the book will have achieved its purpose.

This book developed out of an idea suggested by my friend and colleague Noel Chidwick and I would like to thank him for that original idea and his encouragement throughout the project. (Not to mention the late nights and early mornings which seemed to form an inevitable part of life in recent months!) Thanks are also due to many other friends and colleagues at Telford College, Edinburgh and further afield who have helped and supported me in various ways. I would also like to extend my gratitude to students who attended various classes given by me in recent years. They willingly tried out many of the ideas which finally found their way into this book and provided much helpful stimulation. I am pleased to be able to extend my thanks to Jane Wightwick at Macmillan for her help and support during the lifetime of this project and her understanding when deadlines were missed. Finally, and most importantly, I would like to thank my wife Judy and our children Emma, Lucy and Donald who have put up with an, even more than usual, bad-tempered fifth member of the household! Without their forebearance and encouragement the task of writing would have been much harder.

June 1990   W. Arthur Chapman

1 Beginning with problems

"Some problems are just too complicated for rational logical solutions. They admit of insights, not answers."   J. B. Wiesner

1.1 PRELIMINARIES

In this chapter we will be mainly concerned with the important topic of problem solving. We will be looking at ways in which problems can be tackled and the most productive ways of obtaining solutions – we will be concentrating on problems which can be solved and for which "rational logical solutions" can be found. In the process of working through this chapter you will be introduced to some techniques which enable well structured programs to be developed. This includes the idea of top-down design, the use of stepwise refinement and the writing of algorithms. The fundamental control structures of procedural languages will be introduced and their relevance for C indicated. A method of writing algorithms using pseudocode will be developed and will be applied to some programming tasks which we will be discussing in greater depth in later chapters.

Developing a computer program, whether in C, or in any other language, is a matter of devising a solution to a problem; it involves clear and logical thinking and requires the writing of careful and effective code. Computer programming is a mixture of an art and a science. A computer program can include clever solutions to a problem using obscure elements of the language but if the final program is to be understood, or even used, by someone else then it must have a clear structure and good documentation.

We will be looking at both the art and the science of programming so that by the end of this chapter you will be able to develop an outline solution to most problems. In future chapters these techniques will be extended to enable you to write programs in C. Let us begin, though, by forgetting about the details of computer programming and look first of all at problem solving in more general terms.

> **Computer programming ...**
>
> *involves devising solutions to problems;*
>
> *it requires clear and logical thought*

1.2 PROBLEM SOLVING

The art of problem solving is difficult to define. However the task of problem solving, which is to find a solution to a particular problem, seems all too obvious. This appears easy enough until you start the process. Some problems are easy to solve, others are far more difficult. Problems come in all shapes and sizes. They cover such diverse tasks as: getting up in the morning (a problem to most people), preparing breakfast or making a cup of coffee, existing on unemployment benefit, achieving world peace, saving the tropical rain forests, or solving the all-embracing environmental problems.

We will concentrate on some more mundane tasks and will begin by taking a look at a reasonably simple everyday problem. You are on the pavement at the side of a busy road. You are in a hurry and you need to cross the road. A hundred metres away, in the opposite direction, is a set of traffic lights (see Figure 1.1). What do you do? Think about the possibilities, about what options are open to you (which ones are safest, which ones are quickest) before reading on.

Fig 1.1 *Problem solving ... 'How do I cross the road?'*

Crossing the road

How did you approach this problem? Well, first of all there is no **right** answer; there are many possibilities, most of which have their good and bad points. Perhaps you decided to wait for a break in the traffic and then make a dash for it! This solution is not to be recommended, especially if you have young children or an elderly person with you. Alternatively you may have decided that the traffic was too heavy and so walking up to the traffic lights was the best option – you could afford to be a few minutes late rather than risk ending up in a hospital bed or worse. Again you may have decided that it was rather a silly problem and rather than try to solve it in advance you would wait until you next had to cross a road. Whilst this solution (putting it off) might be satisfactory in this case, it cannot be allowed in computer programming – problems need to be solved before they arise. However you may have decided that this problem was rather silly on the grounds that you were not given enough information. If you came up with this last point then give yourself a pat on the back.

One of the most important points which this seemingly simple problem should have highlighted is that often you are not given all of the necessary facts. For example:

• What day of the week is it?

If it is a Sunday then possibly walking across the road would be the best option – observing the Green Cross Code of course.

• What time of day is it?

The solution will obviously be different if it is the rush hour rather than 1.30 am.

• I neglected to tell you that there is a subway only a few metres away.

Even these few simple and obvious comments should help to underline the important point that a problem may not be well specified and that in deciding on a solution you may need to make some assumptions. If this is indeed the case then these assumptions must be made explicit from the outset. Discovering hidden assumptions, or making explicit assumptions which must be made are part of the task of understanding the problem. Another vital part of the process of understanding a problem involves drawing up a specification of the problem.

A second stage in problem solving is the all-important one of devising a solution. In computing this will generally mean devising an algorithm. We will be looking at one approach to this in the next section andlooking a little more closely at algorithms in 1.4. Once a solution has been devised it then has to be implemented. In computer terms this will involve translating the algorithm into a computer program. Finally the plan is carried out and note taken of its successes (and failures). With a computer program this will mean running it and evaluating the accuracy of the results.

The stages in the problem solving process will generally be carried out in the order given above. However in practice the first two stages may be mixed up and a sufficiently detailed understanding of the problem may only be possible once the process of devising a solution has begun.

Problem   solving   involves   ...

- *understanding   the   problem*

- *devising   a   solution*

- *implementing   the   solution*

- *evaluating   the   solution*

1.3 DEVISING A SOLUTION

There are various approaches to the task of devising a solution. One of the most common involves a 'top down' methodology. This means starting from the problem definition and working step by step towards a solution. At each step in the process the problem is broken up into smaller and smaller 'chunks'. This process of **stepwise refinement** is then continued until a set of easily-solved sub-problems has been arrived at.

Stepwise   refinement   ...

the   process   of   breaking   a   problem into   chunks   which   are   then refined   step   by   step

---

Charlie's   desk

Charlie, a fresher of three weeks' standing, has been pondering the difficulties of working at a tiny table with less than stable legs and is out searching for a desk as a solution to 'all' his problems. Being of slender means (he is still awaiting his grant) he drops into a shop littered with bric-à-brac and second-hand goods of all kinds.

While searching amongst the debris of bird cages, shooting sticks and battered suitcases, he discovers the answer to his prayers. There in the corner, in a dusty plastic bag, is a 'Student Desk', a self-assembly job at what he hopes is a knock-down price. Summoning the shop assistant he enquires the price. 'That's five pounds, sir' is the response to the vitally important question. So, dipping into a pocket of his tattered denims he pulls out five pound coins and, not believing his good fortune, walks out into the chilly October air with his newly acquired possession.

Arriving back at the flat he decides to celebrate his astounding good luck by having filtered coffee – there is just enough to make one last pot. Once the coffee is on he starts the process of unpacking his desk. He carefully lays out the pieces on the not very spacious floor and searches through the odds and ends for the instructions. At last, in a packet containing assorted screws he finds, somewhat tattered and torn, the crucial pieces of paper. He smooths them out and putting on his battered spectacles peruses the words of wisdom.

Charlie is devastated! With a crumpled, torn and incomplete set of instructions (Figure 1.2) how will he ever manage to build his desk? After pondering the problem for a few minutes he has a sudden flash of inspiration. 'Why not try stepwise refinement?' he says to himself. This wonderous method has only recently been introduced to him by his lecturer in programming techniques and now is the time to test out the theory on a real-life problem.

After sorting through the bits and pieces of the kit, checking the contents (luckily nothing appeared to be missing) and after an hour or so's work with the scraps of instructions he finally came up with what seemed like a usable set of instructions.

Charlie's instructions

1. Bookcase

Assemble the carcase using the $1^1/_2$" screws.
Fix the back to the carcase using six small nails.
Glue four dowels into the top of the bookcase.
Leave to set.

2. Cupboard

Glue four dowels into the top of the end panels.

Knock the drawer runners into the end panels.
Glue four dowels into the plinths (one into each end).
Fix the plinths between the end panels using the $1^1/_2$" screws.
Fix the back to the cupboard carcase using six nails.
Attach the front using $1^1/_2$" screws.

Cupboard Door

Screw the hinges to the door using the $1/_2$" screws.
Screw the knob onto the door.
Attach the door with the hinges to the right hand panel using $1/_2$"screws.

Drawer

Glue the drawer wrap at the joints and glue four dowels into the holes
   provided.
Glue the drawer front.
Assemble and leave until the glue sets (24 hours approx.).
When dry wipe over with a damp cloth to remove excess glue.
Fit handle.

3. Final Assembly

Place the top, upside down, on a clean, smooth surface.
Squeeze glue into the eight holes on the underside of the top.
Position the bookcase carcase and press firmly. (A slight tap with a
   mallet may be required to ensure that the dowels are firmly seated.)
Repeat for the cupboard.
Leave for approx. 24 hours to dry.

4. To finish

Wipe the entire desk with a damp cloth.
Cover all exposed screw heads with the screw covers provided.

With the help of his own instructions and after a few bouts of trial and error
Charlie managed to complete the task and a day or two later was seen hard at
work at his newly-acquired masterpiece.

The strategy which Charlie used to solve the problem of assembling the desk,
and which the makers had also suggested, was that of stepwise refinement. The
task was broken up into a number of jobs, each of which could be carried out
separately. Once all the tasks had been completed the problem was solved and the
desk finished.

Fig 1.2 *The desk instructions*

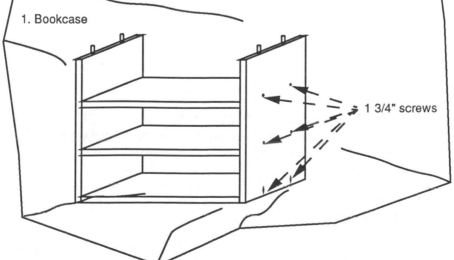

The New Student Desk – Assembly Instructions

You are now the proud owner of a multi-purpose student desk. A four-in-one
give you the ideal working surface for studying but will also provide you with a
and a handy drawer

Follow the instructions given below and you will soon be ready to try out your

Before you begin assembly check the contents of the kit, they are listed below.

CONTENTS

Desk Top		Cupboard Side	2	Cover Cap
Bookcase End	1	Dowel	8	Drawer F
Bookcase Shelf	2	Handle	1	Drawer
Bookcase Base	2	Screw (1 1/2 ")	20	Drawer
Bookcase Back	1	Screw (1")	6	Drawer
Cupboard Side	1	Cupboard Back	1	Cupboard
Door	2	Door Knob	1	Hinges
Glue Sachet	1			
	2			

METHOD

Assemble the desk in the following order:

1. Bookcase   2. Cupboard   3. Top

Follow the step-by-step instructions below and you will

1. Bookcase

1 3/4" screws

1.4 ALGORITHM

"algorithm *a series of instructions or procedural steps for the solution of a specific problem."*

The Penguin Dictionary of Computers

The above example illustrates some of the techniques of stepwise refinement, the breaking up of the task into sub-tasks, the refining of these sub-tasks and the logical nature of the solution. What Charlie ended up with could be described as an algorithm for assembling the desk. This algorithm gives a complete set of instructions which, if followed through in the correct order, will result in a successful solution to the original problem – the desk is assembled. In the context of computer programming the steps of problem definition and analysis, stepwise refinement and the production of an algorithm should ideally be carried out before any attempt is made to write the program itself. These rules are not hard and fast but, if you follow this procedure when writing any program, you are more likely to produce neat, workable and readable code than if you start by 'hammering away at the keyboard'.

Example – kneading the dough!

In order to illustrate how the above procedure might work out in practice we are going to work through a couple of examples. The second example is a computing one and is one which we shall be working on throughout the book. However we begin by applying stepwise refinement to the task of baking bread. You will find that there are surprising similarities between such diverse tasks as making bread and writing a complex computer program.

First of all we need to define the problem or task. How much bread are we going to make? Do we want wholemeal or white, rolls or loaves? If loaves then what kind of loaves? These are just some of the questions which need to be answered before we can even begin to work on a solution.

We will begin by making some assumptions. (Remember what was said earlier about making the assumptions explicit at the beginning.) We will assume that we are going to make wholemeal loaves, using 3lb of flour. We will also assume that the necessary ingredients and kitchen utensils are all available and readily to hand.

We can now start on the process of problem solving by making a list of the various tasks which will form the basis for our 'solution'. In this case there are four main tasks:

1. **Initial jobs**
2. **Making the dough**

3. **Baking**
4. **Removing and cooling the loaves**

Now that this first level of stepwise refinement is complete we can start on the process of further refinement. To do this we look at each step in turn and where possible break it up into smaller steps. This produces our first level of refinement and in this case might result in the following:

1. Initial jobs

Wash hands
Find a recipe
Collect ingredients
Assemble cooking utensils

2. Making the dough

Mix the ingredients
Rising stage
Knock back the dough
Place the dough in the tins
Allow to prove

3. Baking

Switch on oven
Check oven temperature (repeat until correct temperature is reached)
Place tins in the oven
Wait until bread is baked

4. Removing and cooling the loaves

Remove the tins from the oven
Remove loaves from tins
Allow to cool

After this first level of stepwise refinement you will see that we have a reasonably comprehensive algorithm. However there are still lots of details which need to be filled in. One important point about the process of stepwise refinement is that it is not necessary to fill in all the steps in the same amount of detail at the same time. If some of the tasks are still hazy then the steps involved can be filled in later.

Each of the above steps can be expanded as necessary with the help of a recipe. As an example we list the next level of refinement for the important task of making the dough.

2. Making the dough

Mix the ingredients
    Sift flour, sugar and salt into a large bowl.
    Cut up lard and rub into the flour with the fingertips until the
        mixture resembles fine breadcrumbs.
    If using dried yeast
        Add the yeast to the mixture and mix well.
        Add the water to the mixture.
    If using fresh yeast
        Blend yeast with half a pint of the warm water.
        Pour into a well in the centre of the mixture.
        Add remaining water.
    Using one hand work the mixture together and beat until it
        leaves the sides of the bowl clean.
    Knead the dough on a clean lightly floured surface for approx.
        10 minutes.

Rising stage
    Shape the dough into a ball.
    Place in a bowl and cover with a clean damp cloth.
    Leave in a warm place until dough has doubled in size.

Knock back the dough
    Turn dough onto lightly floured surface and knead until firm.
    Divide the dough into two equal pieces.
    Flatten each piece firmly with the knuckles (to remove air
        bubbles).
    Stretch and roll each piece into a rectangle the same length and
        width as the tins.

Place the dough in the tins
    Grease the tins.
    Place the dough in the tins.
    Brush top with lightly salted water.

Allow to prove
    Cover with a clean damp cloth.
    Wait until the dough reaches the top of the tins.

The expanded algorithm for making the dough, given above, is sufficiently detailed to enable the dough to be made. In some cases another level or two of refinement might be required. (Incidently if you want to try the recipe and check whether the algorithm works you can find the complete recipe from which this is adapted in *The Cookery Year*, Reader's Digest, pp. 375 – 6.)

1.5 PROGRAMMING

The examples given above should have started you thinking about how to apply the principles to the task of writing a program, in particular about writing programs in C. In this and the following sections we are going to look at the various tasks which frequently occur in algorithms. This will lead on to a discussion of program control structures and the development of pseudocode.

Let's begin by taking another look at the algorithm for making the dough. An obvious first point is that steps are written down in the order in which they are to be carried out. Notice next that the algorithm is broken up into discrete sections. Thirdly you will notice that some tasks involve repeating something until a certain condition is met. For example 'Cut up lard and rub into the flour with the fingertips until the mixture resembles fine breadcrumbs' or 'Leave in a warm place until dough has doubled in size'. Lastly a selection instruction appears: 'If using dried yeast' and 'If using fresh yeast'. At other points a selection process is implied or assumed. For example, if the oven isn't already on, then switch it on (or light the gas).

These simple examples from a non-computing problem form the basis for program structure and control. They relate very closely to the ideas of **sequence, functions, repetition** and **decisions**. We now take a look at the way these constructs can be applied to programming in C.

The idea of sequence, although no doubt obvious, is crucial to computer programming. In a program execution begins with the first statement and, when this has been successfully executed, control passes on to the next statement. This process continues until the end of the program is reached, the program runs out of data, an error occurs, or the computer is switched off! (A statement can be thought of as performing a certain action. A formal definition with regard to statements in C is given in Chapter 3.) All operations are carried out sequentially and always in the same order as is illustrated in Figure 1.3.

Functions are closely related to the simple sequential structure which we have just been looking at. In fact in Figure 1.3 any statement could be replaced by a function which carries out the same task as the statement being replaced. However functions are by no means confined to such simple uses as we shall see shortly.

Functions more often correspond to a series of statements which perform a specific job as dictated by the algorithm as it is developed using stepwise refinement. Each function is self-contained and can be written and tested independently of other functions or other parts of the program. If the process of stepwise refinement is followed correctly then each section, and thus each function, will perform a specific and well-defined task, or series of tasks.

Fig 1.3 *Simple   program   control*

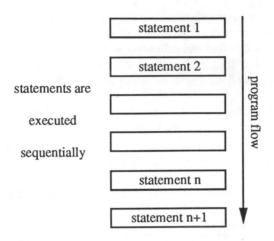

statements are

executed

sequentially

> **A   function   is ...**
> *a   collection   of   statements   which*
> *perform   a   well-defined   task,   or*
> *tasks.*

In C information can be passed into a function (by means of function parameters) and returned to the calling environment. The way in which these tasks are implemented in C will be covered in later chapters. The C language makes extensive use of functions; indeed, as we shall see, every program is itself a function.

The sequential control structure, even with the possibility of functions, allows little versatility since the same sequence of actions is performed each time the program is run. We can achieve more flexibility by incorporating selection. This allows for different paths to be followed through the program at different times. Which path is chosen at any particular time will depend on the value of a controlling expression (or conditional expression). The addition of this one simple control structure (such as the if statement in C) enables more complex and more useful programs to be written. A schematic representation of just one of the infinite variety of possible structures using only the if construct is shown in Figure 1.4.

We noted above that **repetition** played an important role in the dough

Fig 1.4 *Program control with selection*

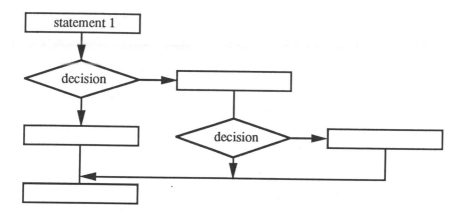

making algorithm and it has a no less important role in program structure. Repetition enables one or more statements to be carried out many times. One consequence is an enormous saving in space. Another is the time involved in typing in a program. Consider the problem of finding the average of a hundred numbers. This involves keeping track of the sum as numbers are read in. This can be achieved by using two expressions such as:

> **read** new_number
> **add** new_number **to** sum

Without repetition we would need to type in these two statements one hundred times. With repetition we can condense the task to:

> **set** sum **to** zero
> **set** count **to** zero
> **while** count is less than one hundred **do**
>   **read** new_number
>   **add** new_number **to** sum
>   **add** one **to** count
> **end_while**

Notice also that with this structure it is a simple matter to change the number of numbers by just altering the while condition (e.g. count is less than 1000).

Repetition is implemented in C in various ways (by means of the `while`, `do ... while` and `for` statements) and we will investigate each of these later on. However no matter which method is used to implement repetition a number of components must be present for correct operation. The most important of these is that there must be some condition which is modified within the loop and which enables the loop to be terminated: for example, stop reading characters when a new line has been entered. Alternatively a counter can be used to keep track of the number of times the loop has been repeated. In such cases the execution of the loop may be terminated when a particular value has been reached.

As we have noted, the constructs which we have been looking at are essential elements in the design of C programs. In fact they are of central importance to any programming language. However, before we look at their detailed implementation in C, we need to examine how they can be used in the development of algorithms.

1.6 PSEUDOCODE

The algorithms which we will be developing will be written for the most part in a semi-formal system known as pseudocode. We have already used some examples of pseudocode when we discussed repetition. For example we used phrases like **while** and **set ... to ...** . The object of pseudocode is to allow these and similar control structures to be represented in a standard way without the formality of the full syntax of the programming language.

Let's return to the bread making algorithm. Recall that we had a couple of examples of selection where the actions taken depended upon the type of yeast which we were using. Other examples of this type might be:

If it is 11am it is time for a coffee break.

The clock has stopped so I must wind it up.

We can represent the first example by the if control structure which, in pseudocode, we will write as:

if it is 11am **then** have a coffee break

At a first glance the second example does not appear to be of this form. However with a little imagination we can rearrange it to fit into our semi-formal structure. Thus we could have:

if the clock has stopped **then** wind it up

So any statement involving a simple decision can be written in the form

if *condition* **then** *do something*

The yeast example could be thought of in this form, in which case we would have two successive selection statements. However a closer look at them reveals that in fact they are alternatives. We will not use both dried yeast and fresh yeast. So a second version of the selection construct has the form:

> **if** *condition* **then** *do something*
> **else** *do something else*

Thus the yeast example becomes:

> **if** using dried yeast **then**
> > Add the yeast to the mixture and mix well.
> > Add the water to the mixture.
> **else**
> > Blend yeast with half a pint of the warm water.
> > Pour into a well in the centre of the mixture.
> > Add remaining water.
> **end_if**

Notice that each sequence of statements is indented below the appropriate keyword (in our pseudocode **if, then, else** and **end_if** are keywords – these will not necessarily correspond directly with the keywords of C). We will be adopting this style throughout as it improves readability and highlights the modular structure of the algorithm.

There are a number of options open to us for representing the repetition control structure. We have used **while ... do** in the pseudocode for summing a series of numbers and we will use this from now on. Thus whenever we wish to use repetition we will use a construct of the form:

> **while** *condition* **do** *task*

Again if the task consists of more than one activity then each activity will be placed on a separate line and they will be indented as for the **if** construct. This loop works by testing the condition and if it is TRUE performing the task. The condition is then tested again and so on until the condition becomes FALSE at which point execution of the loop terminates.

Another pseudocode construct which we have used is **set ... to**. This is used to assign a value to a name. So in the earlier example we had

> **set** sum **to** zero
> **set** count **to** zero

which assigns zero to both sum and count. A value other than zero can be assigned to a name and this value need not be confined to a numerical one.

1.7 A LINE EDITOR

Now that we have outlined some of the stages involved in problem solving and looked at some non-computing examples we can turn our attention to a computing problem. Although we will be using a variety of short programming examples to illustrate the various aspects of C we will also be using a few rather longer programs. These longer examples will appear from time to time in the book and as new control structures and data stuctures are met their relevance to these larger programs will become apparent. By the end of the book you should have three of four fully-fledged programs which might even be of use to you! As part of the learning approach some of the functions will be left as exercises for the reader to develop. You should try writing your own functions before turning to the solutions which appear in the relevant Appendices. We will be developing three main programs and a number of smaller ones. The most important programs are a simple calculator, a bridge tutor and a line editor.

The bridge tutor is introduced in Chapter 2 and the calculator program is covered in Chapter 7. In this section we will outline the specification of a simple line editor and make a first attempt at designing an algorithm for it.

Specification

A line editor is a utility program which is often included as part of an operating system and although limited in power it offers a relatively straightforward means of illustrating many of the concepts and constructs of C which we will be dealing with. We begin by deciding what functions will be required of such an editor. The two most basic functions are the ability to enter and display text. This text will have to be saved for future use or for further editing. Again the editor must provide the facility to retrieve a previously created text file. In this simple editor we will only allow complete lines to be inserted or deleted. However, once you have an understanding of the operation of this program, you could easily adapt it to take account of more sophisticated operations: for example, to insert and delete characters and words, find and replace a string of characters.

A line editor uses line numbers to identify lines of text in the text file and to prevent confusion we need to be able to display a complete line on the screen, which in turn means that we need to think a little about the length of lines. Normal screens will have an 80 character display width which means that, if a line length is greater than 80 characters, we will need to make a decision about what to do with the excess. One option is to not allow a line to be greater than 80 characters and to produce a warning message if this occurs. A second option is to start a new line. This will mean, if we are inserting a line, that subsequent lines will need to be moved down a line and the lines renumbered accordingly.

We will adopt this second option, although to allow for the display of line numbers we will restrict the line length to 75 characters.

The functions outlined above enable us to sketch out a rough diagram of the program structure (see Figure 1.5). We have not mentioned visual representations of algorithms until now, but you will find that often a quick sketch will provide greater insights into how to devise a solution. (Charlie's instructions were greatly helped by the presence of drawings indicating how the various parts of the desk should fit together.) The sketch should indicate the relationship between the various processes in an algorithm and should distinguish clearly between processes and data; in Figure 1.5, for example, data are represented by rectangular boxes whereas processes are represented by ellipses.

Even this very rough sketch is a useful first step in designing an algorithm. It highlights the functions involved and gives an overall picture of the final program. However, many details are left unexplained and a number of questions are raised. These are useful, in fact vital, questions which need to be confronted before much work can be done on designing the algorithm. For example, once the file has been updated are we to exit from the editor or should this be a separate task? What files are we going to use? Ideally we would want to be able to edit any text file. For the moment, though, we will assume that the file to be edited is called data.txt. How is the text to be stored in memory? Do we want a prompt, giving the possible edit options, to be always in view? Some of these questions require a detailed knowledge of C before we can attempt to answer them. However, even if we cannot answer them at present, they are useful in helping us to think through the exact nature of the task and in helping to clarify our thoughts concerning possible solutions and ways of implementing the functions of the line editor.

In addition to deciding on the exact way text is to be stored in memory we have also to decide how the edit commands themselves are to be processed. Before we can do this we need to work out what options are required The summary above gave us a start. We will now expand on those ideas in an effort to arrive at the syntax for the command line of the editor. (The command line is simply a set of abbreviated instructions to the editor to carry out a particular task.)

Since the editor will be working on lines we will need some means of identifying which lines are to be edited. The simplest way is to number each line. This number can either be stored in the file or, better, displayed by the program as and when necessary. The line number is only relevant during the editing process so there is no need to store it with the text. Assume that there are n lines in the text and that we have two integers, n1 and n2, which represent lines in the text ($1 <= n1 <= n$, $1 <= n2 <= n$) then we can edit:

- the whole text (from line 1 to line n)
- selected lines of text (i.e. from 1 to n1, 1 to n2, n1 to n2, n1 to n, or n2 to n)
- a single line

Given that all the lines could be displayed by setting n1 to 1 and n2 to n it might seem that the first option is not strictly necessary as a separate option. However we may not know how many lines there are in the text and so will be unable to set n2 to n. For this reason we need a separate means of informing the editor that we wish to edit one or more lines, including the last line. One way of doing this is to use a special character whenever we wish to edit the last line (e.g. $). This means that we would type the $ symbol instead of a number to mean the last line.

At times we may wish to edit the complete file rather than selected lines. It would therefore be convenient if another special character was set aside for this task (e.g. %). Finally, if we only wish to edit the current line then all that should be entered is the relevant command. If no previous line numbers have been specified then the current line should be defined as line 1. We thus have the valid options shown in Table 1.1 for specifying the lines to edit:

Table 1.1   *Valid line definitions for the line editor*

n1	edit line n1 (e.g. 4)
n1,n2	edit lines n1 to n2 inclusive (e.g. 10, 20)
n1,$	edit from n1 to the end (e.g. 3,$)
,n2	edit from current line to n2 inclusive (e.g. ,12)
,$	edit from current line to the end (e.g. ,$)
%	edit all lines
$	edit last line only
	edit current line (no line specifier)

Having decided upon how we are to specify which lines are to be edited our next task is to decide upon the edit options required. All edit options should be selected by means of a single letter, ideally the initial letter of the chosen option. (This may be case-sensitive, i.e. it may only accept lower-case letters, or conversely only upper-case letters, but it would be better if it were not.) Table 1.2 gives a list of the basic options, based on the earlier dicussions, together with the character associated with each.

The program structure of the line editor given in Figure 1.5, together with the above discussion, enables us to make an attempt at constructing an outline algorithm. This could take the following form:

1. Open the file

Fig 1.5 *The line editor*

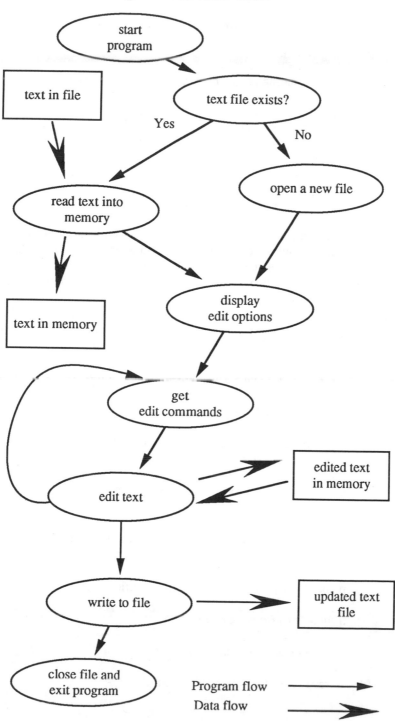

2. Read text from the file into memory

3. Display the command summary

4. Processing section
    while command is not quit **do**
        display command prompt (e.g. :>)
        get the command and line details
        check command and line details
        if error **then** print message and quit
        process the command
    end_while

5. Output section
    quit

This algorithm, although still very bare, provides a useful start in the process of program writing. A number of questions are still outstanding. For example, what happens if the file does not exist? How are we to display the command summary? We will need to consider how to make sense of the command and check for illegal constructs. How are we going to number the lines? Can we make the program versatile enough to allow for the editing of any text file? Most of these questions cannot be answered until we have delved a little deeper into control structures in general and C constructs in particular.

Table 1.2 *The line editor commands*

a   append - add lines to the end of existing text.

d   delete - delete the specified line(s) and renumber
    subsequent ones.

h   help - display information on how to use the
    editor.

i   insert - insert one or more lines before the current
    line.

p   print - display on the screen the specified lines.

q   quit - exit from the editor.

r   read - read text from file data.txt.

s   save - save the edited text to the file.

1.8 THE COMPUTER PROGRAM

We have finally reached the stage where we can begin to think about computer programs and it won't be long before you are deep into the heart of C. However we haven't yet said what a computer program is, so let's rectify that immediately.

So what *is* a computer program?

A computer program is a set of ordered instructions which can be carried out by a computer. The instructions must be in a language which the computer 'understands'. Each instruction will direct the computer to perform a particular task, or series of tasks. In our case these instructions will be written in C. However they will ultimately be translated into sets of single machine code instructions. One of the advantages of high-level languages like C is that they make the task of programming a computer much easier than if only programming in the low-level laguage were allowed.

A computer program goes through various stages during its life and it is to a short discussion of these stages that we now turn.

The Life Cycle of a Computer Program

> *"All the world's a stage,*
> *And all the men and women merely players:*
> *They have their exits and their entrances.*
> *And one man in his time plays many parts,*
> *his acts being seven ages."*
>
> Shakespeare, *As You Like It*

Like all animate objects and like many man-made creations a computer program goes through a particular life cycle. The cycle may not be divisible into seven clearly defined ages but even so there are useful analogies between the ages of man according to Shakespeare and the stages in the life of a program (see Figure 1.6). Some of these stages we have already had a glimpse of; we will be looking at the others later on.

Birth (*Problem Definition*)

The life cycle of a program begins when you decide that a particular problem needs solving, or when you are asked to write a program to do something, or when you suddenly feel inspired and are galvanised into creativity!

At this stage the problem will gradually be tightened up until you know what assumptions are being made and what, if any, extra information needs to be supplied. By the end of this process of problem analysis you will have arrived at a firm definition of the problem and have a reasonably clear idea of what form the algorithm will take. The details may still need to be worked out but the basic form of the solution should be fixed.

Childhood (*Algorithm*)

This is one of the most important parts of the whole process, as is the case with all childhood. It is the formative stage of development and time well spent here will be amply rewarded later on. Various schemes for arriving at an algorithm are available, we have looked briefly at the use of stepwise refinement and pseudocode as one way of doing so. Whatever the exact form, whether it is through stepwise refinement, structure diagrams, flow charts, pseudocode or a combination of them all, each one relies to a large extent on a systematic and logical approach to the problem. The algorithm will be quite general and allow for coding in a variety of languages. However on many occasions the language will have already been chosen and so the algorithm will be written with a specific language in mind. This should not worry you, as a good algorithm should be suitable as a basis for coding the solution in any similar computer language.

Adolescence (*The Program*)

At last the stage has been reached when the code can be written and the program in all its glory springs to life! Although much of the hard work has been done, the program still needs to go through one very important sub-stage before it really 'comes of age'. This involves the testing and debugging of the program. All programs should be thoroughly tested before being let out into the big wide world. This is often tedious and the most frequent question on the programmer's lips at this stage is 'Why?' Even in the most carefully written programs bugs are sure to appear – little eccentricities, or not so little – which need to be ironed out by careful and systematic testing. Don't skimp this stage but make sure that you always rigorously test each and every program. You will find that in the long run it will be well worth while.

Adulthood (*The Program – final form*)

The fully fledged adult program is now released on an unsuspecting world and is ready to perform all manner of wonders at the press of a key or the click of a mouse button! Although it is fully operational there may be times when you wish to delve into its depths or when some other talented programmer wishes to pick your program's brains! Whatever the reason, program documentation should go hand in hand with program development. Exactly what is contained in the documentation will depend to some extent on the type of program that has been written. However, at the very least, there should be a statement of the problem (or the purpose of the program), a list of any assumptions made and any extra

Fig. 1.6 ***The life cycle of a computer program***

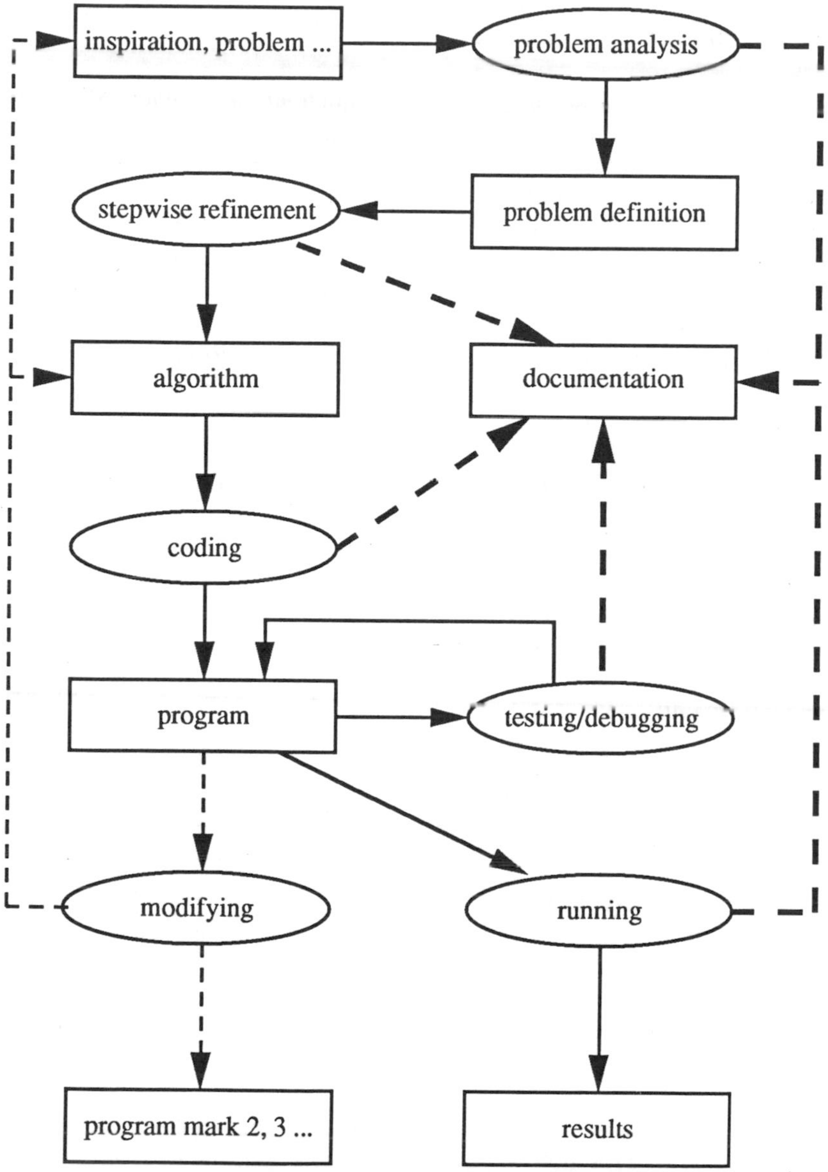

information required, test data and test results should be included as well as the algorithm and a program listing annotated with comments.

Old age   (*Program version 2,3, ...*)

During this period of life changes to the program are often made. Maybe you decide that there are other tasks which the program could perform and so you make some modifications. Whatever the reasons are for changing the program, you should always start with the algorithm, except in the simplest of cases. Make the necessary changes to the algorithm before moving on to modifying the code itself. It is at this time that the benefits of a well-structured algorithm become apparent. You will find that changes can more easily be made without causing disastrous problems with the logic of the program. Time and money will also both be saved at this stage if a well structured algorithm is at hand.

Death

Strictly speaking, old programs never die, they just become obsolete. By the time the program has reached this stage it has carried out the tasks for which it was designed. Perhaps it was only wanted for a 'one off job' and is now surplus to requirements. The program is now being superseded either because of software developments, new languages, better implementations, or because of advances in the hardware. Its use now is confined to the occasional nostalgic glance or to some gentle cannibalism when a well-tested routine is resurrected for use in another program.

SUMMARY

In this chapter we:

> • saw that one of the first steps in problem solving involves defining exactly what the problem is, what is known, what is unknown, and what assumptions are made.

> • were introduced to stepwise refinement as an important tool in problem solving.

> • saw that an algorithm is a crucial stage in the development of a solution.

> • were introduced to the basic control structures represented by sequence, functions, selection and repetition.

> • were introduced to pseudocode as an aid to program design and for writing out algorithms.

• made a first attempt at an algorithm for a line editor.

• examined the life cycle of a computer program and saw the importance of the processes of problem analysis, stepwise refinement, testing and debugging.

• noted that in a complex program the algorithm should be modified before the code is altered to ensure that the logic of the program is not altered in·an unintended manner.

EXERCISES

1. Devise algorithms as solutions to the following problems. Remember to make sure that the problem is well defined before you start and state any assumptions which you make. Once you have done that you can begin the process of top-down design. Start by breaking the problem into chunks, each of which can be treated as a separate entity. Use the process of stepwise refinement to gradually develop an algorithm and use pseudocode to construct it. If all has gone according to plan your algorithm should provide a step by step solution to the original problem.

  a. Make a hot drink. (Think about the various alternatives.)

  b. Mow the lawn. (What about the weather?)

  c. Wallpaper a room. (Assume that you already have the wallpaper, paste etc.)

  d. Produce a table of squares and cubes for numbers from 1 to 9.

2. Devise an algorithm for working out how many times one number divides into another by using repeated subtraction. Take care of any special cases.

3. Devise an algorithm to search a line of text for the occurrence of a given sequence of characters and give the character position of the first character found. Use -1 to indicate that the search was unsuccessful.

4. The following algorithm is intended to find the minimum of a series of integers. What is wrong with it? Correct any mistakes and devise a correct solution.

```
read in an integer
if integer is greater than minimum then
    set minimum to integer
end_if
```

```
while not end of list do
    read an integer
    if integer is less than minimum then set integer to minimum
end_while
print minimum.
```

5. Try the following short questions to make sure that you have understood the last section.

Fill in the missing word(s).

    a. The first stage in designing a computer program is _____ _____.

    b. _____ should be a continuous process and not a last minute creation after the program has been written.

    c. An algorithm is produced by a process of _____ _____.

6. Use the methods developed in this chapter to derive algorithms for the following problems.

a. Wash up the breakfast dishes.

b. Organise a charity fun-run.

c. Produce a chart enabling acres to be converted to square yards. (Allow for a minimum measurement of a quarter of an acre and a maximum of ten acres.)

② Towards C

"Really good programs live forever ... at least as long as the hardware, maybe even longer."   Charles Simonyi

2.1 INTRODUCTION

This chapter introduces C. We begin by examining a very basic program which will serve to introduce some of the keywords of C. The C language may at first appear strange, perhaps more strange than any other high-level programming language. However you will soon find that as you work through this book this new language will become more and more familiar to you. It will not be long before you are quite happy with a statement such as

```
for (j = 0; j < m; ++j)
    s += b[j];
```

One of the aims, then, of this chapter is to introduce the basic structure, and some of the key elements, of C programs. A second aim is to take you through the various stages involved in moving from a program written in C to code which can be executed by a computer. We will take a broad look at the processes of editing, compiling and linking. Finally you will have an opportunity to take a closer look at these processes as they are implemented on your own system.

2.2 THE FIRST C PROGRAM

Let us examine the structure of about the simplest C program. (You will find variations on this program in most books on C, so why change now? Even in computing there are traditions!)

Program 2.1

```
/* greeting.c */
/* The first c program - greetings */
```

```
#include <stdio.h>

main()
{
    printf(" Welcome to ");
    printf("the world of C.\n");
}
```

Even if you have no previous experience of programming (in any language) you may well be able to guess what the result of running this program would be. You will have the chance to try the program for yourself later on and to see if your guess was correct. Meanwhile we will go through the program line by line to get an idea of the structure of the program and to find out what each line means.

```
/* greeting.c */
```

The program begins with a comment. In the C language comments are enclosed within the two combinations of a slash and an asterisk, that is /* and */. Anything appearing between these pairs of symbols is ignored by the C compiler and has no effect on the execution of the program. However comments are extremely useful to the programmer as well as to others who might be reading the program. Comments should be used as often as necessary within a program. They form a very necessary part of the program documentation which we discussed very briefly in the previous chapter. This particular comment (greeting.c) indicates the name of the source file of this program. (The source file is the file containing the coded program as typed into the computer, and as it appears above.)

Note that the name of the program consists of a (meaningful) name plus a .c extension to the name. The .c indicates that the file is a C source file. You will find that this is common practice in C programming and it enables you to see at a glance which files contain C programs. In addition most C compilers look for filenames with this .c extension when starting the compilation process. The filename should as far as possible be meaningful. Filenames such as a1.c, b6.c etc. are not very helpful. However it is not always possible to use the name we would like since in most operating environments there is a restriction on the length of a filename (e.g. a maximum of 8 character in MS-DOS). Within these restrictions, though, try to use meaningful names and only shorten them when necessary.

```
/* The first c program - greetings */
```

The second line is also a comment; it doesn't tell us much – well, there is not a lot to say about this first program anyway! More informative comments would be used in more advanced programs. It is often useful at the beginning of a program to have a comment giving the date when the program was written, the version of the program and, especially if the program is likely to be used by other people, the author. Remember, though, that if the date and/or the program version is included then these should be updated as necessary. Additional comments would be used to supply the purpose and possibly the input required and the output expected.

There are two more points worth noting before we leave the topic of comments. Firstly, comments need not be restricted to a single line; remember that all characters (including a newline or return character) are part of the comment until the */ sequence is encountered. Thus we could have written the first couple of lines of the program as

```
/* greeting.c
The first c program - greetings */
```

However the original form is slightly clearer, in that it separates off different types of comment (the program name from its description).

Secondly, comments can be placed on the same line as other program statements. They can therefore be used to comment on an obscure or important line of a program. Following the two comments at the beginning of the program we have a blank line. This simply serves to separate off the comments at the beginning from what follows. You should adopt the practice of using blank lines in a program whenever they enhance the legibility of the code. As with normal text, dense areas with no white space makes for difficulty reading, and in the context of programming it is just as important to make the program readable. Use blank lines, then, to separate off the various logical elements of the program. You will soon recognise the benefits which stem from this approach when after a few months you come back to the program to make some modifications.

```
#include <stdio.h>
```

This line is not in fact a C statement at all. It is a command to the C preprocessor, which is a program that performs some operations on the source file before compilation as such begins. This particular command informs the preprocessor that information is to be included from a file called stdio.h. This file contains information on basic input and output (stdio stands for standard input/output). The syntax of this statement is

```
#include <filename> or #include "filename"
```

If angle brackets are used then the compiler will search for the file (filename)

in an implementation dependent manner. If quotation marks are used then the search begins in the directory where the source code is situated. On many systems this statement is not necessary for such a simple program but it is included here for completeness. You may be asking why something as basic as input and output is not included as part of the basic C language. The reason is that one of the fundamental principles of C is to keep the language as small as possible; and, since not all programs will need to use the input/output facilities within `stdio.h`, why include them? The extension `.h` indicates that the file is a header file which is placed at the beginning of a C program. Such files are used to group together functions which have already been written and tested and which can then be used in other programs.

`main()`

C programs consist of one or more functions and all programs must contain one function bearing the name `main`. This is the main program, which will use any other functions you define. All function names must be followed by a left and a right bracket (parenthesis) even if the function requires no arguments. Functions are at the heart of C and naturally follow on from our consideration of problem solving in the last chapter. They comprise one of the building blocks of C programs and represent chunks of code which perform a specific, well defined task.

`{`

The left brace (`{`) marks the beginning of the body of a function definition, the right brace (`}`) the end. So this left brace marks the beginning of the main body of the program (it performs a similar function to that of `BEGIN` in a Pascal program). Braces are also used to group statements together to form one compound statement, but more of this later.

`printf(" Welcome to ");`

This is the first executable statement in the program. This statement refers to a function `printf()`, it has the form *function-name()*. Here it is not a function definition as is the `main()` function reference, but a function call asking the computer to perform the function. So this statement uses the function `printf()` to perform a task which in this case is simply to print on the screen whatever appears between the pair of double quotes. Thus when the program is executed (or run) the words `Welcome to` will appear on the screen of the computer.

Notice that this line ends in a semi-colon. All C statements either end in a semi-colon or include a number of statements which are terminated by a right brace. So the whole C program consisting of `main()` `{ ... }` can be thought of as one compound statement. We will be looking at the structure of statements in more detail in a later chapter. For now, remember that at the simplest level C statements must be terminated by a semi-colon.

```
printf("the world of C.\n");
```

It is not difficult to imagine what this statement will do. If you expect the world of C.\n to appear on the screen then you are not far wrong. However there are a couple of important points to note about the printf() function and about this statement in particular.

Firstly, printf() outputs data to the screen in one continuous stream. Thus the characters within this second call of printf() will appear on the same line as Welcome to . Secondly the pair of characters \n do not appear on the screen. These two characters actually represent a single ASCII character, the newline character. They are one of a number of escape sequences which consist of a backslash (\) and one other character.

Thus the net result of the two printf() function calls in this program is to display on the screen the truly exciting sentence

```
Welcome to the world of C.
```

(Well, we had to start somewhere!)

The cursor on the screen is then left at the beginning of the following line, owing to the effect of the escape sequence \n.

```
}
```

This is the matching right brace which indicates the end of the function definition main() and in this example the end of the program.

2.3 C PROGRAM STRUCTURE

Now that you have seen a simple C program we can sketch out the basic structure of all programs written in C. Figure 2.1 illustrates the main components which will be present in all C programs. As you can see, there aren't too many! One point to note is that the function definitions can precede the main program, however we will adopt the layout indicated here throughout this book.

The simplest possible C program would consist of the single function main() together with a left and right brace, that is

```
main()
{
}
```

This minimal C program is sufficient to tell us that a reference to the function main() is an essential part of all C programs. When this, or any C program, is run the computer looks for and obeys the definition of main(). However such a program would not achieve very much, except use up some disk space on your computer! In order for something to happen we must include some statements which will actually perform one or more operations. So the next crucial part of our basic C program is some statements within the function main(). Without these statements the program is just an empty shell.

Fig 2.1 *Simple C program structure*

```
/* comments   here and throughout the program */

preprocessor instructions
/* main program */
main()
{
statement1;
statement2;
...
statementn;
}
/* function definitions */
function1()
{
...
}
...
functionp()
{
...
}
```

We have now arrived at the minimal useful program. However, depending on the particular program, there are two more parts which most C programs will contain. These are the preprocessor instructions and the function definitions.

The preprocessor instructions are generally grouped together at the beginning of the program. These instructions all begin with the hash character (#) and control the use of libraries of predefined functions, such as stdio.h, and the definition of symbols which are used within the program. Other operations carried out by the preprocessor enable conditional compilation of certain pieces of code and can be helpful in testing and debugging a complex program.

A C program ...

    must contain the function main()

and ...

the program statements must be enclosed within { and }

The function definitions are generally collected together at the end of the main program, following the right matching brace of the function main () (see Fig 2.1). As we pointed out in the last chapter, functions are an important aspect of program design. In many cases the sub-problems (strictly speaking methods for solving them) arrived at by stepwise refinement can be coded directly as functions. These functions can be written and tested before being used in the main program. This approach enhances the readability of the final solution and makes maintenance and modification easier. In the next section we will take a quick look at the way functions are declared and used.

2.4 FUNCTIONS – A FIRST LOOK

The basic structure of a function has the form

```
type function_name(parameter_list definitions)
{
        local declarations
        statements
        return(value)
}
```

The items in italics are optional and so the simplest (useful) function will have as a minimum the following structure:

```
type function_name(parameter_list definitions)
{
        statements
}
```

The latest ANSI (American National Standards Institute) and the British Standard Specification (ISO/IEC DIS 9899) adopt this specification for functions while, for the present, also allowing the original version, i.e.

```
function_name()
   {
              statements
   }
```

(Note that even if there are no parameters in the function the two parentheses are still required – and note that there is no space between them.) Whilst you may find many programs written using this form you should adopt the ANSI standard in your programming and we have endeavoured to use this standard in the examples in this book.

Notice that a semi-colon is not used at the end of `function_name()`. The left brace ({) marks the beginning of the body of the function and this must be matched by the right brace at the end of the function definition. Between this pair of braces is at least one statement – essential if the function is to do anything useful!

We have encountered already the most important function in C – that is the function `main()`:

```
main()
   {
              statements
   }
```

which forms the skeleton of all C programs. Thus **all** C programs are themselves functions with one thing in common – they are all called `main`.

Another example with which you are already familiar is the standard function used for outputting data to the screen – namely `printf()`. This function, as we have seen, has the form:

```
printf(conversion_string, parameter_list);
```

This example illustrates that, in general, a function needs to be:

        i) defined,

and

        ii) called (or executed)

to be of any use! If the function is not defined anywhere, the compiler will not recognise it when it is referenced, and without it being called (executed, or used) there is no point in declaring or defining it. (Of course the function need not be in the main program, it could be in a header file, which would be loaded if requested at preprocessor time. Or it might be in a library file, in which case its object code could be linked just prior to the production of the final executable code of the program.) Notice that when a function is called **on its own** a semi-colon follows the right bracket – this is because in such a situation the function call is in fact a statement and so must be terminated with a semi-colon.

In order to illustrate how functions work consider the following problem. Many programs are of the menu-driven variety in which a list of options is displayed on the screen; from this the user can select his or her choice by pressing a single key. As part of this program we need a function which will display such a list. The function is required to carry out two tasks. First the list of options has to be displayed. A second task is that of reading a character from the keyboard and executing the chosen option. This task can be left until later, so for now we will concentrate on what options we require. We need a specific program in mind so let's write a function for the bridge program which we alluded to in Chapter 1. The list of options for the Bridge Tutor program might be as follows

> shuffle
> deal
> display the hands
> count the points
> bid
> play
> quit

I have included an option entitled 'play' – programming a computer to play a hand of bridge is not a simple task. We will not get around to writing this function but it can be left in and we can easily modify the program to ignore this option. One other option is worth mentioning at this point – namely the 'quit' option. This option, or a similar one, will be found in practically all menus. Without this there would be no way to get out of the clutches of the program, except by resetting the computer, or switching off the power – neither of which is to be recommended! A similar option in a sub-menu would allow the user to move back to the previous menu – another task which is necessary in all but the simplest of programs.

We need to think a little about the layout of the screen before we start writing the code. Even in this simple example a little thought at the early stages pays off in the end. One possible display is given in Figure 2.2.

Now we can write the function to produce this display on the screen. We need to give it a name, so why not `main_menu` – there is no need to be imaginative at the moment! The text can be output to the screen in a number of ways, each of which have their pros and cons. We will stick to the method with which we are familiar, i.e. by using the `printf()` function. We can now write the function as follows (Program 2.2).

Fig 2.2 *Bridge Tutor main-menu screen*

```
********************************
          BRIDGE TUTOR
********************************

                1. shuffle
                2. deal
                3. display the hands
                4. count the points
                5. bid
                6. play
                Q. quit

Press a number (1-6) or Q to quit.
```

Program 2.2

```c
void main_menu(void)
{
    printf("\n              ********************************");
    printf("\n                        BRIDGE TUTOR");
    printf("\n              ********************************\n\n");
    printf("                1. shuffle\n");
    printf("                2. deal\n");
    printf("                3. display the hands\n");
    printf("                4. count the points\n");
    printf("                5. bid\n");
    printf("                6. play\n");
    printf("                Q. quit\n\n\n");
    printf("Press a number (1-6) or Q to quit.\n");
}
```

You will notice that this function has no parameters and no declarations, it is in fact one of the simplest of functions possible. However, to make it clear that the function requires no arguments and does not return a value, the keyword void is used in place of the parameter-list and the type respectively (compare with the function skeleton on page 33). (These aspects will be discussed in more detail in the next chapter.)

The function consists of a series of printf() function calls used to generate the desired layout. However despite being simple, it still performs a useful task, and what is more this task can be easily performed from anywhere within the program simply by executing the statement

```
    main_menu();
```

hence saving a lot of time and energy!

Using `main_menu()`

Before we can use the function we need to include it in a program, called `main()`.
A very simple program to achieve this is shown below.

Program 2.3

```
/* Bridge tutor - version 1.0 */
/* name: bridge.c */

#include <stdio.h>

main()
{
    main_menu();
}


/* the function main_menu() should be typed in here */
```

2.5 FROM CODE TO RESULTS

The earlier sections of this chapter have introduced the basic ideas concerning C
program and function structure and have given a glimpse of some of the basic C
statements. It is now time to get to work on the computer, but before reaching
for the switch and typing in a program we need to take a quick look at the
processes involved in moving from the C code to a working program. All
programs written in a high-level language need to be converted from the code –
the C language, or Pascal, or modula 2 – into a form which the computer can
'understand'. This form ultimately consists of a series of binary numbers which
represent instructions to the hardware and addresses in memory where the data is
stored.

The process of conversion, or translation, can be achieved in two ways:

- through an interpreter
- by means of a compiler

Interpreters and compilers are themselves programs which take as input the
source code and eventually produce an object code (in binary or hexadecimal
numbers) which, after passing through one further stage, can be executed or run
by the computer.

An interpreter translates a line of source code, checks for any syntax errors (i.e. mistakes in the arrangement of the 'words' in the 'sentence') and if there are no such errors executes the translated code. The process is then repeated for the next line of code and so on until the end of the program is reached. On the other hand, when using a compiler, the whole program is translated to produce the object code before any attempt is made to run the program. An additional task is also usually carried out which adds in or links other files which are required by the program. These library files are linked to the program prior to the final production of the executable code. Library files might contain object code for input/output functions, mathematical functions (e.g. trigonometric functions) or more specialised functions required for a particular task.

The route in C

The exact means by which the C source file is translated into an executable file which will produce results is dependent on the operating system of the computer and the version of C which is being used. However the majority of C implementations will be compiled. Assuming that this is so in your case we will go through this process step by step (see Figure 2.3).

Entering the code

Once you have successfully negotiated the stages outlined in Chapter 1 and have produced a program written in C (or 'coded' as programmers are wont to term it) then you need to enter your masterpiece into the computer. To do this you will need some form of text editor. This program allows text to be entered into the computer and then saved for future editing or further processing. The text of the program which you enter is known as the source code and in the C language such files are distinguished from other files by the extension . c at the end of the source filename.

Compiling

The next stage is to translate the source code into object code. Before the compilation itself takes place the compiler performs a task known as preprocessing. During this stage the header at the beginning of the C program is processed. One example of a preprocessor instruction which we have already encountered is the #include   <filename> command. When the preprocessor encounters this type of instruction the line is replaced by the contents of the specified file. We will be revealing other preprocessor instructions as and when necessary.

Once the preprocessor has done its work the compiler takes over. The task of the compiler is twofold: to check the code for syntax errors, and to translate the source code into object code. The first task is analogous to checking that the

Fig 2.3 *From code to results - the likely route in C*

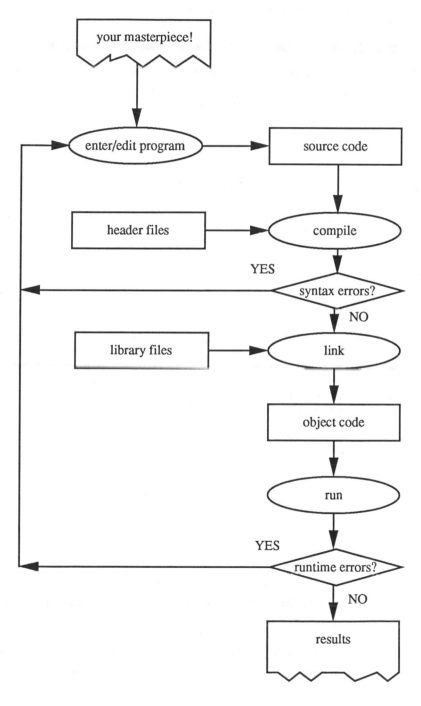

words in an English sentence follow the rules of the language. So misspelt keywords, or missing words, or the incorrect use of these words are located and a list of the errors maintained. The programmer then has to return to the editor and correct the errors in the source code before going any further with compilation.

Provided that the source code is syntactically correct the compiler then proceeds to translate the source file into an object file. The program is now almost ready to be tried out but there is one more stage which it has to pass through.

Linking

The linker is a program which combines the object code of the compiled program with other files which may be required and produces the final executable file. Now the program can be executed, or run, and the real fun begins!

Running

When a program is run, or executed, a variety of different results can ensue. The most desirable result is that it runs correctly and the desired processing occurs with output produced as required. This will not always be the case! A runtime error may occur; for example, an attempt has been made to divide by zero, or to index past the end of an array. The program may also run without producing any errors but with incorrect output. In either of these situations the program will require editing and the 'bugs' eliminated. At this point a well thought out and well documented program is invaluable. (Although if it is really well thought out, there will be no bugs!)

SUMMARY

In this chapter we:

> • looked at the structure of a simple C program and noted that all C programs must contain the function `main()`.

> • saw that functions are fundamental to the structure of C and noted how simple functions could be written and used.

> • were introduced to the `printf()` function and used it to display text on the computer's screen.

> • looked at the compilation and linking processes which are used in C.

EXERCISES

1. The following program contains a few errors, what are they?

```
/* greeting.c *
/* The first c program - greetings */

#include stdio.h>

man ()
{

  printf(" Welcome to ")
  printf("the world of C.\n");
}
```

2.What output will be produced by each of the following combination of printf() statements.

a.
```
printf("1\n This is line one -");
printf("or should it be two?\n");
```

b.
```
printf("AbCdEfGhIj\nKlMnOpQrSt/nletters\n");
printf("1234567890/numbers\n");
printf(\n that was all rather silly!\n");
```

3. There are a number of errors in the program below. Type it in and compile it. Finally, link and run it. What happens?

```
/* Another simple program
with lots of mistakes */

  #include (stdio.h)

main[]
(
print(" This is another very simple\n);
printf(" P\n")
printf(" R\n);
printf(" O\")
print{" GRAM\n");
}
```

4. Enter the first program (greeting.c) exactly as it appears earlier in this chapter. Go through the stages of compiling and linking to produce the executable code and then run the program and see if it does what you expect.

5. Remove the `#include  <stdio.h>` preprocessor instruction from the greeting program and see if the program still compiles and runs successfully.

6. Modify the greeting program to produce on the screen your initials using asterisks, call the new program initial.c.

7. Write a function to print on the screen your name, address and telephone number. Make it appear like a business card. Embellish it as much as you wish, using asterisks or plus signs to add a border.

8. The `main_menu()` function we developed for the bridge program could be made neater if we could clear the screen prior to printing the menu. The easiest way to achieve this is by means of a system call. Most C compilers will be working in an environment which allows a system call to clear the screen. In MS-DOS it is just cls. So the command to clear the screen is simply:

```
system("cls");
```

(However if you use this you should also include the DOS header file by inserting `#include <dos.h>` at the start of your program.)

Investigate the command for your particular implementation and see if you have a comparable command. If not, can you think of any other way of achieving a similar effect?

3 Of words and objects

"...language itself is the most remarkable tool that man has invented, and is the one that makes all the others possible."   *The Story of Language*, C.L. Barber

In this chapter you will be introduced to some important and fundamental elements which form part of the structure of the C language. These elements are concerned with the semantics and syntax of C. We will be discussing the various categories of valid 'words' and how they can be joined together to form meaningful 'sentences'.We will also be looking at some simple programs which will help to consolidate this material. By the end of this chapter you will be able to write simple interactive programs in C.

3.1 LANGUAGE

All languages, whether natural languages like English or Russian, or computer languages like Pascal or C, use words which have particular meanings, and rules for combining these words into meaningful statements. At least some of the words and rules need to be learnt before you can communicate easily and successfully in any language. With your own natural language these are learnt from birth and, to the majority of children, come as second nature. Learning another natural language comes easily to some, but others (like me) find it much harder. You will be pleased to know that learning C is much easier than learning a second, or third..., natural language. One important reason for this concerns the number of basic words which you need to learn. In English there are many thousands of words; in C there are approximately 30 keywords. Although there are many fewer words in C than in a natural language these are sufficient to provide great versatility – you can still do a lot in C!

A computer **language** can be thought of as providing a method of manipulating certain objects by means of well defined rules. A computer **program** consists of sets of instructions which obey these rules and which, once the program is executed, produce new objects from the old ones. A program is therefore just a set of rules for manipulating data. The data are the objects which the C language manipulates; the rules define the language and therefore the instructions which can be used. This chapter introduces the basic data types which C manipulates. We will be exploring their form and answering the question 'What are valid objects in C?'; we will be taking an overview of the ways in which they can be manipulated; and how the basic elements are gathered together to produce a program.

Characters

Before we take a close look at what objects can be manipulated we need to step back and examine the fundamental building blocks of the C language out of which both instructions and data are made. These are the characters which can be used in C. Some of these were introduced in the previous chapter. Many of them will require no introduction, but for completeness we list them all here. These characters, out of which everything is built, are:

lower case letters	a b c .... z
upper case letters	A B C .... Z
digits	0 1 2 9
punctuation and	! @ £ $ % ^ & * ( ) −_ + = ~ {
special characters	} [ ] ` : ; ' " < , > . / ? \	
non-printing	
characters	e.g. space tab newline null

Tokens

Tokens are valid combinations of characters which fall into six categories; keywords, identifiers, constants, string literals, operators and separators (see Figure 3.1). The tokens, grouped together by means of the rules of C, form a program. The category which any one token falls into will depend mainly upon its structure and in some cases upon its position in the program (i.e. its context). We will be explaining some of the most important types of token in this chapter. This will enable you to become familiar with these different categories and their importance. Program 3.1 identifies some occurrences of each of these six categories in a simple program.

What are valid objects in C?

The objects which a C program manipulates are variables, symbolic constants, constants and string literals. All valid objects in C will fall into one of these categories. Variables and symbolic constants are identified by names. Constants and string literals have a value which does not change within the program.

Fig 3.1 *From characters to a program*

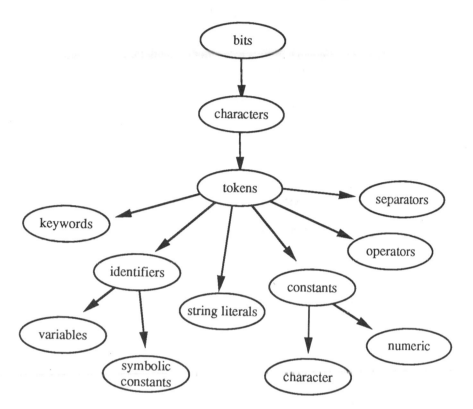

Identifiers

An identifier is a sequence of characters which is used to represent (name) an object (data) which will be manipulated by the program. The name given to an identifier cannot be any combination of characters. The construction of identifier names must follow certain rules. Just as in English there are certain rules for constructing valid words so in C there are a few simple rules and restrictions, as well as some conventions, which govern the construction of valid names. These are listed below.

Restrictions on identifier names

- Names consist of letters, digits and the underline character (_)

- The first character must be a letter or the underline character

- Certain words cannot be used as variable names or symbolic constants – these are the keywords of C (e.g. if, for, int)

Conventions – not hard and fast rules

- It is advisable to avoid using underline as the first character in a name. Often standard library functions begin with this character, and so to avoid the accidental duplication of names it is best to follow this convention.

- Use meaningful names wherever possible.

> **An identifier is ...**
>
> *a sequence of characters used to represent data*

Variables and Symbolic Constants

You will have already noted that there are two types of identifier which can be manipulated in C – variables and constants. Variables are used to identify storage locations which may vary in value during the execution of the program. Although the value of the variable may vary, the place in memory where it is stored (i.e. its address) remains the same. Symbolic constants, on the other hand, are used to identify data objects which will remain the same all the time the program is being run. These are referred to as 'symbolic constants' because each name is a symbol which stands for an actual constant (i.e. is just another name for it). Another convention in naming identifiers is that upper-case letters are used for symbolic constants and lower-case for variables. This makes it easy to distinguish between the two in functions and programs.

Program 3.1

```
/* circle details */
/* this program computes the area */
/* and circumference of a circle*/
```

```
#include <stdio.h>

#define PI 3.141592                /* PI - symbolic constant  */

main()
{                                  /* { , ; - separators      */
      float radius, area, circum;  /* float - keyword         */
                                   /* radius, area, circum -  */
                                   /* variables               */

      printf("\n Area and circumference of a circle \n");
                                   /* "\n Area ... " - string */
                                   /*    literal              */
      printf("\n Enter the radiius : ");
      scanf("%f", &radius);
      area = PI * radius * radius; /* asterisk (*) - operator */

      circum = 2.0 * PI * radius;  /* 2.0 - a constant        */

      printf("\n Radius - %f, Area = %f, Circumference = %f\n",
             radius, area, circum);
}
```

You may be wondering why constant names are used when the value of the data object itself would do. One answer is that it is much easier to identify a symbolic name in a program than a string of numbers. So, for example, PI in the above program is more immediately recognisable than 3.141592. Secondly if the value of the constant requires changing, this can be achieved by simply altering one statement: the one which defines the symbolic constant. All occurrences of this constant will then be replaced by the new value before compilation begins. A third reason, connected with the previous one, concerns the laborious task of modifying each occurrence of numerical constants, with the risk of missing one or, perhaps worse, altering the wrong one!

Keywords

As mentioned above there are some words which are reserved and cannot be used for variable names or as symbolic constants. These are the **keywords** of C and have definite meanings which cannot be altered. They are the words which enable data to be manipulated and useful tasks performed. Without the keywords we would have data but no means of manipulating them. A programming language devoid of keywords is like a cook with all the ingredients for a banquet but no pots, pans or other kitchen utensils - or an experimental physicist with no apparatus. Table 3.1 lists the keywords of C.

The keywords in parentheses are not included in the original definition of the

C language (i.e. in *The C Programming Language* by B W Kernighan and D M Ritchie, Englewood Cliffs, NJ: Prentice Hall, 1978) but are now part of the ANSI standard and should be included in the most recent implementations of C. There are also other keywords which may appear in some versions of the language but they are not specified by the standard.

Table 3.1   *The keywords of C*

auto	break	case	char
(const)	continue	default	do
double	else	(enum)	extern
float	for	goto	if
int	long	register	return
short	signed	sizeof	static
struct	switch	typedef	union
(unsigned)	(void)	(volatile)	while

The keywords, together with variables and symbolic constants, and of course constants (e.g. 2, 45.8, 0.0001, 'a', " a string ") enable the programmer to write a program to perform almost any procedural-type task. The various keywords listed above will be dealt with where necessary in the text – by the time you have worked through this material, you will be familiar with all these keywords and so be able to write quite complex C programs.

3.2 DATA TYPES

We now need to take a more detailed look at variables and symbolic constants. We mentioned above that variables could store numbers, or characters, but we need to be more explicit about what is meant by numbers, and what kind of numbers can be manipulated in C.

Data are stored as a binary number, i.e. a series of 0s and 1s, which may take up a byte, a word, or a number of words. The variables and symbolic constants which we have just been discussing must at some stage during the execution of a program be assigned a value which will be represented as a binary number; as a number of binary digits (see Figure 3.2).

Fig 3.2 *Bits, bytes and words*

A BIT is a BInary digiT and can have a value of 0 or 1 – it is the basic unit of (digital) computer memories.

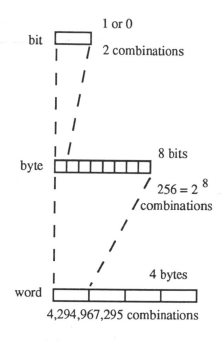

A byte consists of eight bits. This enables a wider range of numbers to be represented than the two which are possible with a single bit.

A word is generally a whole number of bytes (e.g. 1, 2, 4 or 8) and is the basic unit used by a computer. The word length of a computer depends on the architecture of the machine; an 8-bit microcomputer will have a word length of 8 bits, or just one byte, with a 16-bit machine each word will equal two bytes, and with a 64-bit machine the word length will be eight bytes.

Binary numbers are capable of representing a wide variety of data; from simple integers (5, 99, -356) to real (floating point) numbers representing the rest mass of an electron, 9.1083×10^{-31} (kg), or the speed of light, 2.99793×10^{8} (ms^{-1}), or even characters ('a', '!', '8') or strings of characters ("Welcome to the world of C\n"). This task is achieved by using different codes to translate the various types of data into binary numbers.

The keywords out of which the fundamental data types in C are constructed are:

```
char        double      float       int

long        short       signed      unsigned
```

In the following sections we will look at the various data types available. We begin with the most fundamental set – the data type int.

In some computer languages, a distinction is drawn between the number types integer and float. (That is between whole numbers like 1, 289, -62 on the one hand and 3.14159, 6.8, 0.003 on the other). The most basic data type in C is int and it is used when working with the positive and negative whole numbers. The range of numbers which can be represented by a variable declared as int depends on the word length. The normal arrangement is for such data to be stored as a whole number. So on a computer with a word length of 16 bits any integers in the range of -32768 to +32767 could be represented by an int variable. Where do these two numbers come from? Since we need to use one bit to represent the sign of the integer there are 15 remaining bits which can be used to represent a range of numbers. This range will be from -2^{15} to $2^{15}-1$ (i.e. from -32768 to +32767). On a computer with a word length of 32 bits the range of integers will be increased accordingly.

Program 3.2

```
/* program illustrating the int data type */
/* simple addition */

#include <stdio.h>

main()
{
        int num1, num2, sum;                    /* integer variables */

        printf("\n Enter two integers : ");
        scanf("%d %d", &num1, &num2);
        sum = num1 + num2;
        printf("\n The sum of %d and %d is %d \n",
        num1, num2, sum);
}
```

The keywords short, long and unsigned can be used to modify the data type int. The allowable combinations are:

```
        unsigned int
        short int
        long int
        unsigned short int
        unsigned long int
```

You may well be able to guess the effect of using unsigned as a prefix to int – it limits the range of permissible integers to those greater than or equal to zero, i.e. to positive integers. Since there is no need to use one of the bits to indicate sign, the effect of using the data type `unsigned` is approximately to double the largest positive integer which can be represented, compared with that for an int data type (from 32767 to 65535 when using 16 bits). When might you use such a data type? One use might be as a counter; for example the program which I am using as a wordprocessor also provides a word count. The number of words in a chapter will never be less than zero – even if it is still to be written!

The prefixes `short` and `long` also affect the range of integers which can be represented. The type `short` `int` can be used when storage space is at a premium; with this data type "a smaller if possible" amount of memory is used to store an integer. For example two bytes might be used instead of four. Conversely the data type `long` `int` allows a larger range of integers to be used, e.g. eight bytes instead of four. The use of `unsigned` as a prefix with the `short` `int` and `long` `int` data types has the same effect as when it is used with `int` alone, i.e. it restricts the range to positive integers.

There are a couple of important points to remember about these various `int` data types. First of all, they may be abbreviated by omitting the keyword `int` wherever possible. A second point to note is that the range of integers spanned by the data types `int`, `short` and `long` may overlap. On one computer the data types `int` and `short` may mean the same thing, whereas on another the `int` and `long` data types may extend over the same range. The reason for this is based on the 'natural' word size of the machine in question. So on a machine where the normal word size is 16 bits `short` and `int` may use the same amount of storage (16 bits) whilst `long` will utilize 32 bits. On the other hand, on a machine with a natural word size of 32 bits, `long` and `int` may both use 32 bits to store an integer and `short` will use 16 bits.

The data types float and double

We saw above that a natural data type in C is `int`. However if we were restricted to only these types it would be very difficult, if not impossible, to write any moderately useful programs. For example, it would be possible, but not simple, to write a program to find the area of a circle. (How would you write *pi*, and how accurately could you compute the answer?) So, in addition to the `int` data type, C provides a type `float` to deal with real (floating point) numbers. Examples of real numbers are 3.141592, -9.1083×10^{-31} and 299793.0. These examples show that real numbers can be just integers with a decimal point and a zero fractional part, simple real numbers, like *pi* above, or numbers which are very small or very large, positive or negative. Real, or floating point, numbers can be represented in various ways in C and it is worth spending a short time describing the form that such numbers may take.

Let us begin by reviewing the exponential notation. As we saw earlier, the rest mass of an electron (in kg) is usually expressed in scientific notation (i.e. as 9.1083×10^{-31}), with an integer followed by a decimal point, the fractional part, a multiplication sign, the integer ten and a superscript representing the power of ten (-31 in this case). In C the latter part of the number is abbreviated to 'e−31' (equivalent to '$\times 10^{-31}$'). Thus the rest mass of an electron would be written as 9.1083e−31. So a real number written as 5.3e6 is equivalent to 5.3×10^{6} and represents the number 5,300,000.

A floating point number therefore contains the following four elements (see Figure 3.3):

> an integer part
> a decimal point
> a fractional part
> an exponential part

Not all of these four parts need be present, but certain of them must be. A floating point number must contain either a decimal point or an exponential part, or both. If a decimal point is used, then either an integer part or a fractional part, or both, must also be present. If an exponential part is used and no decimal point is included, there must be an integer part in addition to the exponential part. These rules will become clearer if we list a few examples:

```
6.367e3    /* these are all valid   */
6367.0     /* representations of the */
0.6367e4   /* mean radius of the earth */
6367e0     /* in kilometres   */
```

Similarly we could write a million as 1e6, 1000.0e3 or 1000000.0. Notice that no commas are used as separators to signify thousands and millions and that in the last case a decimal point is required. Can you think why?

Fig 3.3. *Float   numbers*

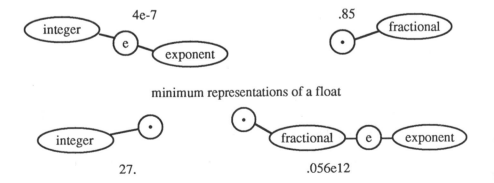

27.   .056e12

Range and precision

So far we have restricted our discussion to the way in which real numbers (or floating point numbers) are represented in C. Two other important factors which affect the representation of these numbers are the range of values which can be used and the accuracy (or precision) with which they can be stored. The typical range of floating point numbers lies from about 10^{-37} to 10^{38} and the precision, when 32 bits are used, is approximately 6 or 7 significant figures. The precision is limited by the number of BITS available for storing the (binary) fraction. The range is limited by the number of BITS available for storing the (binary) exponent.

   Both the range and the precision can be increased by using the data type `double` instead of `float`. The word `double` is used here because the number of bytes used to store data of type `double` is twice that used by `float` data. The `double` data type increases the range typically to 10^{-307} to 10^{+308} and the precision to around 16 significant figures. Check your version of C and find out the range and precision for `float` and `double` in your implementation.

The data type `char`

This data type is used to represent a single character; that is, each of the standard keyboard symbols (letters, digits, punctuation, special characters) as well as a number of non-printing characters such as newline and tab. One byte (i.e. 8 bits) is normally used to store each character, which means that there are a total of 2^8 or 256 different codes available - more than enough to encompass the normal set of characters. Each character is coded as an integer which is then used to represent that character in all subsequent occurrences. The precise code used will depend on the particular implementation; the most common one being the ASCII system in which the character 'a' is represented by the decimal integer 97, and 'A' by the integer 65. Furthermore digits do not represent themselves, so '0' is represented by the integer 47, and '9' by 57. (See Appendix A for a list of the ASCII character set.) In the new standard the keyword `signed` can be used with a `char`. This facility has been included to aid portability where, for example, data other than character data is to be stored in a `char` variable. This keyword can also be used with other data types (e.g. `int`) but it is not necessary as they are signed by default .

Other data types

In addition to the data types we have mentioned above there appear, in certain implementations of C, a number of other data types. We will examine one or two of these later on, but for the moment you may like to check which other types are supported in your particular implementation.

Real numbers - some consequences

The limited range and precision of real numbers in C means that not all numbers can be represented. Very large and very small numbers can obviously not be represented because of the limited range allowed; but also many numbers which do lie in the permitted range can still only be approximately represented. Normally this latter difficulty will not prove too much of a handicap. However one consequence of this inability to store all numbers to an arbitrarily high precision is to introduce rounding errors when very large numbers of computations are being performed. Such problems occur when solving large systems of differential equations, for example. You will not need to be concerned with these problems in an introductory course in programming - such topics are covered in detail in textbooks on numerical analysis. Nonetheless it is worth bearing in mind such problems whenever you examine output from, or predictions based on, very large numerical computations. Treat the results with care!

3.3 MAKING DECLARATIONS

Having examined the various fundamental data types in some detail we can now turn to the process of declaration. Before variables can be used in a C program they need to be declared. This process enables room in memory to be set aside so that values can be stored in the variables. As we have seen, the amount of storage which a variable is allocated depends on the type of data which the variable is to represent. A single character such as 'A' or a variable of type short (perhaps used to store integers in the range 0 to 100) will be allocated less room than a number representing the speed of light or the rest mass of an electron.

All declarations, whether of variables or symbolic constants, come near the beginning of a program or a function.

In a program the layout is:

```
#include<stdio.h>
```

```
      /* symbolic constant declarations here */

main()
{
      /* variable declarations here */
      /* main body of the program */
}
```

The way in which a declaration is made depends on whether the object being declared is a variable or a symbolic constant.

Variables

A variable declaration has the form:

data_type variable_list;

Some examples are:
```
            int day, month, year;
            char   initial;
            float electron_mass, velocity;
```

These declarations associate identifiers with a particular data type; so `day`, `month` and `year` are all `integer` variables; `initial` represents a `character` variable; and `electron_mass` and `velocity` are specified as variables of type `float`. Variables can be initialised at the same time that they are declared. This is most commonly done for variables which are used as counters, or for holding running totals. So for example we might have:

```
            int i = 0, j = 100;
            float sum = 0.0;
```
which will set the integers `i` and `j` to 0 and 100 respectively and the float variable `sum` to `0.0`.

Symbolic constants

A symbolic constant is always defined, that is declared and given a value at the same time. This is achieved by using the preprocessor instruction `#define` at the beginning of the program before the function definition `main()`. For example,

```
            #define PI 3.141592
            #define ME0   9.1083e-31 /* electron rest mass */
```

Notice the form of this declaration/definition:

- There is no equal sign;

- There is no semi-colon at the end of the definition.

Not all the fundamental data types are available for use with symbolic constants; usually they are restricted to the data types `char`, `int` and `double`. The way in which the numeric value is written determines the data type of the number and, in addition, the data type of its associated symbolic constant. The new standard allows a constant to be coerced into a `float` by appending f or F, or into a `long double` by appending l or L. Also ints may be coerced to `long` integers in the same way. An integer constant may also be coerced to `unsigned` by appending a u or U. Both L and U may be appended to the same constant. In addition the derived data type `string` is also available for use with symbolic constants. (Strings will be described later.)

The list below gives a few examples of the fundamental data types which can be used to specify symbolic constants.

int	37	0	1782	-260
long	37L	0L	1782L	-260L
double	37.0	8.15	2.99793e8	-2.6
char	'a'	'H'	'\n'	'-'
unsigned long	37LU	0LU	1782LU	

Either the upper-case or lower-case L can be used to designate a `long` constant but because of the similarity between the digit 1 and the lowercase *l*, it is obviously preferable to use the upper-case version. If a constant is not specified explicitly as a `long` data type but is too large to be stored as an `int` then it will automatically be alloted the data type `long`.

When defining a constant of type `char` (either one of the standard keyboard characters or one of the non-printing characters) the character must be enclosed in single quotes, e.g. 'a'. Most of these examples are obvious enough, but the '\n' requires further explanation. We saw earlier that there are some non-printing characters in C which are used, for example, to format the output from a program. These 'characters' are treated as a single character although they consist of two characters: a backslash (\) followed by a single character. The example given above ('\n') is the code used to generate a newline.

Charlie's musings

It was a bright sunny afternoon and, as Charlie had no lectures, he decided to explore the cobbled back streets of his adopted city. The 'exploration' was not up to much; he was wandering aimlessly around, only occasionally looking up to check where he was, while he juggled a motley collection of thoughts around in his head.

The lecture the other day on programming, and the subsequent discussions with his tutorial group, had left him still rather uncertain about where variables and constants, identifiers and data types fitted into the jigsaw puzzle of programming which was slowly beginning to assemble itself. The street dipped down and curved round in an arc to Charlie's right. As he continued his journey he paused now and then to glance at the antiques in the equally antique-looking shops which lined both sides of the narrow street and seemed to populate most of this part of the city.

His thoughts turned to the chemistry book he had been browsing through the night before. He was getting more and more fascinated by the structure of matter and particularly by the fact that the fundamental building-blocks of all matter were so few and apparently so simple(!). Just from a few basic particles (or were they waves - he was still uncertain about this), like protons, neutrons and electrons, the complex matter which made up the universe could be built. As he was mulling this over he glanced up. The late afternoon sun lit up an ancient-looking shop window, and with the help of its rays he could make out, in the gloomy recesses of the shop, some shelves of jars containing liquids of various colours. Lower down and to the right of these jars he saw others containing crystals - white and blue and black. Pausing and looking over to the left he could just make out a bank of drawers, all labelled but too much in the shadows for him to decipher the writing. Why, this shop had altered hardly at all in over a hundred years! (See Figure 3.4.)

Then he began to make connections. The lecture on programming, his musings about the stuff of the universe, were all brought together in that chance glance through the chemist's (or should it be alchemist's) window. Now the talk about variables and constants, bits, bytes and identifiers all became as clear as crystal. The 0s and 1s, the bits which all digital computers manipulated were the fundamental building blocks of all programs just as protons, neutrons and electrons were the fundamental building blocks of matter (or was it quarks, he still wasn't sure about this). The characters were analagous to the atoms - different combinations of 0s and 1s making up different characters just as different combinations of the three particles made up different atoms. Which is where the chemist shop came in. The labels on the jars and drawers could be thought of as the identifiers. (They identified the contents!) The jars and drawers corresponded to the variables.Whereas the contents of the jars were analogous to the constants: to the various data types, to int, float, double and char.

Charlie stayed for a while in the rapidly fading twilight, staring through the window with a look of enlightenment on his face, but he was brought sharply back to reality by a sudden chilly gust of wind which eddied down the darkening

Fig 3.4   *The   apothecary's   window*

street. He began his trek back to his flat feeling much happier and looking forward eagerly to his evening meal.

3.4 DOING A LITTLE CALCULATING

Although we haven't covered all the aspects of C which are needed to write a moderately useful program we have covered enough material to enable you to understand simple programs. At this point you could usefully look back at the two programs given so far in this chapter and check that you understand their structure and purpose. (Some of the keywords and functions will not yet be familiar to you, but you should nevertheless be able to grasp their purpose.)

We will develop a simple program to help reinforce some of the topics covered so far. Once we have written the program we can return to our discussion of the ins and outs of C syntax. In Chapter 1 you were asked to develop an algorithm which would provide a chart to enable acres to be converted to square yards. Let us take a simplified version of this example and write a program to convert an area given in acres to its equivalent in square yards. First of all we begin by devising an algorithm. A possible algorithm is given below.

Acres to square yards - algorithm

> **declare** constants   (i.e. no. of square yards per acre)
> **declare** variables (acres, sq_yards)
> **read in** the area in acres
> do the calculation
>   **set** sq_yards **to** acres x no. of square yards per acre
> **print** the result

This is a very simple problem so we are able to write down the algorithm with very little thought, and without the need for stepwise refinement. However you must not forget the importance of stepwise refinement - we will soon be dealing with more complex programs which will require a little more planning before the code can be written.

(An acre - original definition)

> *"2. A definite measure of land, originally as much as a yoke of oxen could plough in a day; afterwards limited by statutes 5 Edw. I, 31 Edw. III, 24 Henry VIII, to a piece 40 poles long by 4 broad (= 4824 sq yards), or its equivalent of any shape."*
> *Oxford English Dictionary*

One of the pieces of information which we need is the conversion factor. The definition above is no longer used, although it is interesting to know how the measurement originated. The current definition lists 640 acres to one square mile. We can find the number of square yards per acre as follows:

> There are 640 acres in 1 square mile (according to current tables)
> 1 mile = 1760 yards
> So 640 acres = 1760 x 1760 square yards
> Hence 1 acre = 1760 x 1760/640 square yards
>   = 4840 square yards.
> So the conversion factor we require is 4840.

We could simply use this value as a symbolic constant, however it is not immediately obvious where the number 4840 comes from, so it is better to leave the computer to work out the arithmetic. In order to define a symbolic constant we can simply use the #define preprocessor statement to assign the conversion factor to a suitable identifier. Thus the line in the program which achieves this will be:

```
#define SYPA 1760.0*1760.0/640.0
```

This calculation will be performed at preprocessing time and the resulting value substituted for all occurrences of SYPA at compile time. Remember that there is no equal sign in this (preprocessor) instruction and there is no semi-colon at the end of the line. The identifier I have used (SYPA) stands for Square Yards Per Acre - any other valid identifier could have been used but this is reasonably short and acts as a sensible mnemonic.

The 'heart' of this program is the simple multiplication which uses this conversion factor (SYPA) to convert acres into square yards. This calculation is accomplished by the line:

```
sq_yards = acres*SYPA;
```

Notice here the use of an asterisk (*) for multiplication, rather than a cross which could only be represented by the letter x and thus lead to confusion. The = operator is known as an **assignment operator** and is used to place the result of computing the expression to its right into the variable on its left.

The final task required in this program is a means of printing the result. The printf() function can be used to achieve this, as follows:

```
printf("%f acres equal %f square yards\n", acres, sq_yards);
```

The printf() function, as it appears here, works in the following way. The string between the pair of double quotes is printed out exactly as it appears **except** in the case of special characters, known as formatting characters (i.e. %f and \n). The first occurrence of %f is replaced by the value of the first variable in the list which follows the section in quotes, the second %f is replaced by the value of the second variable. The %f also governs the way in which the variable is printed out, in this case the output is in floating point form. Thus if the variable acres has the value 1.0 then a line similar to the following would be printed out:

```
1.0 acres equals 4840.000000 square yards.
```

The effect of the \n at the end of the *control-string* is to move the cursor (or print head) to the beginning of the next line.

Example program so far

Stage1:

```
/* acres to square yards conversion program */
```

```
/* ****** incomplete version one ****** */

#define SYPA 1760.0*1760.0/640.0
                        /* SYPA - square yards per acre */
main()
{
    float acres, sq_yards;

/*  require to input the area in acres - see below */
    sq_yards = acres*SYPA;
    printf("%f acres equal %f square yards\n", acres, sq_yards);
}
```

Notice that the numbers 1760 and 640 are written as real numbers even though they have no fractional parts. This ensures that SYPA is of type double. The element missing from this program is a fairly crucial one: some means of entering the data into the program. We need a function which will allow us to enter, in acres, the area which is to be converted to square yards. You have already come across the function we require, in the circle and add programs, it is is the scanf() function. This, like printf(), is part of the standard i/o library of C and has the form

scanf(control-string,argument-list)

This function is quite straightforward. However there is one very important point which you need to know before you use it. The elements in the *argument-list* do not represent the variable names, but point to the addresses in memory where the data are stored. To refer to the address of a variable, rather than the contents of the variable, the variable name is prefixed by an ampersand(&). Thus &acres represents the address in memory where the variable acres is to be found. So the statement which we need to read in the area in acres is simply

```
scanf("%f", &acres);
```

The %f format string causes the scanf() function to interpret the string of characters entered as a floating point number just as, when it is used in a printf() function, the output is formatted as a floating point number. Other format strings which can be used with both scanf() and printf() will be introduced later on in this chapter.

This statement on its own is still not very helpful to the potential user. Can you think why? If you can't then enter the program listed below, compile, link and run it - and see if that helps! If you are still stuck, ask a friend to run the program and watch their reaction!

Stage 2:

```
/* acres to square yards conversion program */
/* ****** incomplete version two ******  */

#define SYPA 1760.0*1760.0/640.0
                    /* SYPA - square yards per acre */
main()
{
    float acres, sq_yards;

    scanf("%f", &acres);
    sq_yards = acres*SYPA;
    printf("%f acres equal %f square yards\n", acres, sq_yards);

}
```

When the above program is run the computer awaits an entry from the keyboard before continuing. The problem is that without some indication of what should be entered the user is liable to be in the dark - you should know what needs to be entered, but you will be very lucky if anyone else does, and after all your ultimate aim is to write programs which anyone can use! To overcome this problem all we need do is to insert a prompt to the user before the value is read in by the scanf() function. We can achieve this quite straightforwardly by using a printf() statement, for example:

```
 printf("\n Please enter an area in acres for conversion : ");
```

The prompt can be as verbose or as concise as you wish as long as it gets the message across. Having introduced the scanf() function we have arrived at the final version of the program which is reproduced below.

Program 3.3

```
/* acres to square yards conversion program */
/* ****** final version ****** */

#define SYPA 1760.0*1760.0/640.0
                    /* SYPA - square yards per acre */
main()
{
    float acres, sq_yards;
    printf("\n Please enter an area in acres for conversion: ");
    scanf("%f", &acres);
    sq_yards = acres*SYPA;
    printf("%f acres equal %f square yards\n", acres,sq_yards);
}
```

Notice that the first printf() statement leaves the cursor at the end of the prompt, it doesn't move to a newline. This is very convenient when prompting for the entry of data. Once a number is entered, and the Return key is pressed, the variable acres is assigned the entered value, the computation is carried out, and the result is printed out on the following line.

3.5 OPERATORS

The program we have just developed, as well as introducing the scanf() function and using variable identifers and a symbolic constant, also uses a couple of arithmetic operators (namely = and *). These are just some of a number of operators of various kinds which form a link between keywords, variables and symbolic constants. These, together with the rules for combining them, enable valid C statements to be produced. For the moment we will restrict our attention to the arithmetic operators - in later chapters we will introduce other kinds, such as logical and pointer operators.

The fundamental arithmetic operators consist of the five symbols

$$= \quad + \quad - \quad * \quad /$$

In the next few sections we will be covering the use of all these operators as well as a few other useful ones, but we will begin our tour with the assignment operator.

The assignment operator =

The = operator in C does not perform the same task as the 'equals sign' in mathematics, as for example in the equation

$$x^2 + 3x - 2 = 0$$

In mathematical terms this expresses the fact that the left hand side of the equation is numerically equal to zero. In C the equals sign (=) is used to assign the value of whatever appears to the right of the equals sign to the variable which is on the left of the sign. What is the difference? The difference becomes apparent when we examine a common programming expression which is used to increment a variable. Consider the expression:

$$i = i + 1$$

In mathematical language this does not make sense. How can a quantity be equal to one more than itself? In the terminology of computing, however, it does make sense. It in fact states that a new value of the variable i is to be obtained by adding one to the old value (see Figure 3.5).

Fig 3.5 *Incrementing*

expression	value	
i	62	<-- old value of i
i + 1	63	
i = i + 1	63	<-- new value of i

N.B. The right hand side is worked out first
and then put in the left hand side

Another expression which is mathematically correct but which is invalid in C is x + 1 = 6; mathematically this is equivalent to the equation x = 5, but in C it is syntactically invalid – it is not allowed as an expression in the C language. The reason why x+1 = 6 is not allowed is that the left-hand side of an assignment statement must be a single identifier – a single variable. The right hand side is evaluated and then placed in the variable to the left of the = operator; x+1 is not a single variable and so the value 6 cannot be assigned to it. The rules for using the assignment operator are summarised in the box below.

• The leftmost token in an assignment statement must be a single identifier.

• The left hand side of an expression containing = must consist of a single identifier, or an identifier preceded by another assignment operator.

• The rightmost token must consist of either
  i) Variable(s) and/or constant(s) related by a valid arithmetic expression, or
  ii) A constant (e.g. a number – 3.141592)

All the following are valid assignment statements, provided that the variables are all declared as type int.

```
x = 6;
month = 12;
i = count = total = 0;
```

The last statement may appear somewhat strange; most computer languages do not allow multiple assignment statements like this one. However in C such statements are perfectly valid and are quite common. This statement also illustrates the order in which arithmetic assignments are carried out, that is from right to left. Thus the variables are assigned the value zero in the order: `total`, `count`, `i`. The following are also valid assignment statements:

```
h = a*a + b*b
energy = mass*v*v/2.0
```

Note, however, that garbage will result unless the variables to the right of the assignment operator have previously been assigned a value.

Operators and operands

Before we go on to discuss the arithmetic operators we need to define the terms 'operator' and 'operand'. An **operator** is a symbol (like *) which performs a particular operation on an object, or objects. The objects upon which these operations are carried out are called **operands** (e.g. `mass`, `v`). There are two common types of operator, unary and binary. A unary operator has only one operand, whilst a binary operator has two. Examples of binary operators are =, + and * (multiplication) and examples of unary operators are & (the address operator - used in `scanf()`) and − (minus sign).

The arithmetic operators + - * and /

As in ordinary arithmetic and as we have seen above, two tokens are added together by placing the + sign, or addition operator, between them. The layout is unimportant in that it is irrelevant whether or not the operator is surrounded by spaces. So all the following are equivalent expressions.

```
total=total+8;
total = total + 8;
total = total     +        8;
```

Obviously the legibility of the program is improved if the second option is used. However in long expressions this can become cumbersome. The important point to remember is that spaces may be used to separate operators but they must not be used within identifiers themselves. Thus

```
total = total + 8;   /* valid */
```
is valid, but
```
t o t a l = t o t a l + 8;   /* invalid */
```
is invalid.

Precedence and associativity of arithmetic operators

The order of evaluation (associativity) of an arithmetic expression depends on the operator. The addition (+), subtraction (−), multiplication (*) and division (/) operators have a left to right associativity, meaning that the operand to the left of the operator is operated on by the operand to the right. The assignment (=) and the negation (−) operators have right to left associativity. In other words the expression to the right of these operators is evaluated before the appropriate operation is performed.

The rules for precedence operate first, so in expressions which have a mixture of operators with different precedence those with the higher precedence are evaluated before those of lower precedence. If the precedence of two operators are equal then the rules for associativity are implemented. The rules for all the arithmetic operators are summarised in Table 3.2. The remaining operators are dealt with in the next section.

Table 3.2 *Associativity and precedence of the arithmetic operators*

Operator(s)	Associativity
()	Left to Right
− (unary) ++ −−	Right to Left
* / %	Left to Right
+ − (subtraction)	Left to Right
=	Right to Left

Note: the operators with higher precedence are above those with lower precedence

The multiplication and division operators have a higher precedence than the addition and subtraction operators and so an expression involving either of these operators is evaluated before an expression involving either addition or subtraction. To force evaluation in a different manner, and to clear up any ambiguities which may be present in the user's mind, parentheses can be used, i.e. (and). These have the highest precedence, which means that any expression enclosed within round brackets will be evaluated first, even if this expression includes only addition or subtraction. The following example (Figure 3.6) will help to illustrate the effect of parentheses on the evaluation of an arithmetic expression. Assume that a has previously been assigned the value 2.4, and b the value 1.2.

Fig 3.6 *Using brackets to change the order of evaluation*

Without brackets	With brackets
x = 2+a/b*5	x = 2+a/(b*5)
x = 2+2.4/1.2*5	x = 2+2.4/(1.2*5)
x = 2+2.0*5	x = 2+2.4/6.0
x = 2+10.0	x = 2+0.4
x = 12.0	x = 2.4
Division done first	Brackets done first

Other arithmetic operators

There are four more arithmetic operators which you will find invaluable. These are:

```
-        (unary) negative, or negation
%        modulus
++       increment
--       decrement
```

The (unary) – operator affects the operand immediately to its right and simply reverses the sign of that operand.

The modulus operator is used in integer arithmetic to determine the remainder after an integer division. So 15 % 6 (read as "15 modulo 6") produces the result 3, since 15 divided by 6 equals 2 with a remainder of 3. The whole part (in this case 2) is found by simple integer division. The result is truncated to the next whole number below. Exactly how integer division and the modulus operator behave with negative operands is implementation dependent. Program 3.4 illustrates this point.

Program 3.4

```
/* some integer arithmetic */
/* illustrating the division and modulo operators */

#include <stdio.h>

main()
{
        int n1, n2, i;
```

```
        n1 = 17;
        n2 = 3;
        printf("\n  n1    n2  n1/n2 n1%%n2\n");
        /* the two % characters are necessary in the above */
        /* see section 3.9 for the reason */

        for( i = 0; i < 4; i++) {
             printf("%4d   %4d   %4d   %4d\n");
             n1 = - n1;   /* change the sign of n1 each time    */
             if( i == 1 )        /* if i is equal to 1 the next  */
                                 /* statement is executed        */
                    n2 = -n2;    /* change the sign of n2 on the */
        }                        /*       2nd and 4th time        */
}
```

The output I obtained from this program was:

n1	n2	n1/n2	n1%n2
17	3	5	2
-17	3	-5	-2
17	-3	-5	2
-17	-3	5	-2

Check the result by running the program for youself.

The next operator is the increment operator which performs the incrementing operation which we mentioned briefly earlier in this chapter; it is used to perform the very common task of adding one onto a variable. This operator can be placed either before or after the variable. In the former case it is known as the prefix incrementing operator, whereas in the latter case it is called the postfix (or suffix) incrementing operator. The following short program illustrates how it works.

Program 3.5

```
/* Using the increment operator */
main()
{
   int  i, j, n;
   i = j = 0;
   printf("These are the initial values of i and j");/* line 1*/
   printf("\n i = %d : j = %d \n",i,j);              /* line 2*/
   printf(" Now i and j are incremented\n");
   printf(" ++i = %d : j++ = %d \n",++i,j++);         /* line 4*/
   printf(" and these are the new values of i and j");
   printf("\n i = %d : j = %d \n",i,j);              /* line 6*/
}
```

Enter this program, then compile and link it. Once you have successfully obtained an executable file run the program. You should obtain the following output:

```
These are the initial values of i and j
i = 0 : j = 0
 Now i and j are incremented
++i = 1: j++ = 0
 and these are the new values of i and j
i = 1 : j = 1
```

Notice the difference between the values printed out for i and j in line 4. The prefix incrementing operator (++i) tells the compiler to increment i before performing any further operations; in this case before printing out the new value of i. Thus i is increased to 1 and this new value is printed out. However when written in its postfix form (j++) the value of j is first used and then it is incremented. So the current value of j (i.e. 0) is output and only then is it increased by one. The sixth line of the output shows that both i and j are set to one following the execution of the commands ++i and j++. Another example of how this operator works is given below.

```
int i, j;

i = 1;
j = 2*(++i); /* j = 4 */
             /* i = 2 */
```

```
int i, j;

i = 1;
j = 2*(i++); /* j = 2 */
             /* i = 2 */
```

The decrementing operator (--) works in a similar manner to the incrementing operator and, again, it can be used in two ways, either as a prefix, or as a postfix operator. (See Exercise 5 at the end of this chapter.)

Note that the incrementing and decrementing operators can only be used with variables; the following are incorrect usages of these operators.

```
++8   /* cannot increment  a constant*/
#define PI 3.141592
PI++ /* ....nor a symbolic constant */
```

3.6 SOME NEW OPERATORS

All of the arithmetic operators which have been introduced in this chapter have their equivalent **arithmetic assignment operator** and they are listed in

Table 3.3. These operators can prove very useful in shortening a piece of code and you will soon find that they become second nature to you and that you will be using them in preference to their longer equivalents.

Table 3.3   *The arithmetic assignment operators*

operation	assignment operator	example	equivalent to:
addition	+=	i += 5	i = i + 5
subtraction	-=	k -= 12	k = k - 12
multiplication	*=	k *= epsilon	k = k * epsilon
division	/=	n /= 2	n = n / 2
modulus	%=	num %= 10	num = num % 10

(i.e. the remainder after division by 10)

3.7 TYPE CONVERSION

Consider the following program fragment:

```
int i;
float x,y,z;
i = 5;
x = 6.4;
y = x/5;
z = y + i;
```

In many computer languages, such as Pascal and Modula-2, the last two lines would cause an error because both statements consist of a mixture of data types, i.e. int and float. However in C mixing data types is perfectly legal. Let's deal with these two cases in turn. The first case involves the division of a floating point number (6.4) by an integer. The evaluation of the right-hand side of the statement (i.e. x/5) is performed by converting the integer to a float and then carrying out a floating point division. This produces the result 1.28 which is then assigned to the variable y. In the second case because the variable y is of type float the value of i is converted to a float before being added to y. Note that i is still stored as type int; its value and type are unchanged in memory. Finally the result is assigned to z, giving it the value 6.28. These two examples illustrate the process known as type conversion. This feature of C can be very useful, but at least to begin with you should treat it with care.

Type conversion is performed according to a series of rules which depend on the ordering of the data types. They are ordered as follows, from lowest to highest

highest
```
            double
            float
            unsigned long
            long
            unsigned int
            int
            unsigned short
            short
            char
```

It is a good rule of thumb to avoid mixing types if at all possible. However if you do need to mix them in a statement, make sure that the variable which is being assigned a value is of a higher type than any variables, or constants, in the remainder of the expression. This is necessary to ensure that promotion will occur rather than demotion, as explained below.

Promotion

In an operation which involves two types both the values are converted to the 'higher' of the two types before evaluation. Normally no problems will be encountered when this process of promotion occurs.

```
int i;
char c;

...

c = getchar();  /* read a character from the keyboard  */
if ( c > '0' && c < '9')          /* if c is a digit     */
    i = c - '0';                  /* convert to integer */
```

This fragment is used to convert a digit, read in as a character, to a decimal digit The character ' 0 ' is subtracted from the character c to produce another character (in the range 0 to 9). This is then promoted to an integer before being assigned to i. This next fragment illustrates promotion from int to float.

```
float average, sum;
.
average = sum/count; /* count is promoted to type float,
                    the division performed, and the result
                    assigned to the variable average */
```

Demotion

When an assignment statement is involved and the types are mixed the final result of the calculations is converted to the type of the variable on the left of the equal sign. This may cause no problems, particularly if the type of the assigned variable is 'higher' than the other types involved. However if this type is 'lower' then the process of demotion will occur. Thus a float type may be assigned to a variable of type int. This can cause problems, since the assigned variable may not be big enough to hold the result, or it may be truncated to an integer.

```
int count, average;
float sum;
...
average = sum/count;
```

In this example count is promoted to type float. The division is then performed and the result demoted to int. Finally this result is assigned to the variable average - this would in most cases cause truncation and thus loss of accuracy.

Casts

In addition to the above implicit conversions between data types C also provides explicit conversion by means of casts. So, for example, if n is of type int then it can be casted into a float by the expression

```
(float) n
```

and any expression of which this is a part will now use the float version of n instead of the original int version. The cast operator is a unary operator and has right to left associativity and the same order of precedence as other unary operators. So

```
(int) x + 5 * i
```

is equivalent to

```
((int) x) + 5 * i
```

Thus the conversion is carried out before the other arithmetic operations. Some other examples are

```
(int) (PI * r * r)
x * (float) i / (float) n
(char) (n = i - (int) c)
```

```
y = (double) (3 * x * x - 2 * x + 6)
```

Notice that, although the third of the above expressions is valid, an expression of the form

```
(int) x = 2 * y
```

is invalid. The reason for this is that the process of casting forces a temporary change in the variable, or expression, involved. The variables themselves still retain their declared data types and their current values. If we wished to assign the integer part of 2 * y to x, we would need to write it as follows:

```
x = (int) (2 * y)
```

3.8 EXPRESSIONS

Throughout this chapter we have referred to 'expressions' without giving a precise definition. Now is the time to rectify the matter. At its simplest an expression is just a constant. For example,

```
365
3.141592
1e21
'e'
"A string of some sort"
```

are all instances of simple expressions. A variable, or a symbolic constant, can also be an expression, e.g.

```
c
PI
year
count
```

Expressions, though, will usually be more complex than these simple examples. They will normally consist of a combination of operators and operands. The operands can be constants, as above, variables or symbolic constants, or even other expressions (often called subexpressions). The operators may be arithmetic operators, arithmetic assignment operators, logical operators and so on.

Examples of more complex expressions are:

```
365/12
v*v/(c*c)
```

```
s=u*t+0.5*a*t*t
x*(u=v+5)+z
```

Most of these are perfectly straightforward and, given the values of the variables, you could easily evaluate them. But what about the last example? This looks rather odd and would not be allowed in most other programming languages, but by now you will not be surprised to learn that in C it is perfectly valid! Although such expressions are perfectly valid it is considered poor style to include assignments within other expressions unless it is absolutely necessary. It is better to keep assignment statements separate so that it is clear where assignments occur. However this example does illustrate an important feature of expressions in this language, namely that all expressions have a value. This means that, in the last example, the expression u=v+5 has a value which is then multiplied by the variable x. But what value do such expressions have? The value of an expression as a whole is simply the value which the variable to the left of the assignment operator (=) has following the evaluation of the complete expression. So, for example, the expression u*t+0.5*a*t*t, (with u=0, t=1, and a=9.8) evaluates to 4.9, the variable s becomes 4.9 and thus the value of the whole expression (s=u*t+0.5*a*t*t) is also 4.9. Now in the last example above, if x=2, v=14 and z=3, then the variable u becomes 19, which is therefore the value of the whole expression in parentheses and so the complete expression becomes 2*19+3, which produces 41 as the value of the complete expression.

3.9 STATEMENTS

So far in this chapter we have looked at tokens, variables, symbolic constants, data types, and just now at expressions. All these elements of C are used to construct statements which form the main building blocks of a program. As an analogy you could think of the tokens (variables, symbolic constants, the data types int, float etc.) as the words of C; expressions as phrases; and statements as the sentences of C. However, in C statements can be made up of a number of other statements, and so there are two types of statement which can be formed.

The two types of statement are known as **simple** and **compound**. A simple statement is a complete instruction which ends in a semi-colon; whereas a compound statement consists of two or more statements enclosed within braces ({}). A complete instruction is an expression which performs some task. The semi-colon and the braces form part of another group of tokens called separators, you could think of these as the punctuation marks of C.

Simple statements

The following are all simple statements:

```
int count,n,m;
float s;
count=5;
s=u*t+0.5*a*t*t;
p=x*(u=v+5)+z;
printf(" Welcome to the world of C\n");
scanf("%d %d",&n,&m);
```

The first two are declaration statements which allocate space in memory for the various variables; the next two are simple assignment statements; the fifth is a more complex assignment statement, made up of a number of sub-expressions; whilst the last two statements consist of function calls. All of these types of statement were present in the conversion program. Look back at that program now and make a note of which statements belong to which category (remember, the catogories are: declaration, simple assignment, complex assignment and function).

There is one further basic type of statement which you will need to be familiar with. These statements are sometimes known as **structured** statements. Examples include:

```
for (i = 0; i < n; ++i)
     ++a;

if (a >= max)
     max = a;

while (count++ < 100)
     ++a;
```

These statements perform an action, but their structure is more complex than a simple assignment statement. The details of these structured statements will be left until later. However we will be dealing with the if statement in the next chapter, so you will not have long to wait. Note the structure of the for statement:

```
for ( expression1 ; expression2 ; expression3 )
              statement
```

There are no statements within the parentheses - there are three expressions each separated from the next by a semi-colon.

Compound statements

A compound statement consists of two or more statements which are enclosed by braces. They are also referred to as blocks. We have already met one example of a compound statement - the block of statements which make up the function `main()`. A compound statement can be used anywhere that a simple statement can be used. So, for example, a `for` statement used in the process of computing the sum of squares of integers might take the form:

```
for (count = 0; count < 10; ++count) {
    ++a;
    ++b;
    c = a*a + b*b;
    printf("%d   %d\n", count, c);
}
```

In this example all the statements enclosed by the braces ({ and }) are part of the `for` statement and are executed in sequence each time the `for` statement is executed, that is so long as the variable `count` is less than 10.

We will find many more uses for compound statements as we come across other structured statements in subsequent chapters.

Layout

The exact position in which the right and left brace appear is not crucial. Obviously the left brace must be placed at the beginning of the compound statement and the right brace at the end. However the above `for` statement could equally well be written as

```
for (count = 0; count < 10; ++count)
{
    ++a;
    ++b;
    c = a*a + b*b;
    printf("%d   %d\n", count, c);
}
```

A number of other possibilities exist but these two are the most usual. Whichever approach you use be sure to : (1) be consistent; and (2) adopt a style which allows compound statements to stand out clearly in the code, e.g. indent the statements between the braces by a fixed amount.

3.10 FORMATTED INPUT AND OUTPUT: *SCANF()* AND *PRINTF()*

In this final section we are going to take a further look at the way in which formatted input and output can be achieved by using the functions `scanf()` and `printf()`. You have already been introduced in this, and the previous, chapter to various ways in which these two functions can be used. The object of this section is to bring together what you have learnt so far concerning input and output and to extend it a little.

Both functions for formatted input and output have a similar syntax, i.e.

printf(control-string, argument-list);
scanf(control-string, argument-list);

As you saw earlier there is a minor difference in the construction of the *argument-list*: for `printf` this just consists of a list of variable names, whereas for `scanf` the list is made up of the addresses of variables. The *control-string*, as its name suggests, controls the way in which data is transferred between the computer's memory and the standard input/output device (a keyboard for input and generally a screen for output). The structure of this string varies slightly for the two functions but they both consist of a string of characters enclosed between double quotes. In the case of `printf` the string can contain text for output as well as format information, while with `scanf` only formatting information is allowed. Some examples are

```
"Welcome to the world of C\n"       \* printf() *\
"total = %d, \naverage = %f"        \* printf() *\
"%d %c"                             \* scanf(), or printf()
                            -but not very informative!*\
```

Notice that the `printf()` *control-string* can contain either or both text (e.g. `Welcome to the world of C`), or format strings (or conversion specifications) (e.g. `%d %c`). White spaces can also be included in the *control-string* of a `printf` function. You have already encountered one of the white spaces, i.e. \n for newline. However there are a number of other nonprinting characters which can be represented by a backslash followed by a character and these are listed in Table 3.4.

Table 3.4 *White spaces — nonprinting characters*

\0	null	used to indicate the end of a string
\b	backspace	move back one character
\f	form feed	advance one page (or clear the screen)
\n	newline	start a new line
\r	carriage return	move to the beginning of the present line
\t	tab	move the cursor to the next tab position

Conversion specification

At its simplest a conversion specification consists of the % symbol followed by a single lower-case letter. We will leave until later more complex conversion specifications which consist of numbers as well as characters and allow for the input and output of data with a particular field width and a predefined number of decimal places. The lower case letters are known as conversion characters and the most useful ones are listed in Table 3.5 below, together with the effect on input and output data.

Table 3.5   *Common conversion specifications*

	printf()	**scanf()**
Conversion character	*The argument is printed*	*Characters are converted to*
c	as a character	a character
d	as a decimal integer	a decimal
e	in scientific notation	not used
f	as a floating point number	a floating point number
g	in e, or f format, whichever is shorter	not used
lf	not used	a floating point number (double)
s	as a string	a string

Note that to have a % appear the string %% is required. The reason for this should be obvious since as this symbol is used to indicate a conversion specification ambiguities would be bound to arise.

One other useful method of printing a character is to send the octal code preceded by a backslash. Thus \101 in a control_string would print the letter A (assuming the standard ASCII codes) and \007 would ring the bell.

The program below illustrates the use of some of the *control_strings* which we have just been looking at.

```
/* program to illustrate the use of conversion */
/* specifications with printf() and scanf()   */

main()
{
        char c1, c2;
        int  i1, i2;
        float x;
        printf("Using conversion specifications\n");
        printf("\nPlease enter the following:\n");
        printf("%s\n%s\n%s\n%s\n%s\n",
                "an integer",
                "a character",
                "a float",
                "a character",
                " and finally another integer");
        scanf("%d ", &i1);
        scanf("%c %f %c %d", &c1, &x, &c2, &i2);
        printf("\n\nYou entered :\n");
        printf("\t%d\t%c\n", i1, c1);
        printf("\t%f\t%c\n", x, c2);
        printf(" and\t%d\n", i2);
        printf(" The first character was (%c)\n ", c1);
        printf("and is represented by the integer %d\n", c1);
        printf("..and the second character (%o)\n",c2);
        printf("is represented by the integer %d\n", c2);
}
```

A typical run of this program might produce the following output:

```
Using conversion specifications

Please enter the following:

an integer
a character
a float
a character
and finally another integer
25 P 5.73
z
14


You entered :
  25      P
```

```
5.730000 z
14
  The first character was (P)
and is represented by the integer 80
..and the second character (z)
is represented by the integer 122
```

Program analysis

The first couple of printf() statements should have given you no problems, but the third one looks a bit strange. First of all it contains an odd assortment of characters in the *control-string* (%s\n%s\n%s\n%s\n%s\n), and secondly the *argument-list* is spread over a number of lines. Let's dissect the *control-string* first. If you look closely you will see that it is made up of five strings of %s\n. The \n is simply the escape sequence for a new line, and the %s is just the format expression for a string. So the effect of the complete *control-string* is to output five strings on successive lines. This means that the *argument-list* must contain five string constants; and indeed it does – if it did not then the output would be undetermined. Note that these five string constants need not have been written one to a line – the layout is unimportant so long as the number of strings match the number expected. Both of the following are valid constructs for this statement and would produce exactly the same result.

```
printf("%s\n%s\n%s\n%s\n%s\n",  "an integer",
        "a character",
        "a float",
        "a character",
        " and finally another integer");

printf("%s\n%s\n%s\n%s\n%s\n",
        "an integer", "a character",  "a float",
        "a character",  " and finally another integer");
```

The data are input to the program via the two scanf() statements. The first of these, scanf("%d ", &i1);, is used to assign an integer constant entered at the keyboard to the variable i1. The integer is terminated as soon as a 'white space' is entered at which point control moves on to the next statement. (That is as soon as a space, a tab, or a new line is encountered.) The second scanf() statement contains a *control-string* to read in the remaining items - a character (%c), a float (%f), another character (%c) and an integer (%d). Notice that the items read in must correspond to the formats defined by the *control-string* but the exact layout is immaterial. So the following two input strings would also be read correctly by the pair of scanf() statements.

```
25 P 5.73 z  14 /* here the separator is a space (or blank) */
```

```
25          /* here the separator is the newline character (\n) */
P
5.73
z
14
```

The data are output by the `printf()` statements using the white space character tab (`\t`) to produce a rudimentary formatted layout. A later chapter will detail how to produce a more fully structured layout.

The last two `printf()` statements show how a character can also be displayed in its (decimal) coded form (in this case ASCII), that is by using the `int` conversion character (`%d`) instead of the one for `char` (`%c`).

SUMMARY

In this chapter we:

- examined some of the fundamental building blocks of C.

- explored the differences between keywords, variables and symbolic constants.

- discussed the data types `int`, `float` and `char`.

- looked at one class of operators, the arithmetic operators, and noted their rules of use.

- examined the construction of expressions and found that in C every expression has a value.

- saw that there are two catgeories of statement: simple, ending with a semi-colon, and compound which, contain other statements enclosed within braces.

- were introduced to the input function `scanf()` and noted the use of format strings to control input and output.

EXERCISES

1. Check your own documentation and find out the particular set of keywords which are used in your implementation. You will find that the minimum you have will be the 27 listed in Table 3.1 (i.e. all those apart from the ones in parentheses).

2. Which of the following are valid names for variables, or symbolic constants, and which are invalid? Give the reason(s) for your answer.

a. `lower`   b. `E`   c. `time`

d. `+factor`   e. `int`   f. `integer2`

g. `TAX_RATE`   h. `count1`   i. `%interest`

j. `SUN'S_DIAMETER`

3. The program listed below uses the operator `sizeof()` to compute the number of bytes taken up by the various data types. This operator takes the item immediately following it and computes its size in bytes. The item can be a data type (which must be enclosed in parentheses) - as in this example - or a variable name. So `sizeof(area)` would compute the number of bytes occupied by the variable `area` **not** the value of the variable `area`. (Note that in the ANSII standard the function `sizeof` returns a `long int` so the conversion specification `%Lf` is required in the `printf` statements to produce the correct result.) Enter the program, compile and link it. Finally run it and compare the results with the answers you expected.

```
/*  Finding the number of bytes occupied by */
/*  the various data types */
main()
{
        printf("\n\tData Type\tSize in bytes\n");
        printf("\n\t=========\t==============\n");
        printf("\n\tshort int\t%Ld", sizeof(short));
        printf("\n\tint\t%Ld", sizeof(int));
        printf("\n\tlong int\t%Ld", sizeof(long));
        printf("\n\tchar\t%Ld", sizeof(char));
        printf("\n\tfloat\t%Ld", sizeof(float));
        printf("\n\tdouble\t%Ld", sizeof(double));
}
```

4. Which of the following are valid assignment statements, and which invalid, and why?
```
a.  2x = 6;
b.  year = 1988;
c.  total + 6 = 8;
d.  elephant = giraffe = monkey = 0;
e.  sum = sum + 4;
```

5. Modify the incrementing program (Program 3.5) by replacing the increm operator (++) by the decrement operator (--). Before running the program try to

work out what the output should be. Once you have done that, run the program and see how the results compare.

6. Write down the output which you would expect from the `printf()` statements below, given the following information.

```
int i, count; float x, y; char c;
i = 10; count = 55; x = 6.8; y=4.5e9; c ='a';
```

a. `printf(" \nThe sum of the %d floats entered is: %f\n",i,6.8);`

b. `printf("count = %d, maximum = %e, i = %d", count, y, i);`

c. `printf("The character %c has the ASCII value ", c);`
`printf("%d \n%d were found in the text\n", c, count);`

7. One of the options of the line editor program discussed in Chapter 1 is a help option which is used to provide information about the various commands available to the user, how to use them and their syntax etc. Design a suitable display based on the list which we developed earlier and then write the code to produce it. (For the moment this can be coded as a program; later on you will be able to modify it so that it becomes a function.) Note that this problem requires that a % symbol is displayed on the screen. There are two ways of doing this: what are they?

8. Modify the conversion program (Program 3.3) to output the area in square miles and hectares, as well as square yards.

9. The owner of a local cycle shop has just bought a microcomputer to help deal with accounting and stocktaking. She is also keen on programming and has been dabbling in C. One problem which she decided was worth tackling is the following.
    The gear ratio of a cycle is defined as the ratio between the number of teeth on the chain wheel to the number on the rear sprocket (i.e. gear_ratio = chain/rear.) Write a program to work out the gear ratio. Use the following values to test your program: chain 34, rear 14, 16 and 18.

10. Extend the above program to work out how far the cycle will travel for each revolution of the pedals - assume a wheel diameter of 27 inches.

11. Write a program to calculate the reciprocal, square and cube of a given integer (in the range 1 to 20). Hint: think about what data types you should use.

12. Write a program to convert a time in seconds to hours minutes and seconds. Produce the output in 24 hour format, e.g. 16:45:20.

4 Selection in C, or 'Which way next?'

"...to be or not to be, that is the question..." William Shakespeare, *Hamlet III i*

4.1 INTRODUCTION

In Chapter 1 we dealt in general terms with the fundamental control structures which are found in any procedural programming language. In this chapter we are going to be concentrating on just one of these control structures, the various ways in which C allows choices to be implemented. The alternatives open to us are perhaps not as daunting as those open to Hamlet, but without the ability to modify the flow of control within a program C programming would be extremely boring and very unproductive! Before looking in detail at the ways in which these structures are implemented we will need to consider the nature of conditional expressions and how logical expressions are used.

4.2 CONDITIONAL EXPRESSIONS

In Chapter 1 we introduced one version of the pseudocode for selection, i.e.

if *condition* **then** *do something*

The operation of the if statement depends on the value of the *condition*, or in terms of C the conditional expression. We also saw in Chapter 3 that all expression have a value. It might therefore be reasonable to assume that any expression could be used to control the selection process. This is in fact the case. Often, however, the value of the conditional expression will be determined by comparing values using relational operators. We will investigate these before examining more complex examples.

> **Any valid C expression ...**
>
> *can be used as the test in a conditional expression*

Relational operators

These operators are used to compare two expressions and they produce the `int` value 1 (TRUE) or 0 (FALSE). (Remember the discussion in the last chapter when we noted that an expression can be a single variable, a constant, or any combination of valid tokens.) The complete list of relational operators is given in Table 4.1.

Table 4.1 *The relational operators*

relational operator	meaning	precedence
==	equal to	Low
>	greater than	High
<	less than	High
>=	greater than or equal to	High
<=	less than or equal to	High
!=	not equal to	Low

The first and last of these operators (== and !=) are often referred to as equality operators, for obvious reasons. These relational operators are all **binary** operators which means that they have two operands. The syntax of a relational expression is therefore:

expression1 relational-operator expression2

Some examples of expressions involving relational operators are:

```
i <= 100
x > max
(x * x - 2x + 4)  != 0
ch != '\n'
```

The first expression will have a value of 1 as long as `i` is less than or equal to 100 but it will take on the value 0 once `i` becomes greater than 100. In the third example the whole expression is evaluated and then compared with the `int` constant 0. In the last example a character is compared with the `'\n'` character to test for the end of a line.

When using the operators consisting of two characters make sure that no spaces are inserted between them. Thus > = and ! = are not relational operators.

The precedence of these operators enables some expressions to be written without parentheses; expressions involving operators with the higher precedence are evaluated first. However such constructs should not be used as they can cause confusion. Again the moral 'use brackets whenever they improve the clarity' is well worth adhering to.

One final point concerning relational operators concerns the accidental substitution of the equality operator (==) by the assignment operator (=). The expression n = 10 is very similar to the expression n == 10, but their effect is totally different. The first sets n equal to 10 whereas the second compares the current value of n with the constant 10 and produces and int result of 1 or 0. It is very easy to make the mistake simply through haste of writing = when == is intended. It is for this reason that some compilers will flag as a warning conditional expressions which have the form of an assignment expression such as the expression (z = 3.5 * x - 5). This is perfectly valid and makes sense. The result of evaluating the expression 3.5 * x - 5 will be assigned to z. If the result is zero then the conditional expression will be FALSE. Any other result will yield a value of TRUE. Although the assignment is intended it might have been the case that we wished to **test** whether a previously assigned value of z was equal to 3.5 * x - 5; if this is the case, we must use the form:

```
if (z == 3.5 * x - 5)
```

Since the arithmetic operators have a higher precedence than the relational operators this is in fact equivalent to:

```
if (z == (3.5 * x - 5))
```

This second form is preferable since it makes it clear that the variable z is being compared with the expression (3.5 * x - 5).

4.3 LOGICAL OPERATORS

In addition to the relational operators which we have been discussing there are a number of **logical operators**. There are three of these operators, ! (NOT), && (AND) and || (OR). They are typically used to test sets of conditions. So, for example, I might base my decision on whether or not to go for a walk on whether there is enough time before tea and whether it is fine. The expression might then take on the form

(time until tea **is greater than** 1 hour) **AND** it is fine

In C we could code this as:

```
int fine;       /* TRUE if fine or FALSE if raining etc. */
float time;     /* in minutes */

if (( time > 60 ) && fine)
        printf("\n You can go for a (short) walk.\n");
```

The NOT operator comes in useful when we want to put on our coat if it is raining. So the expression NOT fine might be coded in C as:

```
if ( ! fine )
        printf("\n You had better put on your raincoat.\n");
```

Finally we might use the logical operator OR when there are alternative conditions to test. So we might want to go for a walk if it is fine or if the rest of the family are watching the television. We would then have

```
if ( fine || tv_being_watched )
        printf("\n Go for a walk to get some peace.\n");
```

The truth value of an expression involving logical operators can be found by means of a truth-table. Such tables list all possible outcomes of the logical function. Table 4.2 below shows the truth-table for the two operators AND and OR for variables x and y. (These variables are arbitrary and are used simply as a means of writing down the expression.)

Table 4.2 *The truth-table for && and || in terms of truth values*

x	y	x && y	x || y
T	T	T	T
F	T	F	T
T	F	F	T
F	F	F	F

Under x the letters T and F are written repeatedly as many times as is necessary. For two variables this means two repetitions, with three it would mean four, and so on. Under the y variable the values are written in pairs. Following this procedure all possible combinations of the two variables x and y will be written down. The columns under the AND and OR operators are then filled in, according to the rules of the appropriate logical operators, to produce the final table.

The truth-table in terms of the integer values of these variables and expressions is given in Table 4.3.

Table 4.3   *The truth-table for && and || for any expression*

x	y	x && y	x || y
non-zero	non-zero	1	1
0	non-zero	0	1
non-zero	0	0	1
0	0	0	0

Notice that each of these operators consists of two identical characters and that there is no space between them (e.g. && is not the same as & &).

One of the examples of the use of these operators involves testing whether a character is a vowel. There are five possibilities and an expression of the form :

```
if (c == 'a' || c == 'e' || c == 'i' || c == 'o' || c == 'u')
```

can be used to test the condition. This is read as

"if c equals 'a' or c equals 'e' ..." etc.

This example illustrates one important fact concerning logical operators. As soon as any vowel is encountered the evaluation of the expression terminates and control passes to the body of the statement. In this case all that this means is that time is not wasted on making further tests. In more general terms, in expressions involving the logical operators && and ||, once the outcome (true or false) of the complete expression is known (tested from left to right), the evaluation process stops and control passes to the appropriate statement.

Suppose we have a test which involves finding the reciprocal of a variable and testing whether this reciprocal is greater than a fixed value. Let the variable be x and suppose we want to continue if 1/x is greater than 0.001. We could use the following expression to perform the test:

```
(x != 0 && 1/x > 0.001)
```

Listing some possible values of x in a modified truth-table (Table 4.4) will help to illustrate how this expression is evaluated.

The most important point to note about this example is that evaluation of the expression (x != 0 && 1/x > 0.001) stops as soon as the first sub-expression becomes FALSE (i.e. when x = 0). This ensures that a runtime error does not occur in an attempt to evaluate 1/0. Whenever you are considering constructing even a very simple logical expression it is well worth taking a few minutes to construct a table similar to the one above, or to Table 4.2, so that it is clear exactly what the expression means and how it is evaluated.

Table 4.4 *Truth-table for the expression* : *(x != 0 && 1/x > 0.001)*

x	A x != 0	1/x	B 1/x>0.001	A && B
10	T	.1	T	T
100	T	.01	T	T
1000	T	.001	F	F
0.0	F	not evaluated	F	F

4.4 THE *IF* STATEMENT

The simplest means of choosing between alternatives in C is to use the if statement. We have mentioned this already in Chapter 1 and we have alluded to it already in this chapter. The syntax is:

```
if (expression)
      statement1
statement2
```

where `expression` is any valid C expression.

The if statement works in the following way:

- `expression` is evaluated and if it is TRUE then `statement1` is executed; control then passes to `statement2` which is then executed.

- if `expression` is FALSE then control passes straight to `statement2` and `statement1` is skipped.

Note that under normal circumstances `statement2` will always be executed. Abnormal circumstances might be when a runtime error occurs during the execution of `statement1` or when `statement1` causes control to be transferred to somewhere else in the program. `statement1` can be any valid C statement and so can consist of a single statement or a compound statement (i.e. any number of statements enclosed in braces {}). Below are some examples of if statements using a single statement for `statement1`.

i) ```
    if (error)
          printf(" Incorrect range given");
    ```

ii) ```
    if (score == 10)
    ```

```
                printf(" Brilliant - well done!\n");

iii)   if (x > max)
            max = x;

iv)    if (c == 'a'||c == 'e'|| c == 'i'|| c == 'o'||c == 'u')
            vcount++;
```

An example using a compound statement is

```
v)    if (c == '\t') {
            tab_count++;
            putchar(SPACE);
      }
```

The examples above use a variety of different expressions as the test condition. In example (i) the value of error is tested to see whether it is TRUE or FALSE (i.e. non-zero or zero). Examples (ii), (iii) and (v) use the relational operators == and > in the conditional expression and example (iv) uses a mixture of both relational and logical operators. The body of the if statement (the single statement in the first four examples or the block consisting of two statements in example (v)) is executed if the corresponding expression is TRUE.

Example - getting the change right

The program given below illustrates a simple use of the if statement. It calculates the change required in a transaction and also a possible combination of coins (and notes) to make up the required change.

Program 4.1

```
/* simple if example */
/* giving change */
/* money.c */

#include <stdio.h>

main()
{
      int five_pound, pound, fifty, twenty, ten,
            five, two, one, pounds, pence, rest;
      float price, money, change;

      printf("\n Enter the price of the goods : ");
      scanf("%f", &price);
```

```c
printf("\n Now enter the money tendered : ");
scanf("%f", &money);
change = money - price;
if( change < 0 ) {
      printf("\n * You haven't given me enough money! *");
      exit(0);
}
/* calculate change */
printf("\n You need %f in change \n", change);
pounds = change;
five_pound = pounds / 5;
pound = pounds % 5;
/* now calculate pence */
pence = 100 * ( change + .005 - pounds);
fifty = pence / 50;
rest = pence % 50;
twenty = rest / 20;
rest = rest % 20;
ten = rest / 10;
rest = rest % 10;
five = rest / 5;
rest = rest % 5;
two = rest / 2;
one = rest % 2;
printf("\n The change can be made up as follows: \n\n");
if( five_pound > 0) {
      printf("\t %d five pound note", five_pound);
      if( five_pound > 1 )
            printf("s");
      printf("\n");
}
if( pound > 0) {
      printf("\t %d pound coin", pound);
      if( pound > 1 )
            printf("s");
      printf("\n");
}
if( fifty > 0)
      printf("\t %d fifty pence coin\n", fifty);

if( twenty > 0) {
      printf("\t %d twenty pence coin", twenty);
      if( twenty > 1 )
            printf("s");
      printf("\n");
}
if( ten > 0)
      printf("\t %d ten pence coin\n", ten);
```

```
    if( five > 0)
        printf("\t %d five pence coin\n", five);

    if( two > 0) {
        printf("\t %d two pence coin", two);
        if( two > 1 )
            printf("s");
        printf("\n");
    }

    if( one > 0)
        printf("\t %d one pence coin\n", one);

    printf("\n Thank you ....\n");
}
```

This program, although rather long, only uses a few simple concepts. We will look at each one in turn. First notice the use of meaningful variable names. This helps considerably with the readability of the program and should help you to understand how the program works. Using names in this fashion provides a certain amount of self-documentation and alleviates the need for comments explaining the purpose of each of the variables.

Next, notice the way the change is calculated. Initially the amount in whole pounds is calculated by simply assigning the `int` variable `pounds` to the `float` variable `change`. Truncation of the floating point number occurs thus providing the correct whole number of pounds. However if we rely on truncation to obtain the amount of `pence` required we run into difficulties. Since the floating point number `change` may not be stored exactly, in order to make sure that the correct arithmetic is carried out we need to add half a pence (.005) onto `change` to obtain the `int` number of `pence`.

The third point to note is the way we have used integer division and the modulus operator to compute the number of coins for each denomination.

Finally we come to the use of the `if` statements! The first one simply prints a message out if we have failed to hand over enough money. The program is then terminated by use of the `exit ()` statement. This function returns the value of its parameter to the calling process (e.g. the system). By convention 0 is used to indicate that the program ran correctly and a non-zero value is used to indicate abnormal program termination. The main use of the `if` statements occurs in the output section. We could produce a very rough and ready output without the use of these statements, but that would result in output of the form:

```
You need 3.570000 in change
```

```
The change can be made up as follows:
```

```
        0 five pound note
        3 pound coins
        1 fifty pence coin
        0 twenty pence coin
        0 ten pence coin
        1 five pence coin
        1 two pence coin
        0 one pence coin
```

```
Thank you ....
```

The majority of the if statements simply test whether the relevant variable is greater than zero and if so print the appropriate message. But notice how we have employed an if statement within another if statement to add an 's' on when necessary. This code can be further simplified by using the keyword else, to which we now turn our attention.

4.5 THE *IF ... ELSE* STATEMENT

If you are at all familiar with programming, you will not be surprised to learn that C provides a means of extending the usefulness of the if statement by means of the keyword else. The syntax of the if ... else statement is:

```
if (expression)
        statement1
else
        statement2
next_statement
```

where, as before, statement1 and statement2 can be single statements or compound statements. This control structure works in a similar manner to the basic if statement. The expression is evaluated and if it is non-zero (i.e. TRUE) then statement1 is executed, otherwise (i.e. if expression is 0, or FALSE) statement2 will be executed. Following the execution of either statement, control passes to next_statement. Thus in the following example the if ... else construct allows us to print out a different message, depending on whether a number is zero or not.

```
if (a != 0)
        printf(" a is positive or negative \n");
else
        printf(" a is zero \n");
printf("The End\n");
```

We can modify our change program using if ... else as follows. When the possibility arises of more than one coin being given we need to cater for adding an 's' to the end of the message e.g.

```
3 pound coins
```

We can achieve this by using a character which can be either the letter s or a space. (Since the extra character will come at the end of the line the space won't affect the appearance of the output.) We can then output this character as part of the main print statement. So we might have, for the pound coin case:

```
if( pound > 0) {
        if( pound > 1 )
                plural = 's';           /* char variable plural */
        else
                plural = ' ';           /* space character */
        printf("\t %d pound coin %c\n", pound, plural);
}
```

Since an if statement is itself a statement it can be used in the body of another if statement as we have seen. A construct of this type produces a form known as a **nested** if statement. However we may not need to use braces if the if statements themselves only contain one statement. Consider the following example in which we have a series of if ... else statements forming the body of the first if statement. The appropriate counter is incremented unless the character read is the EOF character, signifying the End Of File, in which case the message "End of input stream" is displayed.

```
if ((c = getchar()) != EOF)
        if (c == '\n')
                line_count++;
        else if (c == '\t')
                tab_count++;
        else if (c == ' ')
                space_count++;
        else
                other_count++:
else
        printf("End of input stream \n");
```

This whole program fragment is in fact one single statement. There is only one semi-colon and no braces. Now consider the following example:

Program 4.2a

```
if (a != 0)
        if (b == 0)
                printf(" a is non-zero and b is zero\n");
```

```
else
        printf(" a is zero \n");
printf("The End\n");
```

The intention is, and the layout implies, that if a is zero then the message "a is zero" is displayed. If a is positive or negative **and** if b is zero then the message "a is non-zero and b is zero" is displayed, whilst if b is non-zero no message should be displayed. However what actually occurs is that in this last case (both a and b non-zero) the message "a is zero" appears - not what we might have expected or intended! How can we explain this? A close look at the code of Program 4.2a will show that the else is in fact part of the second if statement and not the first as was intended. This brings us to the following rule:

An *else* attaches itself to the nearest *if*

So this example is equivalent to:

Program 4.2b

```
if (a != 0)
        if (b == 0)
                printf(" a is non zero and b is zero\n");
        else
                printf(" a is zero \n");
printf("The End\n");
```

This makes it clear to the reader what the code is doing - even though it is not doing what was intended. How can we rectify the matter, since Program 4.2b although laid out correctly will still not produce the intended result? There are a number of ways to avoid this pitfall, two of which are illustrated below.

Program 4.2c

```
/* first correct version */
if (a != 0) {
        if (b == 0)
                printf(" a is non-zero and b is zero\n");
} else
        printf(" a is zero \n");
printf("The End\n");
```

This piece of code uses braces to force the required association – because of the braces the nearest if to the else is the first one, as required.

Program 4.2d

```
/* second correct version */
/* illustrating the use of the empty statement */
if (a != 0)
        if (b == 0)
                printf(" a is non-zero and b is zero\n");
        else
                ;                       /* an empty statement */
else
        printf(" a is zero \n");
printf("The End\n");
```

In this example we have made use of another else, which will be associated with the inner if, and the empty statement. The empty statement is necessary because the else on its own is a keyword, not a statement. It is normal practice, and good practice, to position the semi-colon as in this example, rather than on the same line as the else. This helps to make it clear that an empty statement is indeed intended. If this statement is reached, because both a and b are non-zero nothing happens but control passes directly to the statement following (i.e. The End is displayed).

4.6 THE *SWITCH* STATEMENT

When the choice between alternatives only amounts to two or three, the if . . . else construct which we have been looking at will probably suffice. However, as the number of alternatives increases, this construct can become very cumbersome. In such cases the switch statement is a useful alternative. The basic syntax has the form:

```
switch (integral_expression) {
case integral_constant_expression1 :
        statement1     /* can be one or more statements */
case integral_constant_expression2 :
        statement2
...
...
...
default :
        default_statement
}
next_statement
```

The integral_expression must evaluate to an integral value – if necessary the usual arithmetic conversions will be carried out. Each *integral_constant_expression,* as the name implies, must consist either of an integer constant, a character constant, or a constant expression. Examples include: 'c', 'Y', 10, 25, EOF (a symbolic constant). Each statement (*statement1, 2* or the *default_statement* in the generalised layout above) can be an empty statement, a single statement, or a compound statement.

The operation of the switch statement proceeds as follows:

- If the integral_expression matches the value of the
  integral_constant_expression in a case then
  control is passed to the statement immediately following that
  case label. If no matches occur and a default case label is present
  then control passes to that statement. If no matches are found and
  no default case label is present then control passes to
  next_statement.

- Once a case matches, and the following statement has been
  executed then control passes to the next case statement in the
  list (i.e. the one immediately following). This process is known
  as 'falling through' and unless care is taken it can produce
  unwanted side-effects (see the discussion below).

Consider the task of identifying 'white spaces' in a stream of data and keeping count of the number found and the total of other characters in the data. A switch statement which would accomplish this task is:

```
switch (c) {
case '\n' :
case '\t' :
case ' ' :
        ws_count++;
        break;
default:
        other_count++;
        break;
}
next_statement
```

If the character c is either a newline, a tab, or a space, the two statements ws_count++; and break; are executed. The break keyword causes control to be passed to the statement following the switch() statement, i.e. next_statement. If the break; statement happened to be missing then the variable other_count would also be incremented. Thus control would 'fall through' from one case statement to the next. 'Falling through' can be useful when a number of alternatives require the same action to be taken - as in this example when we want ws_count to be incremented whenever a 'white_space' is encountered. However 'falling through' can sometimes be disastrous so be sure to use break when necessary to prevent this happening.

Note that, strictly speaking, the last break; statement is not necessary as control will fall through to next_statement after other_count has been incremented. However if you adopt this convention then if further case statements are added the presence of this break will prevent the unintended execution of the new statements. As an illustration, suppose we wish to add to the above a case statement which will enable a count to be made of the number of occurrences of the % character and that other_count will be used to count any other character not already counted. We then have:

```
switch (c) {
        case '\n' :
        case '\t' :
        case ' ' :
                ws_count++;
                break;                  /* break #1 */
        default:
                other_count++;
                break;                  /* break #2 */
        case '%' :
                p_count++;
                break;                  /* break #3 */
}
next_statement
```

Without the presence of break #2 the variable p_count would be incremented whenever the character read is anything other than a 'white space' and not just when the % character is read.

Example – the line editor

In the line editor program we require a function to check whether a valid command has been entered. The function returns TRUE (1) if the command syntax is correct and FALSE (0) if the command is invalid. The inputs to the function are the command (a single character) and two integers (n1 and n2) specifying the range of lines to edit. If the command is to insert then n1 should be equal to n2. Other checks are simply to see that a valid character has been supplied (i.e. one of a, d, h, p, q, r, s). One way of writing this function involves the use of an if ... else statement and a number of OR operators (i.e. | |) as used in Appendix B (Program B.4 p. 278). It takes the form:

```
/* function check_command()
** this function simply checks for valid commands
```

```
** and returns TRUE if the syntax is valid, FALSE otherwise
*/
int check_command(char cm, int n1, int n2)
{
    int valid = FALSE;

    if(cm == 'i' && n2 == n1) valid = TRUE;
    else if( cm == 'a' || cm == 'd' || cm == 'h' || cm == 'p'
    || cm == 'q' || cm == 'r' || cm == 's')
        valid = TRUE;
    return(valid);
}
```

An alternative way of coding this is to use a switch statement, as follows.

Program 4.3

```
int check_command(char cm, int n1, int n2)
{
    int valid = FALSE;
    switch (cm) {
        case 'i':                          /* insert text   */
            if (n2 == n1)
                valid = TRUE;
            break;
        case 'a':                          /* append text   */
        case 'd':                          /* delete text   */
        case 'h':                          /*     help       */
        case 'p':                          /* print text    */
        case 'q':                          /*     quit       */
        case 'r':                          /* read from file*/
        case 's':                          /* save text     */
            valid = TRUE;
    }
return(valid);   /* value of valid (int) passed back to main() */
}
```

Here we have used the 'fall through' facility to allow each of the valid options to set valid to zero at one point rather than repeating the assignment statement for each case.

This function uses arguments in its parameter list (cm, n1 and n2) and returns an integer value which is then used in main() to control subsequent program action. Although we haven't formally discussed these details you will at least be familiar with the former through the use of printf() and scanf() and we mentioned the latter in Chapter 2. We will be dealing with functions in more detail in Chapter 6.

Another part of the line editor program is the one used to process the chosen option. This function can easily be developed at this point. Recall that the process function is required to transfer control in order that different processes can be performed (Table 1.2). The options are: append, delete, help, insert, print, quit, read and save. Assuming that the character variable com holds the relevant character, the pseudocode becomes:

> **if** com is equal to 'a' **then** append to existing text
> **else if** com is equal to 'd' **then** delete text
> **else if** com is equal to 'h' **then** display help screen
> **else if** com is equal to 'i' **then** insert text
> **else if** com is equal to 'p' **then** print text
> **else if** com is equal to 'q' **then** quit
> **else if** com is equal to 'r' **then** read text from file
> **else if** com is equal to 's' **then** save text.

This algorithm can be implemented very easily using the if ... else construct or alternatively by using the switch statement. The exact nature of the actions taken once a condition is satisfied are not specified at present. However we can leave the details until such time as we are able to code the functions or program fragments. (See Appendix B for the complete function.)

SUMMARY

In this chapter we:

> • investigated ways in which the control structures involving selection were implemented in C.

> • examined the form of conditional expressions.

> • used the relational operators ==, <=, >=, <, > and !.

> • were introduced to the logical operators !, && and ||.

> • were introduced to the syntax of simple if statements, if ... else statements and nested if statements.

> • saw how the switch statement is used.

> • examined the use of the break statement.

EXERCISES

1. Construct a truth-table for the following logical expressions:

      a.   !a && !b || c.

      b.   a && ok || (b && !last).

      c.   b || !c || d || (e && !EOF).

2. A line editor program uses a function to check that a valid range of line numbers has been entered in the edit command. Two line numbers are required (n1 and n2) which may be in the range 1 to last, where last is the last line number of the current text; n1 must be less than or equal to n2. There are a number of ways of coding this. Write down a version using a single if statement and one using switch.

3. Write a program to take as input a character which should be either a, s, m, or d, followed by two integers and perform the appropriate arithmetic calculation (i.e. add, subtract, multiply and divide).

4. Write a program to determine whether three numbers entered from the keyboard make up a triangle. For any three numbers a, b and c a triangle will be formed provided that a + b > c and a + c > b and b + c > a. If they do form a triangle then determine what kind: i.e. scalene, obtuse, acute, isosceles, equilateral, right-angled. Note that these are not all mutually exclusive. The lengths of the sides of the triangle, together with the type of triangle should be displayed.

5. Write a program to convert a year given as a four-digit integer to its equivalent in roman numerals. You will need to use integer division and the modulo operator as well as various selection control structures.

6. In the bridge program we require to count the number of points in a hand. These points are allocated as follows:

      each Ace counts 4 points,
      each King counts 3 points,
      each Queen counts 2 points,
      each Jack counts 1 point.

Other cards do not contribute to the point count. In addition extra points are allocated depending on the distribution (i.e. the number of cards held in each suit). These extra points are added as follows: if a suit has more than four cards then 1 point for cards five and six, 2 points for the seventh and subsequent cards.

For example, a hand consisting of:

♠ 2 J   ♥ A K 6   ♦ A K J 10 9 5 2   ♣ 4

would gain a total of 20 points.

Write an algorithm which will calculate the total number of points held in a hand of thirteen cards.

7. One system of bidding in bridge lists the point count requirements for various opening bids. The table is given below. By using `switch` and/or `if / if ... else` statements write a program fragment to simulate this table and print the appropriate bid. For the purposes of this exercise you do not need to know the definitions of the various terms involved. Allocate variable names for terms such as balanced hand, powerful distribution (these are mutually exclusive), vulnerable etc. and test their values to select the appropriate action. Base your program on opening bids up as far as two in a suit, ignore the three and four bids.

POINTS NEEDED FOR AN OPENING BID

Opening Bid	Qualifications
One No trump	15 to 17 points, balanced hand
One in a suit	13 to 20 points
Two No Trumps	20 to 22 points, balanced hand
Two Clubs	23 points up, balanced hand, or 21 points up, powerful distribution
Two Diamonds, Two Hearts, Two Spades	18 to 22 points, at least eight playing tricks
Three No Trumps	Solid suit of Clubs or Diamonds, little else
Three in a suit	Seven playing tricks if vulnerable, six if not vulnerable, less than 13 points
Four in a suit	Eight playing tricks if vulnerable, seven if not vulnerable, less than 13 points

From: *How to play a good game of Bridge*, by
Terence Reese & Albert Dormer, Pan Books, 1971

5 Doing it again and again!

" 'You are old, Father William,' the young man said,
    'And your hair has become very white;
And yet you incessantly stand on your head -
    Do you think, at your age, it is right?'

'In my youth,' Father William replied to his son,
    'I feared it might injure the brain;
But now that I'm perfectly sure I have none,
    Why, I do it again and again.' "

Lewis Carroll

5.1 INTRODUCTION

We continue our investigation of control structures by examining the implementation of repetition in C. There are three statements which can be used to perform tasks repeatedly, namely while, do ... while (sometimes just referred to as do) and for. In general all of these constructs require the initialisation of a variable, its modification within the statement and a test condition which will allow for exit from the loop. Although all three constructs have many similarities, there are important differences between them which will obviously affect the way they are used. In many cases when deciding on the choice of loop there may seem to be little to choose between them. However on other occasions one version will be more appropriate than the others. For this reason it is important that you are clear about the differences as well as the similarities which exist between them. This chapter covers the last of the major control structures in C so that once you have worked through this chapter you should have enough knowledge of the language to tackle more substantial programming tasks.

5.2 THE *WHILE* LOOP

The while statement has the following syntax:

$$\text{while } (\textit{expression })$$
$$\textit{statement}$$

Some examples include:

```
time = 0;                          /*  (i)  */
while( time < limit )
        time++;

while((c = getchar()) != EOF)      /*  (ii)  */
        putchar(c);


i = -100;                          /*  (iii)  */
while(i <= 0){
        printf("%d\n", i);
        i += 10;
}

scanf("%lf", &n);                  /*  (iv)  */
while(n > 0){
        printf("The square root of %lf = %lf\n",n, sqrt(n));
        scanf("%lf", &n);
}
/* note in this example the sqrt() function requires, and
returns, a double so n needs to be declared as a double and
%lf is needed in scanf() and printf() */

                                   /*  (v)  */
while((c=getchar()) != EOF && c != '\n')
                char_count++;
```

Notice that in all of the above examples the expression part of the `while` statement consists of a relational or logical expression – i.e. an expression which tests a condition the result of which determines whether or not the body of the loop is to be executed. If the test proves TRUE then the statement (perhaps a compound statement) in the body of the `while` loop is executed and control passes again to the expression, which is tested once more and the whole process is repeated. In some cases (e.g. (ii) and (v)) the test incorporates a modification to the variable being tested – in these examples a character is read from the input device by means of the `getchar()` function. In the other examples the variable tested is modified in the body of the `while` loop (by `time++;`, `i += 10;` and `scanf("%f", &number);` respectively).

The `while` statement performs the test at the beginning of the loop, which in turn means that the statements in the body of the loop may not be executed at all.

In general it is important, in order that the loop may terminate, that it is possible during the execution of the loop for the expression being evaluated to become FALSE (but see below for an exception). Thus in example (iii) above if the value of i were to be decreased by ten each time (i.e. i -= 10), then the condition i < 0 would always be TRUE and as a consequence the loop would never terminate - we would have an infinite loop. Exit from the loop could still be achieved, but this would require the use of another statement employing the keyword break. At times this can be useful (for an example see below) but obviously in this particular example there would be something wrong with the logic of the algorithm and so it would be more appropriate to correct the algorithm rather than add an *ad hoc* line of code to correct the mistake.

Whilst it is generally the case that a while loop contains a statement, or statements, that perform a certain task it is sometimes useful to write a while statement which **appears** to do nothing. Consider the following construct:

```
while( (c = getchar()) == ' ')
        ;                       /* do nothing */
```

All the work done by this statement is performed by the *expression* part of while - the body itself 'does nothing' and to an uninitiated observer this might appear as a useless statement. The expression c = getchar() reads a character from the standard input device; this character is then compared with the character ' ' and the loop continues while spaces are read in. Notice that we could also lay out this particular loop as:

```
while( (c = getchar()) == ' ');     /* do nothing */
```

but this is more confusing than the former version. Whenever a null or empty statement is used it is much better to make it obvious that this is indeed intended by placing the semi-colon on a separate line.

Before leaving the while statement it is worth comparing it with the if statement which we looked at in the last chapter. Both have a similar form, i.e.

```
if(expression)                  while(expression)
        statement1                      statement1
next_statement                  next_statement
```

where *statement1* can be a single or a compound statement and is executed if *expression* is TRUE. The difference, however, lies in the fact that *statement1* is only executed once in an if statement, whereas, as we have seen, the body of the while loop may be executed repeatedly.

Example – counting vowels

As a means of illustrating the use of a `while` loop in a more substantial problem we will consider the task of reading in a piece of text from the keyboard and keeping a count of the number of vowels of each type. This basic algorithm, as well as much of the code, can be used as a basis for a more complex program which might be used in a number of different ways. For example, with only a slight modification, we can arrange for the text to be read from a file instead of from the keyboard – which would obviously make the program more useful. Again, with only a slight adaptation, we could change the program so that the number of words in the text is counted. We will look at these options later on, but for the moment let us concentrate on the basic vowel count algorithm.

With just the very brief outline given above we can write down the essential elements of the algorithm.

```
        declarations
        set vowel counters to zero
        read character
        while character not End-Of-File do
                if character is 'a' then increment a_count
                if character is 'e' then increment e_count
                if character is 'i' then increment i_count
                if character is 'o' then increment o_count
                if character is 'u' then increment u_count
                read next character
        end_while
        print a_count, e_count, i_count, o_count, u_count
```

Before we start coding let's decide upon the layout for the summary. This is not a very difficult task, but it is worth thinking about the output before coding, especially in the case of more complex programs. One layout might be:

```
                      COUNT OF VOWELS FOUND

                      a       e       i       o       u
        number found: 12      23      10      8       0
```

There are many other possibilities, and you might like to modify the program to suit your aesthetic tastes later on!

The next task is to decide on what variables are required; we need one to represent the value of the character read (say ch) and then a counter for each vowel. We have called them a_count, e_count etc. in the algorithm; these seem to be reasonable names, so we will stick with them.

The algorithm we have at present can be further improved by considering the nature of the problem again. Notice that each **if** statement is mutually exclusive. If we have encountered an 'a' then we test for any other vowel until a new character is read. Consequently the **if** statements (apart from the last one) can be replaced by **if ... else** statements. This will speed up the program slightly although you will not be able to see the difference. However it is important that you use the **if ... else** construct in cases like this as it also improves clarity.

There is one further point we need to address before starting to code the algorithm and that concerns how we tell when the stream of characters has been terminated. With a file the EOF marker will be used (typically ' \n ' followed by a CTRL D, but this is system-dependent); with the keyboard this will not be the case. Various solutions can be found, but let us suppose that the presence of two successive newline characters signifies the end of the input stream. This presents us with another problem - the program needs to 'remember' the previous character read - so we need to introduce another variable (say last_ch). Two conditions therefore have to be met before we exit from the while loop, both ch and last_ch must be newline characters. How can we set up a conditional expression to achieve this control? One approach is to use a flag which is set to FALSE when these conditions are both met. This involves the use of an if statement to test the values of ch and last_ch. We can now write a refinement of our original algorithm.

```
vowel count algorithm

declarations
        integer a_count, e_count, i_count, o_count, u_count, more
        character ch, last_ch
set vowel counters to zero
set more to TRUE
read character
while more do
        if character is 'a' then increment a_count
        else if character is 'e' then increment e_count
        else if character is 'i' then increment i_count
        else if character is 'o' then increment o_count
        else if character is 'u' then increment u_count
        set last_ch to ch
        read next character
        if last_ch is newline AND ch is newline then
                set more to FALSE
end_while
print heading lines
print a_count, e_count, i_count, o_count, u_count
```

This algorithm enables us to write the complete program (Program 5.1).

Program 5.1

```
/* vowel count program */
/* vcount.c   */

#include <stdio.h>
#define TRUE 1
#define FALSE 0

main()
{
     char ch, last_ch, more = TRUE;
     int    a_count=0, e_count=0, i_count=0, o_count=0,
            u_count=0; /* declare and initialise counters */

     printf("\n Please enter text (as much as you like).\n");
     printf(" Indicate the end with two successive Returns\n");
     ch = getchar();        /* get the first character */
     while ( more ){
             if (ch == 'a')
                     a_count++;
             else if (ch == 'e')
                     e_count++;
             else if (ch == 'i')
                     i_count++;
             else if (ch == 'o')
                     o_count++;
             else if (ch == 'u')
                     u_count++;
             last_ch = ch;
             ch = getchar();
             if( ch == '\n' && last_ch == '\n' )
                     more = FALSE;
                     \* set more to FALSE if no more text */
     }
     /* now output the results */
     printf("\n The VOWEL COUNT PROGRAM\n");
     printf("\n\t\ta\te\ti\to\tu\n");
     printf("number found:\t");
     printf("%d\t%d\t%d\t%d\t%d\n",
             a_count,e_count,i_count,o_count,u_count);
}
```

Notice that the program does not follow the algorithm exactly. We have initialised the vowel count variables to zero and the flag (more) to TRUE at the same time as declaring them. We have also added a few more print statements.

A comment on `break`

We mentioned at the beginnning of this section that the keyword `break` could be used with the `while` statement. (In fact it can be used with any of the looping control structures.) Its function is the same as when used within a switch statement. Once it is encountered control passes to the next statement outside the enclosing looping statement. Its main use is to allow exit from the loop from a point in the middle of the loop. Consider the following program fragment.

```
while( (c = getchar())!= '\n') {
    ...
    if( count >= 1000 )
            break;
    ...
}
```

Exit from the while loop can be achieved in two ways. Either a newline character is read or the variable count exceeds 1000.

On many occasions it is possible to replace the use of `break` with a slightly more complex conditional expression. So it might be possible to use a conditional expression of the form

```
(c = getchar())!= '\n') && ( count < 1000 )
```

However this would depend upon the logic of the program.

5.3 THE *DO ... WHILE* LOOP

We noted above that it is possible for the body of a while statement not to be executed. This is because the condition is tested on entry to the `while` loop, and if it is found FALSE then control passes directly to the statement following the body of the `while` loop. However there are a few occasions when it is necessary for the statements in the body to be executed at least once. For such cases the do `...` `while` is the obvious choice. This loop, which is often just called a do loop, has the form:

```
        do
                statement
        while (expression);
```

which means that the loop (i.e. *statement* and *expression*) is executed at least once - because the test is not carried out until the end of the body of the loop.

In Chapter 1 we wrote out an algorithm which, as part of a menu driven program, was intended to display a list of options on the screen from which to choose (the main_menu function). One of these options was the quit option and this provides us with a ready example of the use of the do statement. Consider the logic of the algorithm; the menu must be displayed until the quit option is chosen, in which case the program terminates. The algorithm takes the form:

> **do**
>> **execute** main_menu()
>> **read** option
>> **if** option is '1' **then execute** shuffle()
>> **else if** option is '2' **then execute** deal()
>> **else if** option is '3' **then execute** display()
>> **else if** option is '4' **then execute** count()
>> **else if** option is '5' **then execute** bid()
>> **else if** option is '6' **then execute** play()
> **while** option not equal to 'Q'

This form ensures that the menu will be displayed on the screen until the Quit option is selected. (We have introduced one further pseudocode keyword, i.e. **execute**. This is used to indicate that a function (or an as yet ill-defined series of statements) is to be carried out.)

This particular control structure can be very useful for specific tasks. At other times the while construct is more appropriate. It is a good rule to use whichever most naturally expresses the problem concerned. One instance where you should not employ the do loop is illustrated by example (iv) in the previous section. Here there are two uses of scanf(): one prior to entry into the while loop, and one in the body of the loop. At first sight it might appear that this structure could be replaced by the following using do ... while:

```
/* illustrating when not to replace a while loop */
/* by a do ... while loop */
do {
    scanf("%f", &n);
    printf("The square root of %f = %f\n", n, sqrt(n));
} while(n > 0);
```

A close examination of this piece of code should reveal the error which has been made. We now only use the scanf() function once, which is one step forward, but because the test is carried out on exit from the do loop it is possible that a negative number may be entered and an attempt made to find the square root - at least two steps back! We repeat the correct version for comparison.

```
/* finding the square root - correct method */
scanf("%f", &n);
```

```
while(n > 0){
        printf("The square root of %f = %f\n",n, sqrt(n));
        scanf("%f", &n);
}
```

The layout of do ... while

One final point worth making before we leave this control structure concerns the form of the body of the loop. Even when the body consists of only a single statement it is considered good programming practice to enclose it within braces. This prevents the `while` keyword at the end of the loop being confused with a simple `while` statement. Thus

```
do c = getchar(); while (c == ' ');
```

whilst being a perfectly valid C statement, is much better written as:

```
do {
        c = getchar();
} while (c == ' ');
```

5.4 THE *FOR* LOOP

The final method used to perform repetitive tasks in C is the `for` statement. Consider example (iii) of section 5.2 in which a variable (i) is initialised to -100 (i = -100), modified (i += 10), and compared (i <= 0). These three operations of initialisation, modification and comparison are crucial to the correct operation of this and many other similar loops, but they are distributed over three lines of the program. It would be much neater and clearer for these operations to be collected together in one place. The `for` loop enables us to achieve this, so we can rewrite the `while` loop of this example as:

```
for( i = -100; i <= 0; i += 10)
        printf("%d\n", i);
```

The loop behaves in exactly the same way as the `while` loop in the original example, but it has the advantages that it is both more compact and easier to interpret.

The syntax of a `for` statement is:

```
for( expression1 ; expression2 ; expression3 )
                statement
next_statement
```

and its structure is given in Figure 5.1.

Fig 5.1   *The structure of a for loop*

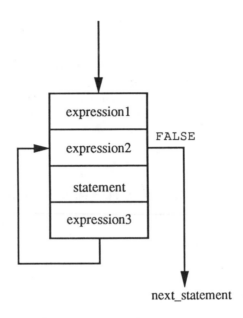

next_statement

The various expressions have the following, general, meanings:

- *expression1*   is an initialising expression
- it is used to set a variable (or variables) on entry to the for statement.

- *expression2*   is a conditional expression

- a variable is evaluated at the beginning of each time round the loop.
  This must produce a TRUE/FALSE result. So long as the condition
  results in the truth-value TRUE the body of the loop will be executed.
  Once the truth-value becomes FALSE execution of the loop stops and
  control passes to *next_statement*.

- *expression3* is an expression which is evaluated at the end of each
  time round the loop

- this is typically used to modify a variable being tested in
  expression2.

- *statement* can be a single statement or a compound statement.

In the remainder of this section we will be examining the `for` loop in some detail. Once you have worked through this material and the exercises at the end you should be familiar with a rich variety of uses for this particular control structure and you will have discovered that it is much more versatile than the standard `for` loop in many other programming languages.

If you are conversant with other languages (e.g. Pascal or BASIC) then the essential idea of a `for` loop will already be familiar to you. You will be aware, for instance, that such loops are often used to perform a predetermined number of iterations, or repetitions, of one or more statements. So, for example, we might wish to produce a table of squares and cubes of whole numbers from 1 to 20 in steps of 1. This could be achieved by the program fragment:

```
for( num = 1;   num <= 20; num++)
        printf("%4d%10d%10d\n", num, num*num, num*num*num);
```

The variable `num` is first initialised to 1, this value is then tested for being less than or equal to the constant 20 and, this expression being TRUE, the number itself, its square and cube are displayed. The value of `num` is now incremented (num++) and the test applied again. This process continues until `num` reaches the value 21, at which point the second expression (num <= 20) becomes FALSE and so the `for` loop is exited.

This, perhaps rather obvious, structure can be extended to give even more flexibility. We will examine a few possibilities. Take a look at the diagrammatic representation in Figure 5.1. The structure of a `for` loop does not in fact dictate what type expressions 1, 2 and 3 should be. All that is specified is when these expressions are evaluated. The diagram helps to make this point clearer - the `for` loop continues execution and thus the repetition of *statement* continues until *expression2* is FALSE. Note that *expression3* can be any valid expression, although most usually it will be used to update a control variable. Since there are no restrictions on what this expression can be we have at our fingertips a wide variety of ways of modifying the control variable. Some examples are given below using the various arithmetic assignment operators introduced in Chapter 3:

• The variable can be increased/decreased in an arithmetic progression, e.g.

`num++`	`num--`	increase/decrease `num` by 1 at the end of each pass
`i = i + 5`	`i -= 5`	add/subtract 5 to/from `i` at the end of each pass
`k = k + 12`	`k += 12`	add/subtract 12 to/from `k` at the end of each pass

• The variable can be increased/decreased in a geometric series, e.g.

```
n *= 2                          n /= 2   n is multiplied/divided by 2
                                         at the end of each pass
```

• The variable can be modified by another variable, e.g.

```
n += delta               n -= delta   delta  is added
                                       to/subtracted from n at the
                                       end of each pass
k *= epsilon          k /= epsilon   k  is multiplied/divided by
                                       epsilon  at the end of
                                       each pass
```

It will not have escaped your notice that *expression2* will require some modification if the control variable is being reduced rather than increased (i.e. by means of subtraction or division). Thus to produce a loop which starts with i equal to 100 and steps down by 5 while i remains positive we might have the following for expression:

```
for( i = 100; i >= 0; i = i - 5)
         . . . . . . . . . . . . . . . . ;
```

More about for

In the basic structure of the for loop, any of the expressions within the first set of parentheses can be omitted; the modification of the test variable can be performed within the body of the loop; the variables can be initialised outside the loop, or can be non-existent.

The case of the missing expressions!

In the following example all three expressions are missing from within the brackets:

```
for (;;)
          statement
next_statement
```

You may be asking what this achieves. The statement within the body of the loop will be executed continually; since there is no test expression (*expression2* in the basic form) the test is always considered TRUE and thus there is no means of exiting from the loop. When would such a construct be used? If we wanted to read a character from the keyboard repeatedly, this could be achieved by this type of loop, for example:

```
for (;;) {
        c = getchar();
        putchar(c);
        char_count++;
}
```

Note that a `while` loop could also be set up to perform the same function. An equivalent version to the above, but using `while`, is:

```
while (1) {
        c = getchar();
        putchar(c);
        char_count++;
}
```

Since the constant 1 represents the truth-value TRUE this loop will execute until the program is terminated (e.g. by a run-time error, or by the power being switched off). Although these two examples of control structures are logically correct they should be used with caution as they both give rise to an infinite loop. They are most often used when testing a piece of code and an unknown number of repetitions are required or possibly in conjunction with `break`.

As we mentioned above, a number of other possibilities exist but apart from the one we have just looked at they are considered poor style. Generally an alternative construct using `while` can be substituted for the modified `for` loop. However if any of these forms are used then no matter which expression is missing, the two semi-colons must always be present. This is obvious if you think about it, as the semi-colons are the only means of telling which expression is which if any are missing.

5.5 THE COMMA OPERATOR

The last main topic in this chapter concerns a new operator. The comma operator serves a special function and can be particularly useful in conjunction with the `for` statement. Consider the task of finding the sum of whole numbers and the sum of their squares in the range 1 to 20. This could be achieved as follows:

```
sum = 0;
s_sum = 0;
printf("\n\t i\t sum \t sum of squares");
for (i = 1; i <= 20; i++){
        sum += i;
        s_sum += i*i;
}
```

The comma operator allows a number of variables to be initialised in one expression. Thus we can rewrite the above program fragment as:

```
printf("\n\t i\t sum \t sum of squares");
for (sum = 0, s_sum = 0, i = 1; i <= 20; i++){
    sum += i;
    s_sum += i*i;
}
```

This version, making use of the comma operator, keeps the initialising of the three variables, `sum`, `s_sum` and `i` together in one place in the `for` statement and makes it clear that these variables belong in the same section of code.

One further aspect of the comma operator is illustrated by the program below which represents two attempts at calculating the first five terms of the series defined by the equation

$$x_i = x_{i-1} + y_i , \quad i = 1, 2, \ldots. 10$$
$$y_i = y_{i-1} + 1$$
$$\text{where } x_0 = 10, \quad y_0 = -1,$$

which has 10, 11, 13, 16, 20 as its first few terms.

Program 5.2

```
/* an illustration of the comma operator */
/* calculating a series */

#include <stdio.h>
main()
{
    int x, y;

    /* attempt #1 */
    printf("\nThe series x = x + y, y = y + 1 \n");
    printf("\nWith expression 3 : x += y, y++ \n");
    for (y = 0, x = 10; y < 5; x += y, y++ )
        printf(" y = %d : x = %d \n", y, x);

    /* attempt #2 */
    printf("The series x = x + y, y = y + 1 \n");
    printf("\nWith expression 3 replaced by : y++, x += y \n");
    for (y = 0, x = 10; y < 5;  y++, x += y )
        printf(" y = %d : x = %d \n", y, x);

}
```

These two attempts illustrate the care which must be taken when comma operators are used. The only difference between them concerns the order of the two terms making up *expression3* of the `for` loop. This expression contains two sub-expressions, one of which depends on the other. Thus the effect of

$$(y++, \quad x \mathrel{+=} y)$$

is different from that of

$$(x \mathrel{+=} y, \quad y++)$$

The evaluation of an expression containing a comma operator is from right to left and so in the first example, y is incremented at the end of the loop after which it is added to the current value of x, whereas in the second example the current value of y is added to x, following which y is incremented. The output from the program, given below, illustrates these differences.

```
The series x = x + y, y = y + 1

With expression 3 : x += y, y++
y = 0 : x = 10
y = 1 : x = 10
y = 2 : x = 11
y = 3 : x = 13
y = 4 : x = 16


The series x = x + y, y = y + 1

With expression 3 replaced by : y++, x += y
y = 0 : x = 10
y = 1 : x = 11
y = 2 : x = 13
y = 3 : x = 16
y = 4 : x = 20
```

Notice that we could have changed the order of the sub-expressions in the expression1 (y++ and x = 10) without affecting the calculations, the reason being that x is initialised to a constant (i.e. 10) and so the value of y has no effect on x in this expression.

The comma operator should not be confused with the comma separator which is used for example to distinguish between function arguments. Thus the comma in the expression `sum(a, b)` which refers to the function `sum` which requires two arguments is a separator. However in the expression `sum((a, b), c)` the first comma is a comma operator and the second is a separator. Since the comma operator ensures evaluation from left to right this expression is equivalent to `sum( a, c)`.

5.6 EXAMPLE - PRIME NUMBERS

In order to illustrate a simple application of some of the topics we have covered so far in this chapter we will consider the problem of determining whether a whole number is a prime. (A prime number is a number which only has integer factors of 1 and itself). One way of solving this problem is by repeated division of the number by all numbers from 2 up to and including itself. This is a rather 'brute force' method but it serves as a useful illustration. We can use the modulo operator to test for any remainder; if a remainder of zero is found then the number is not a prime. This test will also tell us what numbers are factors and so we can 'kill two birds with one stone' and print out a list of these as well. A flag will also be required in order to keep track of whether or not the number is a prime so that we can print out a suitable message. One possible algorithm is:

```
Prime number algorithm
declarations
          long integer i, n
          integer prime
print user prompt
read in n
while n is greater than zero do
          set prime to TRUE
          set i to 2
          while i is less than n do
                    if n is divisible by i then
                              set prime to FALSE
                              print i
                    set i to i plus 1
          end_while
          if prime
                    print "n is a prime"
          print user prompt
          read in n
end_while
```

We have made one addition to the algorithm which we outlined above in that we have an outer `while` loop so that we can continue running the program for different values of n. We exit the loop, and the program, by entering a negative number. This algorithm is very easily coded in C now that we have this level of detail. Notice that we have used a `while` loop in the algorithm for the bulk processing. This is perhaps better converted to a `for` loop as indeed we have done in the program (Program 5.3 below).

One of the problems with this program is the time it takes as n gets large - well, I did say it was a brute force program.

Program 5.3

```
/* simple brute force prime program */
/* note the time it takes for large n !!! */
/* e.g. try n = 477777 (which is not a prime) */

#include <stdio.h>

#define FALSE 0
#define TRUE 1

main()
{
        long int i, n;
        int prime; /* used to flag whether or not n is a prime */

        printf("\n A BRUTE FORCE PRIME PROGRAM\n\n");
        printf("\n Enter a positive integer (0 to terminate) : ");
        scanf("%ld", &n);      /* read in a long int */
        while( n > 0 ) {
                prime = TRUE;
                for( i = 2; i < n; i++)  /* try all integers < n */
                        if( n % i == 0) {
                                prime = FALSE;
                                printf("%Ld", i);
                        }
                if( prime )
                        printf("\n %Ld is a prime\n", n);
        printf("\n Enter a positive integer (0 to terminate) : ");
                scanf("%ld", &n);
        }
}
```

Notice the use of symbolic constants (TRUE and FALSE). This helps to make the logic of the program clearer. Notice also the conversion specification for reading and writing long integers.

5.7 ARRAYS - A QUICK LOOK

We will be covering the detailed analysis of arrays and their use in programs and functions in Chapter 8. However arrays fall naturally into a discussion of repetition and it is appropriate to mention them briefly at this stage.

Strictly speaking an array is a data structure which associates an index with a value. It is generally implemented as a block of storage in which data elements of one particular type are stored in consecutive locations in memory. Each of these elements can then be accessed by means of an index. In C the index begins from zero. Thus a simple integer array might be declared as:

```
int a[100];
```

which would declare an array of type `int` capable of holding 100 integers and indexed from 0 to 99.

Example

We can use arrays to make an improvement to the prime program we have just been looking at. One method of computing primes is known as the Sieve of Eratosthenes. This method allows us to compute all primes up to a given integer. It is based on the observation that all numbers which are multiples of n will also be divisible by n and therefore cannot be primes. If we cross out all these multiples, as we progress through the integers only primes will be left. Let's write down the first twenty integers and see how this process works.

1 2 3 4 5 6 7 8 9 10 11 12 13 14 15 16 17 18 19 20

We can ignore 1 so we begin with 2. All integers divisible by 2 cannot be primes. Therefore we can remove them. That gives us:

1 3 5 7 9 11 13 15 17 19

We now move on to 3 and remove all its multiples, giving:

1 2 3 5 7 11 13 17 19

For the numbers up to twenty we have found all the primes. This process would be continued and each time we only need divide by existing prime numbers. An algorithm for this task could be:

```
Sieve of Eratosthenes for primes
declarations
        integer i, j
        short integer array a[1000]
set all elements of a equal to 1
set i equal to 2
while i is less than 1000 do
        print i
        set j equal to i
        while j plus i is less than 1000 do set a[j] equal to zero
        set i equal to i plus 1
        while i less than 1000 and a[i] is zero do nothing
end_while
```

Thus we begin with an array filled with 1s (any other number or character would do). The index of the array is then used to indicate the numbers we are testing. Thus element 2 represents integer 2, element 3 the integer 3 and so on.

The program below provides our final solution.

Program 5.4

```
/* Sieve of Eratosthenes prime program */

#include <stdio.h>

#define SIZE 1000
main()
{
    long int i, j;
    short a[SIZE];  /* short is sufficient as we are only */
                    /* storing the integers 0 and 1 */

    printf("\n *** Sieve of Eratosthenes for primes ***\n\n");
    /* fill array with 1's */
    for( i = 0; i < SIZE; i++)
            a[i] = 1;
    /* 1s will represent primes, 0s not primes */
    printf("All primes less than %d : \n", SIZE);
    i = 2;
    while( i < SIZE ) {
            printf("%d ", i);      /* prime */
            j = i;
            while(( j += i) < SIZE)
                    a[j] = 0;
            while(++i < SIZE && a[i] == 0)
                    ;          /* skip to next prime */
    }
}
```

SUMMARY

In this chapter we:

- examined the ways in which looping is implemented in C by use of the while, do and for statements.

- saw that the body of a while statement might not be executed whereas the syntax of the do statement guarantees that the statements in its body will be executed at least once.

- examined the `for` statement in detail and investigated some of its versatility.

- saw that a `for` statement must include both semi-colon separators even if one or more of its expressions is missing.

- found that the comma operator can be useful in `for` statements, but noted that care has to be taken in the ordering of expressions which use this operator.

- noted how simple integer arrays are declared and used.

EXERCISES

1. For each of the examples above ((i) to (v), p. 104) write down the conditions which would prevent evaluation of the `while` loop, that is the conditions which render the expression being tested FALSE. Write simple programs to test these loops and check your answers.

2. Enter the vowel count program (Program 5.1), compile, link and run it. Test it with some short pieces of text. Modify the conditional expression in the `while` statement so that `&&` is used instead of `||`. Use a truth table to work out the required expression before coding it.

3. In the vowel count program we have used `if ... else` statements. What other alternative is there? Code your solution and test it.

4. The vowel count program discussed above can be modified to use a `do` loop instead of a `while` loop. Is this a better solution? If so why, if not why not? Recode the program using a `do` loop and test it.

5. In one version of a line editor program a test is required to check whether a command is a 'q' or an 's', to quit and save respectively. This can be coded using a `while` loop or a `do ... while` loop. In both cases the body of the loop contains the bulk of the program – all the command options will be called from within this loop. The two tests which are required are (i) the command not equal to q, and (ii) the command not equal to s.

Write a program using both the `do` and the `while` constructs. Within the loops you can simulate the action of the editor by using `printf()` statements to display a suitable message. Which option, if any, is preferable, and why?

6.
a. Enter program 5.3 and compare your results with those given in the text.

b. Now suppose that the expression x = 10 which forms part of the initialising expression in the for loop is replaced by x = 10 + y. Is the order of the two sub-expressions important? If so which version is correct? (That is (x = 10 + y, y++), or (y++, x = 10 + y)). Modify your program to check your answer.

7. Write a program to compute the square cube and reciprocal of integers from 1 to 20.

8. Modify the above program to allow for the start, step and end values to be entered. Use a check to trap a divide by zero error. Include in your program tests and suitable messages for

    a. the starting value being negative;
    b. the end value being less than the start value;
    c. the step being greater than the range (i.e. end - start).

9. The series expansion of sin(x) is

$$x - \frac{x^3}{3!} + \frac{x^5}{5!} \ldots\ldots$$

a. Write a program to evaluate sin(x) using this expansion for 5, 10 and 20 terms.

b. Modify the program to achieve a predetermined accuracy, allow this value to be entered by the user. (Hint: compare two successive evaluations of the series and terminate when the difference is less than the required accuracy.) Experiment with different values for the accuracy. How many terms are required to obtain an accuracy of .001 for $x = \pi/3$? Do the number of terms required change for $x = \pi/2$?

c. Find out about the library function sin(x) and use this function in your program to compare results with the above method.

10. Write a program which computes the sum of a series of integers stored in an array.

6 Functions – making them useful

"Of the Division of Labour."   Adam Smith

6.1 INTRODUCTION

In Chapter 1 we introduced the concept of functions and took a brief look at how they are used in C. The functions which we have written so far have been very simple ones with only a limited amount of communication between the function and the outside world. We have used library functions which are more complex, `printf()` being the most obvious example, and in this chapter some of the finer points of function structure will be explored. In particular we will be looking in detail at means of transferring information between a function and the calling environment (i.e. the program or function which is using it).

Before we start on a deeper exploration of functions, let's recap a little. A function is called by referring to its name and enclosing in brackets any parameters that are required. When a function call is encountered control is directed to the named function and processing continues within the body of the function. At some stage control will generally be redirected back to the calling program or function, at which time processing continues from the statement following the one which called the function.

A function is defined by giving it a name and enclosing within braces the statements which are to be carried out by the function. Within a program functions will generally all be grouped together at the end or at the beginning of the program.

6.2 THE *RETURN* STATEMENT

The keyword `return` is used to pass control back to the calling function. (We will drop the use of program in this context as programs are themselves functions.) This has two forms:

```
return;   and   return(expression);
```

In the first of these forms it is used simply to transfer control back to the calling function. The second form enables a value to be passed back at the same time as transferring control. An example of this use of return is illustrated by the function ch_test() which checks whether the character input is a digit or a letter and displays a suitable message, depending on the value of the character which has been entered.

Program 6.1

```
/* test input for lower-case, upper-case, or digit */
void ch_test(void)
{
    char ch;

    printf("\n please enter a character :");
    ch = getchar();
    if (ch >= 'a' && ch <= 'z'){
        printf("\n a lower case letter was entered \n");
        return;
    }
    if( ch >= 'A' && ch <= 'Z'){
        printf("\n an upper case letter was entered \n");
        return;
    }
    if( ch >= '0' && ch <= '9'){
        printf("\n a digit was entered \n");
        return;
    } else
        printf("\n you entered some other character\n");
}
```

The above use of return simply transfers control back to the calling function - no information (or data) is passed back. Note that a return statement is not required at the end of a function since transfer of control occurs automatically once the closing right brace of the function is reached. This particular function could in fact be written without the use of return. How might this be achieved?

Let's now consider a problem in which a value is to be returned to the calling function and investigate how the return statement can be used to achieve this. Consider the task of finding the sum of a series of non-zero numbers. We are restricting ourselves to non-zero numbers so that we can use a zero to signify the end of the series. This restriction can be lifted later on if we wish. The pseudocode for such a function is:

```
sum()
declarations
        integer isum, number
set isum to zero
read number
while number is not zero do
        add number to isum
        read number
end_while
return isum
```

In C this function has the form:

Program 6.2a

```
/* function sum() */
/* to sum a series of integers read from the keyboard */
/* zero terminates entry */

int sum(void)
{
    int number, isum = 0;

    scanf("%d", &number);
    while (number != 0) {
        isum += number;
        scanf("%d", &number);
    }
    return(isum);
}
```

This example illustrates how the return statement is used to pass back (i.e. return!) the value of the variable isum. In order to test this function we need a program which uses it. One such program is given below.

Program 6.3

```
/* sum test program */
/* s_test.c */

#include "stdio.h"

main()

    int total, sum();

    printf("\n The SUM function \n");
    printf("This returns the sum of a number of integers \n");
```

```
printf(" ... to end the series enter 0 \n");
total = sum();                                    /* A */
printf("\nThe sum of the numbers is %d\n", total); /* B */
}
```

```
/* put the sum function (Program 6.2a) here */
```

Exercise

Enter the program s_test and the function sum(), compile and run it. Use as
test data the integers

$$3, 67, 4, 21, 25, 57, 96, 12, 8, 23, 0$$

and check your answers.

Discussion

Now that you have some results we can take a closer look at the way the sum()
function works.

First the variable isum (which keeps track of the sum of the integers as they
are entered) is initialised to zero. Next we use the scanf function to read in the
first integer and assign the value to the variable number. The while loop is
then entered and a check made to see if the number is zero. If it is non-zero the
body of the loop is executed; the number is added to the variable isum and then
the next number is read in. The test is then carried out again. If the new number
is non-zero the while loop is executed again. Once a zero is encountered
control is passed from within the loop to the statement following, which is the
return statement. Since this particuler return statement contains an
argument (isum) its value is returned to the calling function (in this case
main()). In fact the value of the function sum() takes on the current value of
isum.

The statement in the main program which uses this result is

```
total = sum();
```

and this assigns to the variable total the value of isum. This statement
illustrates an important point concerning functions, which is that all functions
have a specific data type. So what type is the function sum()? It would be
convenient, and sensible, if it was of type int, and this is indeed the case. By
default all functions are of type int, and if any value is returned this will also
be of type int. If the variable being assigned to the function is of a different

type then type conversion will take place according to the rules given in section 3.7.

Functions thus have a data type and, in general, they will also have a value. The value of the function depends on the expression in the `return()` statement which is executed within the function. We have just seen that in our `sum()` function the value returned is the value of the sum of the integers entered. Other functions will return different values. The `scanf()` function for example returns a value after each call. The three possible values it can return are:

a positive integer representing the number of items read successfully

0 if an error occurred while the entry was being read (e.g. because a number of type `float` was entered when an `int` was expected)

EOF if an End of File was encountered.

We can use this information to make the function `sum()` more robust.

Program 6.2b

```
/* function sum() - version 2 */
int sum(void)
{
     int number, isum = 0;

     while ((scanf("%d", &number) == 1) && number != 0)
          isum += number;
     }
     return(isum);
}
```

The `if` statement is used to test for a valid integer entry. If the character(s) entered do not match the *conversion_string* then `scanf()` returns a 0 or an EOF, the test fails and the value of `isum` is returned to the program. If normal termination occurs (through the entry of 0) then the second part of the conditional expression becomes FALSE and again `isum` is returned.

One further modification can be made to this function. Now that we are using the return value of `scanf()` to test for a valid entry we can use any invalid entry to terminate the calculation, thus dropping the need for zero to be used as a stop indicator. So we have for the final integer version of this function:

Program 6.2c

```
/* function sum() - version 3 */
int sum(void)
{
    int number, isum = 0;

    while (scanf("%d", &number) == 1)
        isum += number;
    }
    return(isum);
}
```

6.3 FUNCTION TYPES OTHER THAN *INT*

We mentioned above that the default data type of a function is `int`. What happens if we wish to use a function with some other data type? An obvious answer is that the function is declared in the same way as a normal variable is declared, simply by preceding the function definition with the appropriate data type. So the following are all skeletons of valid function definitions (or declarations).

```
float product(void)
{
    float x;
    ...
    ...
    return(x);
}

double power(float a, int n)
{
    double y;
    int i;
    ...
    ...
    return(y);
}

char change_case(char ch)
{
    char c;
    ...
    ...
    return(c);
}
```

The sum() function (Program 6.2b) can now be rewritten so that the sum of a set of numbers of type float can be calculated. We only need to make a few modifications to the program and the function to achieve this. A first attempt is set out below:

Program 6.4

```
/* sum test program - float version: first attempt */
/* s_test_f.c */

#include <stdio.h>

main()
{
        float f_total;                                  /* A */

        printf("\n The SUM function \n");
        printf("This returns the sum of a number of floats \n");
        printf("to end the series enter 's' or any other char.\n");
        f_total = f_sum();
        printf("\n The sum of the numbers is %f \n", f_total);
}

/* the float version  (f_sum(void) ) */
float f_sum(void)
{
        float number, fsum = 0.0;


        while (scanf("%f", &number) == 1)
                fsum += number;
        return(fsum);
}
```

If this program and function declaration are entered as they stand and compiled a compilation error may occur. This is because the function f_sum() is first encountered in the statement

```
        f_total = f_sum();
```

where there is a mismatch between the data type of the variable f_total and the function f_sum(). Why is this since we have defined f_sum() to be of type float? The reason lies in the fact that this definition comes after the first call of the function and therefore the f_sum() is assumed to be of type int (by default). There are two ways to get around this difficulty. The first (known as prototyping) and most common, is to specifically declare the function at the beginning of the program, either externally (before main()) or internally in the body of the program. Thus we could solve our problem by modifying line /* A */ in Program 6.4 to read:

```
float f_total, f_sum(void);                    /* A */
```

This informs the compiler that a function f_sum() is being used which is of type float.

The second solution is to place the definition of the function f_sum() before the bulk of the program, i.e. before main(). In this case, since the definition comes prior to any use of the function, there will be no problems with mismatching data types. This method is not normally adopted as, especially if a large number of functions are used, the main program is pushed further away from the program heading and preprocessor statements, thus making it harder to understand what the program as a whole is doing.

Expressions and return

Before leaving our discussion of the return statement it is worthwhile pointing out that the value passed back by return need not be the value of a single variable but can be the value of any valid C expression. You will remember from our discussion in Chapter 3 that all expressions have a value, so that an expression within a return statement will possess a value which in turn becomes the value of the function as a whole after it has been called. Some examples using expressions are:

`return(a*x*x + b*x + c);`	which might be used to return the value of a quadratic expression for a given value of x.
`return(-100);`	which returns an integer constant.
`return('Y');`	which returns a character constant.
`return(++c);`	which returns the incremented value of c.
`return(scanf("%d", &x));`	which returns a 1, 0 or EOF depending on the outcome of the scanf() function call.

Remember that the data type returned from a function is that of the function itself, so that if the expression within the return statement is of a different type from that of the function then the normal type conversions will occur.

The form of `return`

In all of the above examples we have enclosed the expression following
`return` in brackets. These brackets are not in fact obligatory and thus
statements of the form:

```
return a*x*x + b*x + c;

return -100;
```

are allowed. However it is considered by many to be poor style to omit the
brackets, as this can lead to confusion, especially when the expression becomes
more complex. We only mention it here because you may come across examples
in this form.

6.4 PASSING DATA INTO A FUNCTION

So far we have dealt with ways in which information is passed back from a
function to the calling environment. The next aspect we need to investigate is
how to pass data into a function for use within it. We are now in a position to
consider the general form of a function which is:

```
type function_name(parameter_list definitions )
{
        /* body of the function */

        return(expression);
}
```

where, as usual, words in italics are optional.

In order to illustrate a simple use of parameters in functions we will develop a
function which can be used with the earlier display_menu function to select a
number of options. The options from which we had to choose were:

> 1. Shuffle
> 2. Deal
> 3. Display
> 4. Count points
> 5. Bid
> 6. Play
> Q Quit

We require a function to read and check for valid characters entered from the
keyboard and a second function to carry out the chosen command.

The pseudocode for the function to read a character from the keyboard is:

> **do**
> > **read** a character
> **while** not a valid option
> **return** (character)

which in C is simply:

Program 6.5

```
char valid_c(void);
{
        char c;

        do {
                c = getchar();
        } while (c !='Q' && (c < '1' || c > '6'));
        return(c);

}
```

Notice that although 1 and 6 are integers in this function they are treated as characters. The reason for this is that they are just being used as symbols to effect a choice and so the numerical values are unimportant. It also means that we can treat the character 'Q' in the same way as the digits 1 to 6, thus simplifying the code. You may be puzzled by the form of the conditional expression c !='Q' && (c < '1' || c > '6'). It is not immediately obvious that this is the correct expression. However a little thought should prove to you that it is correct. If you are still not sure, construct a truth-table such as that outlined in Chapter 4.

Having obtained a valid character from the keyboard you can use it to enable the selection of the appropriate option to be made. An obvious way of doing this is by means of the switch statement which we covered in Chapter 4. We can write down the function almost immediately, viz:

Program 6.6

```
/* Bridge example execute_option() function */
int execute_option(char c)
{
        switch(c)
        {
                case '1':
                        printf("\n Executing shuffle\n");
                        break;
```

```
            case '2':
                    printf("\n Dealing the hands\n");
                    break;
            case '3':
                    printf("\n Displaying the hands\n");
                    break;
            case '4':
                    printf("\n Counting the points\n");
                    break;
            case '5':
                    printf("\n Bidding \*");
                    break;
            case '6':
                    printf("\n playing Bridge! \n");
                    break;
            case 'Q':
                    return(0);
    }
    return(1);
}
```

Note In this example we have used `printf()` statements to simulate the various operations; in practice these would be replaced by, or appended to, the appropriate function calls.

This function is the first one which we have written which passes arguments into the function. Notice that the parameter in the function call is declared in the parameter list. In older implementations of C the declarations would be before the opening left brace of the function body.

Notice that the `return` statement is used twice, once if the Q option is executed, in which case the value of the function (`execute_option()`) is 0, and once when any of the other options are invoked, in which case the value of the function is set to 1. These values can be used to control the program after this function has been called.

The Bridge Tutor program now has the form:

Program 6.7

```
/* Bridge Tutor Program */

main()
{
        void main_menu(void); /* prototyping functions */
        char c, valid_c(void);
```

```
int execute_option(char ch);

do {
        main_menu();
        c = valid_c();
    } while( execute_option(c));
}


/* function main_menu() Program 2.2*/
/* function char valid_c() Program 6.5 */
/* function execute_option(c) Program 6.6 */
```

Prototyping

The first point to note about this program is the way in which prototyping is used for the functions. Two of the functions require no arguments and this is indicated by use of the keyword `void`. The third function returns an integer and because of the fact that the default type of a function is integer it is not strictly necessary to add the keyword `int`. However it is good practice to adopt the typing of functions even if they are of this type. Another point concerns the prototyping of parameters. In the example above we used `char  ch` to indicate that an argument of type char is expected. Note that the scope of the parameter `ch` is restricted to inside the parentheses. Any variable name, or none, can be used, not necessarily the one used in the function prototype. So we could equally well have

```
         int execute_option(char character);,
         int execute_option(char);,
or       int execute_option(char c);
```

The one used in the program is preferable as it makes it more explicit what role the argument is taking.

Notice that by using functions for each well-defined logical process the form of the program becomes very simple. It essentially consists of some declarations and a single `do` loop which calls the two functions `main_menu()` and `valid_c()`. The bulk of the work is done by the `execute_option()` function which forms the conditional expression of the `do  ...  while` loop. We will return to this program later on and add a few more functions to it so that we can get something useful out of it!

6.5 SOME EXAMPLES

In this section we are going to look at a few examples which illustrate the design and use of functions. They cover some of the functions required for the line editor program and a calendar function. We begin with some simple functions for use with the line editor. When entering the commands in the line editor, spaces are irrelevant and it would be useful to have a function to skip over them. We can use the `getchar()` function which we have used already to obtain a character from the keyboard. All we need in addition is some form of loop to allow characters to be read until a non-space is entered. The do ... while provides us with the simplest solution. So we have:

Program 6.8a

```
/* getnextchar() function */
/* This skips spaces in a character stream */
/* It returns the character read */

char getnextchar(void)
{
    char c;

    do {
        c = getchar();
    } while(c == ' ');
    return(c);
}
```

This function can be simplified even further by incorporating the statement `c = getchar()` in the conditional expression. This gives us:

```
        do {
        } while((c = getchar()) == ' ');
```

An even more compact form can be obtained if we use the `while` construct instead of the do ... while loop, i.e.:

```
        while((c = getchar()) == ' ')
            ;
```

Using this last alternative we have for the complete function:

Program 6.8b

```
/* getnextchar() function */

char getnextchar(void)
{
    char c;

    while((c = getchar()) == ' ')
        ;
```

```
        return(c);
}
```

Since in this program a variety of numbers and other characters need to be read in another useful function would be one which tells us whether a character is a digit. This will take a character as an argument and return TRUE if it is a digit and FALSE otherwise. Once again we can write this function down straight away.

Program 6.9

```
/* isadigit(char c) function */
/* This takes a character as an argument and */
/* returns TRUE if it is a digit and FALSE otherwise */

int isadigit(char c)
{
        if( c >= '0' && c <= '9' )
                return(1);        /* TRUE */
        else
                return(0);        /* FALSE */
}
```

The final function we are going to look at from the line editor program is one to read a series of characters and convert them to an integer. The final version which we will be using in the program will differ slightly from this one. We will examine the modifications required later on. For the moment all we are concerned with is that a decimal digit should be returned. We can convert a character into a decimal digit quite simply by subtracting ' 0 ' from the character and assigning it to an integer variable. (Providing of course the digit is in the range ' 0 ' to ' 9 ') What we are in fact doing is subtracting the ASCII code for '0' from the ASCII code for the character. This process can be represented in pseudocode as:

> declarations
>> **integer** i
>> **character** c
> **read in** c
> **if** c is a digit **then**
>> **set** i **to** c - '0'
> **end_if**

Next we have to consider the case of integers which are greater than 9. We may wish to edit line 15, for example. As successive characters are read in, if they are digits we need to modify the existing number in some way before adding the new digit to it. This process is again reasonably straightforward. We simply multiply the existing number by 10 before doing the addition. So the first character is a 1 and the second a 5, then the two together represent 15, which is just 10 times 1 plus 5.

In this function we need to test for a character being a digit. Well we have just written one such function so we can incorporate it in our new function. We therefore finally arrive at:

Program 6.10

```
/* int get_int(void) function        */
/* This reads characters while they   */
/*   are digits and computes          */
/*   the equivalent decimal integer   */
/* Once a non-digit is encountered     */
/*   the converted integer is returned */

int get_int(void)
{
     char c;
     int i = 0;                      /* initialise the number to 0 */

     c = getchar();
     while( isadigit(c)) {     /* execute while c is a digit */
           i = 10 * i + ( c - '0');       /* decimal convert */
           c = getchar();
     }
     return(i);
}
```

These functions although small simplify the task of getting valid characters and processing them for further use.

Now for a little light relief. You may be familiar with the nursery rhyme:

> *"Monday's child is fair of face,*
> *Tuesday's child is full of grace,*
> *Wednesday's child is full of woe,*
> *Thursday's child has far to go,*
> *Friday's child is loving and giving,*
> *Saturday's child works hard for a living,*
> *but the child that is born on the Sabbath day*
> *is bonny and blythe, good and gay."*

We are going to write a program which, given a date, will output the day of the week corresponding to it and the appropriate section from the above rhyme. The hardest part about this problem is finding out which day of the week corresponds to which date. Luckily it has already been worked out for us. Zeller's algorithm performs this task. It works as follows. Suppose we have a date given in the form 19/12/1965, which in general terms has the form D/M/Y. Then, if month (M) is January or February, they are taken as months 11 and 12 respectively of the previous year. Other months are numbered starting with March as month 1 of the year. We now substitute this modified numerical date into the formula:

$$\text{weekday} = \left(D + \frac{13 \times M - 1}{5} + 5 \frac{(Y \bmod 100)}{4} - \frac{7 \times Y}{400} \right) \bmod 7$$

The number returned will be between 0 and 6. A 0 represents Sunday, 1 Monday and so on. Using 19/12/1965 we get from the above formula a 0 which means that the 19th of December 1965 was a Sunday. We can now write a function which returns the weekday (as an integer).

Program 6.11

```
/* function using Zeller's algorithm */
/* to find the day in a week given a date */
/* in the form day/month/year */
/* the function returns the numerical value of the weekday */
/* 0 for Sunday, 1 for Monday etc. */

int zeller(int day, int month, int year)
{
        int zmonth, zyear, wday;

        zyear = year;  /* compute zeller year */
        zmonth = month - 2;   /* and zeller month */
        if( zmonth <= 0 ) {
                zmonth += 12;  /* becomes last or last but one */
                zyear--;       /* month of previous year */
        }
        wday =(day+(13*zmonth-1)/5+5*(zyear%100)/4-7*zyear/400)% 7;
        return(wday);
}
```

All that we need now is a program to test out our function. One possibility is:

Program 6.12

```
/* Birthday program */
/* using Zeller's algorithm */
/* to compute the day of the week */

#include <stdio.h>
```

```
main ()
{
    int d, m, y, week-day, zeller(int d, int m, int y);

    printf("\n Enter your birthday in the form D/MM/YYY : \n");
    scanf("%d/%d/%d", &day, &month, &year);
    week_day = zeller(day, month, year);
    printf("\n You were born on a ");
    switch (week_day) {
    case 0 :
            printf("Sunday \n and you ");
            printf(" are bonny and blythe, good and gay. \n");
            break;
    case 1 :
            printf("Monday\n and you ");
            printf("are fair of face. \n");
            break;
    case 2 :
            printf("Tueday\n and you ");
            printf("are full of grace. \n");
            break;
    case 3 :
            printf("Wednesday\n and I'm sure you");
            printf("are not full of woe!\n");
            break;
    case 4 :
            printf("Thursday\n and you ");
            printf("have far to go. \n");
            break;
    case 5 :
            printf("Friday\n and you ");
            printf("are loving and giving. \n");
            break;
    case 6 :
            printf("Saturday\n and you ");
            printf("work hard for a living. \n");
            break;
    }
}
```

This concludes our look at simple functions. Try them out for yourself and check that they work as expected.

6.6 CALL BY VALUE

Functions in C use the 'call by value' method to pass information from the calling environment to the body of the function. This fact has had no obvious effect on the operation of the functions which we have developed so far, but the next example illustrates what is meant by 'call by value' and how program calls need to be modified in order for a function to operate as intended. We will consider the example of a function which is used to find the maximum value of a set of integers.

One way of accomplishing this task is to set a variable (e.g. max) to -32768 (a large negative integer) or some other similar integer and each time an integer is read in compare the new value to the current value of max. If the number just entered is greater than the present maximum value then it becomes the new maximum. The integer -32768 is a suitable value since on most implementations of C this will be the largest negative integer. Before looking at the use of a function to accomplish this task let's write a program which will find the maximum of a set of 10 numbers entered from the keyboard. The pseudocode is:

```
Maximum algorithm
declarations
        integer i, num, max
set max to the largest negative integer
set i to 0
while i is less than 10 do
        set i to i plus 1
        read in num
        if the num > max then
                set max equal to num
end_while
print max
```

A program corresponding to this algorithm might be:

Program 6.13a

```
/* maximum program */

#define MAXNINT -32768      /* or largest negative int - we will
                               use a function to compute this later
                               */
main()
{
        int i, num, max;

        printf("Please enter 10 integers \n");
        printf(" ...use spaces to separate the integers\n");
        printf(" and end the list with a return. \n");
        max = MAXNINT;
        for (i = 0; i < 10; i++){    /* use for instead of while */
                scanf("%d ", &num);
```

```
        if (num > max)                    /* A */
                max = num;
    }
    printf("\n The maximum number entered was: %d \n", max);
}
```

The function maximum()

Now that we have a working program (type it in and check it to verify that it is correct) we should be able to modify it to use a function to perform the calculation. At first sight the following function might appear to be a suitable solution:

```
/* maximum function - version 1.0 */
/* incorrect version */
void maximum(int n, int cmax)
{
    if (n > cmax)
            cmax = n;
}
```

We also need to modify the if statement at line /* A */ in the original program to read:

```
maximum(num, max);
```

Finally, by adding our new function at the end of the main program we have a program to test it.

Exercise

Modify the original program as indicated above (remember to add the maximum() function). Compile and run the program using the same test data as before.

What is the result?

Discussion

You should have found that no matter what value was entered the result always came to -32768. So max does not in fact alter, even though the program and function appear to be written correctly. In order to investigate how the program and function are working modify the function by adding the printf() statements shown below.

```
printf("\n cmax on entry = %d :", cmax);
if (n > cmax)
        cmax = n;
printf("\n cmax on exit = %d \n", cmax);
```

This modification allows us to keep track of what is actually happening within the function each time it is being called. Once you have modified the function, compile and run the complete program. Use the following data:

$$0, 4, -16, 8, 99, -328, 6352, 12, 42, -37$$

An extract from the output you should obtain is given below:

```
Please enter 10 integers
0
 cmax on entry = -32768 :  cmax on exit = 0
4
 cmax on entry = -32768 :  cmax on exit = 4
-16
 cmax on entry = -32768 :  cmax on exit = -16
....
....
-37
 cmax on entry = -32768 :  cmax on exit = -37

The maximum number entered was: -32768
```

This test shows that the value of cmax on entry to the function is always -32768 and that although the if statement in the function enables this value to be replaced by the new number, as intended, the value of max outside the function does not change. The reason for this is that on entry to the function the value of max is assigned to the local variable cmax, which is then updated; however max is never assigned the new value of cmax, and thus remains at the value of -32768, i.e. its initial value. The problem, then, lies in the fact that the variable max is never in fact updated. How can we solve this problem? One solution involves the use of return which we looked at earlier. All we need to do is return the value of cmax, as we know that this value will be updated. The variable max can then be assigned to the function maximum() in the usual way. The function thus becomes:

Program 6.14

```
/* maximum function - version 2.0 */
/* correct version using return */
int maximum(int n, int cmax)
{
```

```
        if (n > cmax)
                cmax = n;
        return(cmax);
}
```

The statement in the program can be changed to accept this returned value. So the program now becomes:

Program 6.13b

```
/* maximum program */
/* using a function returning the */
/* current maximum value */

#define MAXNINT -32768      /* or largest negative int - we will
                               use a function to compute this later
                               */
main()
{
        int i, num, max, maximum(int n, int max);

        printf("Please enter 10 integers \n");
        printf(" ...use spaces to separate the integers\n");
        printf(" and end the list with a return. \n");
        max = MAXNINT;
        for (i = 0; i < 10; i++){       /* use for instead of while */
                scanf("%d ", &num);
                max = maximum(num, max);
        }
        printf("\n The maximum number entered was: %d \n", max);
}
```

A second solution requires a modification to the function and the function call to allow the parameter cmax to be changed within the function and this new value to be used to replace the current value of the variable max. This method involves the use of pointers and will be covered in Chapter 8.

6.7 FUNCTIONS AND HEADER FILES

All the functions we have written so far have been placed at the end of the main program. This means that the functions have all been part of the same source code as the program which is using them and they have consequently been compiled at the same time as the main program. This means in turn that if the program uses any header files, or symbolic constants (defined using the #define preprocessor instruction), then these will all be accessible to all of the functions which follow in the program source code. For many purposes this state of affairs presents no difficulties. However suppose that a function which we have been using is required in more than one program. This, after all, is one of the main reasons for writing functions in the first place, so that they can be tested independently and then used in a number of programs as and when necessary. When functions are extracted from a program for use elsewhere we need to take care that the appropriate header files and other preprocessor instructions are also included. For this reason it is considered good practice to include all the necessary information in a separate header immediately before the relevant function. This will ensure that the necessary information is maintained with the function and that the function compiles and operates correctly.

As an example consider the case of reading characters from the keyboard and changing all upper-case letters to their lower-case equivalents - all other characters are to be left intact. We will add two further tasks to this function; firstly the changed character should be displayed on the screen, and secondly the function should return a count of the number of characters changed. The function given below will perform the necessary operations:

Program 6.15

```
/* convert upper-case letters to lower-case */
to_lower()
{
      char ch;
      int count = 0;

      while((ch = getchar()) != '\n'){
            if ('A' <= ch && ch <= 'Z'){
                  putchar(ch + OFFSET); /* symbolic constant*/
                  count++;              /*      OFFSET      */
            }
      }
      return(count);
}
```

This example uses the two library functions getchar() and putchar() and thus the standard input/output header file stdio.h must be included in the program. (By means of the #include <stdio.h> preprocessor instruction.) In addition we have used a symbolic constant (OFFSET) to add a constant value to the upper-case letters in order to change them to lower-case letters. Again this constant must also be available to the function and so must be defined within the program. So, in order to make sure that the correct header files etc. are used, we can add the following lines just before the function definition:

```
/* function to_lower()                               */
/* This function converts upper-case letters to      */
/* lower-case letters and returns the number of      */
```

```
/* conversions carried out                              */
/* Header files used :-      stdio.h                     */

#define OFFSET 'a'-'A'
```

As with program titles I have included a brief description of the function to make it clear what it does. Notice the way in which OFFSET is declared; we do not need to know the precise ASCII codes for 'a' and 'A'; we can let the computer work out their separation for us. This does, however, make one assumption. Can you see what it is?

If these lines are included with the function to_lower() itself then all the necessary information is available for use by the function. The header file is not explicitly included here as it may already be loaded, in which case loading it again would be inefficient and could cause confusion. However the #define instruction can remain as this is likely to be local to the function. We can even move this instruction to within the body of the function. These means that it will be local to the function and not available to any other functions. However in this instance that does not matter.

6.8 STORAGE CLASS

As you will by now be aware all variables and functions require to have a data type specified, even if by default (as we saw earlier, functions are by default of type int). In addition to this attribute, variables and functions also have a storage class attributed to them. The storage class governs the availability of the variable (or function) to other functions, other parts of the program, or other programs. In more usual language the storage class affects the scope of variables and functions.

The scope of a function or a variable can be modified by the four keywords:

```
auto extern register static
```

A storage class keyword is combined with a *data_type* keyword as follows:

storage_class data_type identifier

The storage_class keyword is used in the same way for a function, except that the data_type keyword may be absent - if the function is of type int. We now discuss each of these storage classes in turn.

auto

Unless variables are modified specifically by use of a storage class type then they are local to the block (function or program) in which they are declared - they have no effect outside the block. Thus no identifier defined within a function can be accessed from outside that function.This may appear to be a disadvantage but it does in fact have advantages. For one thing it aids the modularity of functions and programs. Each function, including its variables, is self-contained and will not affect other functions or variables unless explicitly instructed to do so. Very often the letters i, j or k are used as `int` variables in the control of program flow, in loops for example, and these variables may well be used in the main program as well in various functions called by the main program. The basic scope (or storage class) rules mean that a variable can be used both in the main program and in a function without one use affecting the other.

Program 6.16

```
/* Illustrating the auto storage class */

main()
{
      int n, i, sum(int num);       /* i local to main() */

      for( i = 1; i < 5; i++){
            n = sum(i);
            printf("\n sum of integers (1 to %d) = %d\n", i, n);
      }
}

int sum(int k)
{
      int i, total = 0;     /* this i is local to sum() */
                            /* i in main invisible to sum() */
      for( i = 1; i <= k; i++)
            total += i;
      return(total);
}
```

Note that the variable i in the function is allocated a different address in memory from that occupied by the variable i in the main program. Although the variables have the same name the variables they identify occupy different storage locations.

The **auto** storage class is the default class for variables declared within a function and is only rarely used explicitly. The scope of such variables is local to the block in which they are declared and so the same variable name can be used in two different blocks without either value affecting the other. One case when this storage class could be used explicitly might be to indicate that a variable is intended to be an `auto` variable and that it is not simply an oversight on the part of the programmer.

An **auto** variable has memory allocated to it when the function containing it is called. Once the function call is terminated and the program moves on to another statement the memory allocated to the automatic variables is freed and available for use by other variables.

extern

One use of the storage class **extern** is to allow the transmission of information from an outer to an inner block (for example, to allow a function access to a variable, or a symbolic constant declared in the main program). All variables declared outside a function and the main program (i.e. before main()) are by default of storage class **extern** and have storage permanently allocated to them. Although this facility allows communication between the calling program and its functions care should be taken if this method is used to alter an external variable. Good programming practice dictates that programs should be modular - that is, they should consist of self-contained units of code with well-defined means of transmitting data between the modules (in C the modules are functions!). We have seen one method of achieving this modularity which is by means of the return statement; the other method uses the argument list.

The **extern** storage class is also used to inform the compiler that a variable or function is external to the present program. An example of when such a declaration might be used is when a set of functions are located in a file separate from the main program and some of these functions use variables which are declared in the main program. The variables would be declared outside the function main() and within the separate functions (in the other file) would be declared with storage class **extern**. All functions have storage class **extern** and as a result are available to all other functions as well as the main() program.

register

The storage class **register** has the same effect as the **auto** storage class except that the compiler is 'advised' to place variables with this storage class in a particular area of memory - the CPU registers if possible. No guarantee can be given that the variables will be placed in these particular locations. The most common use of **register** variables is to speed up the access to these specific variables. Thus a variable which is used frequently in a program could be given the **register** storage class in an attempt to speed the program up.

static

A **static** variable is used when its value is to be retained between uses. An example will help to illustrate how such variables work.

MACMILLAN MASTER SERIES

YOUR CHANCE TO WIN A BOTTLE OF QUALITY FRENCH WINE

We at Macmillan are constantly trying to improve and update the Master Series to suit the needs of our customers. Please help us to do this by answering the following simple questions. The sender of every 100th completed card will receive a bottle of French wine.

Which Mastering title have you bought?

- ☐ Advanced Pure Mathematics
- ☐ Electrical & Electronic Calculations
- ☐ Philosophy
- ☐ C. Programming
- ☐ Basic Management
- ☐ Economic & Social History

Are you studying the subject?

- ☐ for use on a course - please specify _____
- ☐ for use in business
- ☐ for general education
- ☐ other - please specify _____

How did you hear of the Macmillan Master Series?

- ☐ Advertisement
- ☐ Lecturer/teacher recommendation
- ☐ Friend/colleague recommendation
- ☐ Bookshop recommendation
- ☐ Library
- ☐ Bookshop browsing
- ☐ Catalogue
- ☐ Other - please specify _____

Have you ever bought any other Mastering titles?

- ☐ Yes - please specify _____
- ☐ No

Please tick if you would like further details on the Macmillan Master series ☐

Name _____

Address _____

_____ Postcode _____

Thank you for your help

Data Protection Act. The information you provide may be kept on a database and may be used by Macmillan to offer you allied products.
Please tick here if you object ☐

21

Jackie Parry
Macmillan Press
FREEPOST
Houndmills
Basingstoke
Hampshire
RG21 2BR

The function maximum() which we developed earlier in this chapter could be used in a number of different places within a program. In this case the value of max (the current maximum) needs to be retained between calls. This can be achieved by declaring this variable as a **static** variable. This means that the default class of auto will be disposed of.

Program 6.17

```
/* Simple maximum program */
/* using static variables */

main()
{
     int a, b, m, maximum(int num);        /* prototype maximum */

     printf("\n Please enter two integers: ");
     scanf("%d %d", &a, &b);
     maximum(a);
     m = maximum(b);
     printf("\n The largest is: %d \n", m);
}

/* maximum function */
/* - this returns the current maximum integer */
int maximum( int x)
{
     static int max = -32768;      /* making max static means
                                      its value will be retained
                                      between functions calls */

     if (x > max)
           max = x;
     return(max);
}
```

Within the function maximum() the variable max is set to -32768 once only – the first time the function is called. On subsequent calls the value of the variable is the latest value. Thus repeated calls of this function will produce the current maximum value which can be accessed via the return statement. Note that max is invisible to the main program; its value can only be accessed by an expression such as m = maximum(b). One further point concerning this function is that, as it stands, it is impossible to reinitialise max to -32768 within the program – initialisation occurs once only, on the first call of the function. Thus this is **not** a good idea if you need to find maxima twice within one program. So care has to be taken with functions of this type as they are often the cause of hard to find errors.

SUMMARY

In this chapter we:

- looked at ways by which data can be passed between a function and its calling environment.

- saw how the `return` statement can be used to pass control back to the calling program or function.

- used `return (expression)` to pass back a value.

- saw how parameters are passed into a function.

- noted that each parameter must be declared in the function parameter list.

- learnt that all functions have a data type which is `int` by default.

- noted that a function has a value which is that of the expression in the `return` statement.

- saw that variables used in a function are in general local variables whose scope is restricted to the function in which they are declared.

- noted that comments should be added as a header to functions detailing any header files and symbolic constants which are necessary for the correct operation of a function.

- examined the concept of storage class and the use of the keywords **auto, extern, register** and **static.**

EXERCISES

1. Change the original version of `sum()` to version 2.0 (Program 6.2b) and use the following sets of data to test the new version.

(i) 3 8 15 92 0

(ii) -4 9 12 R

(iii) 7 19 45 1 -12 CTRL Z

You should notice that this time characters other than 0 can be used to terminate the entry of integers,

2. Write a function to read characters from the keyboard and return the number of characters read in. Use an asterisk to terminate the string of characters (don't include this in the count).

3. Use the sum() function as a basis for writing a function mean() which computes the arithmetic mean of a set of integers. This time 0 must be a valid entry and not a terminator. Use the value of scanf() to test for the end of the input stream. Test your function thoroughly.

4. Using the skeleton function definitions in section 6.3 (i.e. product, power and change_case) write complete versions of the functions and appropriate test programs. Use suitable data to test each function thoroughly.

5. Write a function, and a test program, to compute the value of a quadratic expression (i.e. a*x*x +b*x + c) for a particular value of x. Allow the user to enter the values of (the integers) a, b and c and the value of x (float or double) for which the solution is required. Use the following data to test your function.

a	b	c	x		
1	2	-2	0	1.5	4
2	-3	1	-1	0	6

6. The maximum() function assumes that the data type int has a range of -32768 to +32767. The sizeof() function can be used to check the number of bytes occupied by int variables and can thus be used to calculate automatically the constant MAXNINT (i.e. the largest negative integer of type int). Work out how to do this and then modify the maximum() function and program accordingly. Thoroughly test the function and program.

7. Write a function double convert(acres, c_factor) which will convert acres to other measures of area (e.g. square mile, hectares) using the appropriate conversion factor (c_factor). (See the example in Chapter 3, Program 3.3.) Write a program to test the function and use suitable test data.

8. The following function is intended to count the number of lower-case letters entered from the keyboard. The value of count needs to be passed to the calling program. However the function in its present form does not work correctly - find out what is wrong and correct it. Write a program which uses the function and then use appropriate data to test both the program and the function.

```
count_lower(int count)
{
```

```
      int i;
      char c;

      while((c = getchar()) != '\n')
            if( 'a' >= c && c <= 'z')
                  count++;
}
```

9. Write a function which will compute the sum of the squares of a set of real numbers entered from the keyboard. Write a suitable program and test the function.

10. Suppose we wish to modify the sum() function (Program 6.2c) to allow it to keep a running total. What step(s) would need to be taken?

⬡7 The calculator

"Does a calculating machine calculate?"   Ludwig Wittgenstein

7.1 INTRODUCTION

At this point we are going to take a short break from our detailed study of C and develop the program for a simple calculator. This should serve to consolidate your understanding of the topics covered so far. In this chapter we will be devising an algorithm and developing the functions required for this task. In the process we will be looking briefly at parsing and recursion. This chapter will provide you with a number of useful functions which can be used in a variety of programs. Furthermore the development of a solution from the initial problem definition through the various stages of stepwise refinement, algorithm design, coding and testing should be helpful in working through problems of your own. There are no exercises as such in this chapter, but you should work through all the functions and test them out on your own system. There are alternative ways of implementing some of the functions and new ones can be written which may improve the modularity and enhance the operation of the final program. So, as you work through this chapter, you should keep an eye open for any enhancements or modifications which can be made.

7.2 PROBLEM DEFINITION

In the days of cheap credit card sized calculators it may seem somewhat pointless to write a program in C to simulate just the basic functions of such a machine. However it is a useful exercise for a number of reasons, some of which have already been alluded to. One additional reason is that anyone reading this book and/or seriously wishing to program in C will be familiar with the operations of a simple arithmetic calculator. So the task of writing the algorithm which involves examining the logic of the way a calculator works can be concentrated upon - there is no need to explain the nature of the problem before we start the problem-solving process. Also the control structures needed in order to emulate a calculator have already been discussed. Therefore this is an appropriate point at which to use some of the constructs in the solution of a more substantial problem. We begin, then, by defining the problem.

Deciding on the notation

To begin with we need to decide how the information is to be passed to the program, what operations are to be allowed, and what final result we require. How the data is to be passed to the program is fairly obvious - we will input data from the keyboard. However we must also decide on the order in which the information is passed to our calculator. One method which is used in some calculators (and in the Forth programming language) is based on a notation known as reverse Polish. In this method the operator follows the operands. Thus if we wish to find the sum of 2.4 and 5.3, using this method we would enter:

$$2.4 \ 5.3 \ +$$

and with luck the display would read:
$$7.7$$

This method is used by Kernighan & Ritchie as an example in their book (*The C programming language*, 2nd edn., 1988, pp. 74 ff) and the reader is referred to their example after working through this chapter.

A more common notation is one in which binary operators are sandwiched between their two operands. Thus to add the two numbers 2.4 and 5.3 we simply enter:
$$2.4 + 5.3$$

Again we would hope to obtain the answer 7.7! This method has the advantage that it is rather more natural than the reverse Polish notation and thus easier to understand. However this it at the expense of an added complication in that parentheses are required for some operations. To illustrate this aspect, consider the calculation:
$$2.4 * 3 + 5.1$$

Unless parentheses are used this calculation could be ambiguous. Does it imply that we should first multiply 2.4 by 3 and then add the result to 5.1, or are we to first add 3 to 5.1 and multiply this result by 2.4? These two possible interpretations in both reverse Polish notation and conventional notation using brackets are illustrated below.

Reverse Polish	Conventional	Result
2.4 3 * 5.1 +	(2.4 * 3) + 5.1	12.3
3 5.1 + 2.4 *	2.4 * (3 + 5.1)	19.44

The way in which an arithmetic expression is entered using conventional notation is rather more natural than the method imposed by reverse Polish notation, and to most people the conventional notation is clearer. We will therefore adopt the conventional approach.

The operations

Now that we have settled which method of calculation we are going to use we can move on to the next stage in the design process which involves deciding upon what operations are to be allowed. We will begin by sticking to the four basic arithmetic operations, remembering that we must allow for the entry of left and right parentheses to resolve the ambiguities which we have just been discussing. One last point on this aspect: we need to decide when the expression has been terminated so that the calculation can be performed. For the moment we will simply assume that an expression is terminated once the Return key is pressed. The use of the = key could be added at a later date as a possible enhancement.

The display should include the expression, as entered, plus on the following line the result of evaluating that expression. We can incorporate a number of other items on the screen if we wish, possibly even a picture of a calculator, but again these frills can be ignored for the moment.

A start on the algorithm

We now have enough information about the basic operation of the calculator to outline the basic structure of the calculator algorithm. This will be very basic, but it will serve as a starting point. One possible outline is :

>**The input section**
>This section is required to:
>>Issue the necessary prompt to the user
>>Initialise any variables

>**The calculating section**
>In this section the operations are:
>>Read characters from the keyboard
>>Perform the specified operations

>**The output section**
>The only operation here is to
>>Output the result

(We may wish to add a facility to output error messages such as an attempt to divide by zero.)

The above skeleton algorithm outlines the tasks involved but we now need to decide on one or two language dependent aspects before we can proceed further. For example, how exactly are we going to input the characters? Later on we could use an array, or a linked list to store the keystrokes - this would mean that the complete expression could be entered before any attempt at a calculation is made. However we have only dealt briefly with arrays and have yet to investigate lists, which means that we will need to process the characters as they are entered, using a minimal amount of storage. At this stage it is worth thinking about the types of valid expression which may be input. Some examples include:

```
(i)        2+3
(ii)       14*2/9
(iii)      2.4*3+5.1
(iv)       12 + 3/2
(v)        -4 * 6
```

It is important that you look carefully at all of these seemingly randomly selected examples. Let's take each one in turn and examine the consequences for our calculator.

(i)   2+3

This is one of simplest of examples; single digit integers are used and the operation is addition. Extending this example we can see that the process of reading in a character is such that we cannot easily use the scanf() function - using it implies that we know in advance the types of tho variables being read. Although it is likely that the first character will be a digit, we cannot guarantee that - it could be a left parenthesis.

(ii)   14*2/9

This second example differs only marginally from the first; however it illustrates that integers consisting of more than one digit may well be entered and that we must take account of more than one arithmetic operation in the same expression.

(iii)   2.4*3+5.1

These two points are further illustrated by this example which mixes integers and real numbers as well as two arithmetic operations. So to generalise we need to treat all numbers as type (at least) float. In fact to deal with as wide a range of numbers as possible it would be best to treat them as type double. We also need to allow for multiple arithmetic operations. Provided we keep track of the current result there will be no need to impose any definite limit on the number of operations.

(iv)   12 + 3/2
(v)   -4 * 6

These two examples illustrate the fact that spaces may, intentionally or inadvertently, be inserted in the expression. We should therefore use a function which will ignore spaces. However we will treat as an error a number which contains spaces. Another point is illustrated by example (v) and that is that a number may be preceded by a minus sign, so we should allow for this eventuality as well.

Operator precedence and parsing

At this point we need to take another look at the way in which various arithmetic operators are used in an expression. Let's return to an earlier example (2.4*3+5.1). In normal arithmetic this would reduce to:

$$7.2 + 5.1$$

to produce the final result:

$$12.3$$

In this case we are able to calculate the expression exactly as it is written down, i.e. from left to right. We simply retain the current value of the first sub-expression (2.4*3) and then add it to the final number (5.1). But what if the expression were to be entered in the form 5.1+2.4*3 ? If we adopt the process just described then we will get an erroneous result (i.e. as if it had been entered with brackets, (5.1+2.4)*3). This leads us to conclude that if the first operation is addition then the first two operands must be retained as well as the '+' operator until the next operator is supplied. If this is an '*' then we need to get the third number. We can then process this last triplet (e.g. 2.4 * 3) and place the result in number2. The process is now repeated. If at a subsequent stage a '+' is encountered then the first triplet can be processed (number1'+' and number2). We can now generalise this a little by noting that the rules governing the evaluation of an expression remain the same when a '-' is replaced by a '+' or an '*' is replaced by a '/'. What this discussion reveals is that multiplication and division should be carried out before addition and subtraction – the basic precedence rules of arithmetic. It also shows that, at most, three numbers and two operators need to be retained at any one time. Let us now write down an algorithm which represents the processing which we have just been discussing (Figure 7.1).

Take a few minutes to look over this algorithm. It looks rather daunting, but the ideas involved are not all that perplexing. The algorithm uses two functions which have yet to be detailed: getop() and getnum(). These functions return the next operator and a number respectively. When we come to code the process()

function we will see that getop() simply needs to ignore spaces and return the next character. The getnum() function is a modification of a function which we wrote earlier (Program 6.10) and can therefore be coded without much effort.

Fig 7.1   *The   process()   algorithm*

The **process** algorithm

This uses x1, x2 and x3 for the numbers being read in,
        and op1 and op2 for the two operators.
That is the syntax of an expression at any one time
        is at most of the form:x1 op1 x2 op2 x3.
set x1 **to** getnum()
set op1 **to** getop()
while op1 not equal to return **do**
        if op1 is equal to + or - **then**
                set x2 **to** getnum()
                set op2 **to** getop()
                while op2 not equal to return **do**
                        if op2 is equal to + or - **then**
                                set x1 **to** evaluate(x1, op1, x2)
                                set op1 **to** op2
                                set x2 **to** getnum()
                        else if op2 is equal to * or / **then**
                                set x3 **to** getnum()
                                set x2 **to** evaluate(x2, op2, x3)
                        else
                                print Invalid operator and **stop**
                        end_if
                        set op2 **to** getop()
                end_while
                set x1 **to** evaluate(x1, op1, x2)
                return x1
        else if op1 is equal to * or / **then**
                set x2 **to** getnum()
                set x1 **to** evaluate(x1, op1, x2)
        else
                print Invalid operator and **stop**
        end_if
        set op1 **to** getop()
end_while
return x1

A final point to consider before we go any further is how to deal with a bracketed expression, for example 2*(4+3*(7-5)/(10-6)). Once parentheses are introduced we need to think carefully about the way the expression is evaluated. One way of setting out the evaluation of this expression is given in Table 7.1, using the variables x1, x2, x3, op1 and op2, as used in Figure 7.1.

Table 7.1 *Evaluation of the expression:* $2*(4+3*(7-5)/(10-6))$

x1	op1	x2						
2	*	(	suspend evaluation					
		x1	op1	x2	op2	x3		
		4	+	3	*	(	suspend evaluation	
						x1	op1	x2	op2
						7	-	5	)
						2	result	
		4	+	3	*	2		
		4	+	6	/	(	suspend evaluation	
						x1	op1	x2	op2
						10	-	6	)
						4	result	
		4	+	6	/	4		
		4	+	1.5	)			
		5.5	result					
2	*	5.5						
11	final result							

A careful study of Table 7.1 will show the processes that are involved when a left bracket is encountered.

> The current value of the expression being evaluated is retained and its evaluation is suspended (e.g. 2*).

> The expression following the bracket is evaluated just as if it were a normal expression (e.g. 7-5).

> The evaluation of the first expression can now continue using the result of the bracketed expression for x3.

> The whole process is then repeated until the complete expression has been entered.

The only position at which a left bracket can validly occur is when a number is expected: e.g. 3*(7-5) is valid, but not 3(7-5). Bearing this in mind, we can carry out the checking for a left bracket in the function which reads a number (i.e. in getnum()).

As soon as a left bracket is encountered we simply suspend the remaining operations within getnum() and call process(). Once a right bracket is found the value which is returned from process() is the value of the bracketed expression.

The process which we have introduced is known as **recursion**. This involves the calling of a function from within itself or from another function which calls it, and can at times be extremely useful, as it is here. However it should be used with care, as any available memory can soon be eaten up by repeated recursive function calls.

Now that brackets have been introduced we will need to modify the process algorithm to take account of the new possibilities. Since the test for the left brackets is made in getnum() we only need to consider a test for closing brackets. This can be achieved by just adding another test to the two while loops, so these become:

> **while** op1 not equal to return and not equal to) **do**

and

> **while** op2 not equal to return and not equal to) **do**

respectively. As soon as a right bracket is found the while loop is exited and the process() function returns the value in x1.

The final version of the process() function, as coded in C, is given in Program 7.1.

Program 7.1

```
/* calculator process() function
        This carries out the processing and bulk of
        the parsing of the entered expression. It uses functions:
        getnextchar(),getnum() and evaluate().
        The value of the expression is returned.
*/

double process()
{
        char op1, op2, getnextchar();
        double x1, x2, x3, getnum(),
                evaluate(double x, char op, double y);

        x1 = getnum();
        while((op1 = getnextchar()) != '\n' && op1 != ')') {
                switch (op1) {
                case '+':
                case '-':
                        x2 = getnum();
                        while((op2 = getnextchar()) != '\n' && op2 != ')') {
                                switch (op2) {
```

```
                    case '+' :
                    case '-' :
                            x1 = evaluate(x1, op1, x2);
                            op1 = op2;
                            x2 = getnum();
                            break;
                    case '*' :
                    case '/' :
                            x3 = getnum();
                            x2 = evaluate(x2, op2, x3);
                            break;
                    default:
                            printf("\n * Invalid operator *\n");
                            printf("    op = %c \n", op2);
                            exit(1);
                    }
            }
            x1 = evaluate(x1, op1, x2);
            return(x1);
        case '*' :
        case '/' :
            x2 - getnum();
            x1 = evaluate(x1, op1, x2);
            break;
        default:
            printf("\n * Invalid operator *\n");
            printf("    op = %c \n", op1);
            exlt(1);
        }
    }
    return(x1);
}
```

getnum()

We now need to consider the other processes in the basic algorithm (Figure 7.1).
Let's take a look at the getnum() function first. This function reads characters
one at a time and converts the resulting stream of digits to a decimal number.
(Actually the conversion takes place as the digits are read.) The process of
converting a series of character digits into an integer has already been discussed
and a program written (see Program 6.10). Read over that discussion now to
make sure that you understand the principles involved.

To continue, the formula we are considering is:

$$num = 10 * num + (c - '0')$$

We will need to modify the function slightly as we are dealing with real numbers not just integers. Thus a decimal point is a valid character in a stream of digits. So how do we cope with the decimal point? One way is to continue the process of shifting the variable (num) which we are building up to the left, with successive multiplications by 10 and at the same time keep track of the number of digits which have been read in since the decimal point. Before reading on, see if you can work out why this additional counter is needed.

Consider a number such as 237.58. Using the above expression we will have read in, up to the decimal point, the digits '2' '3' '7', which will have been converted by the above formula to the decimal number 237. Once the decimal point is encountered we begin incrementing a variable, say nexp, each time a new digit is read. Thus when the end of the number is reached we have a number 23758, and the counter nexp is set to 2. All that is required now is to divide our integer (23758) by 10 twice (i.e. the value of the counter nexp) to shift the number right by two decimal places. Now that we have worked through this process we can write down the algorithm in pseudocode.

```
function getnum() for real numbers
set num to 0
set nexp to 0
set flag to 0
set c to getchar()
while c is a digit or decimal point do
        if c is a decimal point then
                flag = 1
        else
                num = 10 * num + ch - '0'
        if flag == 1 then
                increment nexp
        set c to getchar()
if flag is equal to 1 then
        while nexp is greater than 0 do
                set sum to sum/10
                set nexp to nexp - 1
return sum
```

The algorithm above forms the basis for the getnum() function. However we still need to make one or two refinements for the function we require. These are to check if the number is negative, and to check for the left bracket. The first of these is simple. If a minus sign is read as the first character then we set a flag and read another character (which we will assume is a valid digit). The converted number is then negated just prior to returning it from the function. Checking for a left bracket is also quite simple. Instead of returning a number directly from the getnum() function we do it via a call to process(), i.e.

```
return(process());
```

With these refinements we have the following function:

Program 7.2

```
/* The getnum() function for real numbers.
      This function reads characters from the standard
      input device and converts a stream of digits
      containing at most one decimal point into a number
      of type double. The function is called by means of
              a statement such as:       x = getnum();
              where x is of type double,
/*
double getnum(void)
{
        char c, getnextchar(void);
        double num = 0, process();
        int flag = 0, nexp = 0, minus = 0, isadigit(char c);

        c = getnextchar();
        if( c == '(')
                return(process());
        else if( isadigit(c) || c == '.' || c == '-')
                ; /* valid numeric input - skip */
        else {
                printf("\n ** Numeric digit . or ( expected ** \n");
                printf(" Character is %c \n", c);
                exit(1);
        }
        if( c == '-') {
                minus = 1;               /* minus */
                c = getnextchar();
        }
        while (isadigit(c) || c == '.') {
        switch (c){
        case '.' :
                flag = 1;       /* set flag to compute */
                break;          /* fractions */
        default:
                num = 10 * num + (c - '0');
                if (flag)
                        ++nexp; /* increment negative exponent */
                break;
                }
                c = getchar(); /* notice not getnextchar()        */
```

```
        }
        ungetc(c, stdin);     /* push last character back onto */
        while ( nexp-- > 0)   /*              the buffer        */
                num /= 10;    /* shift decimal point left       */
        if(minus)
                num = -num;
        return(num);
}
```

There is one addition to this function which we haven't yet discussed. That is the purpose of ungetc(c, stdin). This function is a standard library function which 'ungets', that is pushes back onto the input stream, a character just read from the input buffer. Here stdin is a file pointer which is associated with the standard input device (i.e. the keyboard). (A fuller discussion of file pointers and stdin is given in Chapter 9.) The reason that we need this function is that, once a return from getnum() has been made, the character which was just read, and was not a valid character for getnum(), is needed by process() to get the next operator. (An alternative is available; can you work out what it is? If so, try it out.)

Finally we need to write one more function which performs the actual arithmetic calculations. This function requires three arguments: two operands and an operator. It returns the result of the calculation. This can be coded by using another simple switch statement. It is given in Program 7.3, below.

Program 7.3

```
/* the evaluate()  function  */
double evaluate(double x, char op, double y)
{
        switch(op) {
                case '+' : return(x + y);
                case '-' : return( x - y);
                case '*' : return(x * y);
                case '/' : if( y != 0.0 )
                                return(x / y);
                        else {
                                printf("\n** Divide by zero **\n");
                                exit(0);
                        }
        }
}
```

We have now reached the stage where the program itself can be written, since the two remaining functions which we require have already been written. These are the getnextchar() and the isadigit() functions. These are given as Program 6.8 and Program 6.9 in Chapter 6.

So at last we have the calculator program.

Program 7.4

```
/* Simple calculator program */

#include <stdio.h>

main()
{
        double process(), getnum(), evaluate( double x,
        char op, double y);
        char getnextchar();

        printf("\n Enter your calculation \n");
        printf(":>");
        printf("\n = %f \n", process());
}

/* Put the following functions in here:
        evaluate()   Program 7.3
        process()    Program 7.1
        getnum()     Program 7.2
        getnextchar()Program 6.8
        isadigit()   Program 6.9
*/
```

That completes our tour through the development of the simple calculator program. Notice the simplicity of the program itself! All the work is done in the functions. Try the program out and see how you get on with it.

EXERCISES

There are a number of improvements which could be made to the program. For example there is no check that a number being entered is too large, or that two or more minus signs are entered during a getnum() call. The program could also be extended to compute powers. You could even add the trigonometric functions to it.

8 Pointers, arrays and strings

"To me the most important part of a program is laying out the data structure."

Dan Bricklin

8.1 INTRODUCTION

In this chapter we will be concerned with pointers, arrays and strings. If you have done any programming before beginning to study C, you will have already encountered and used arrays and strings. If you have arrived here via assembly language programming, you will already be familiar with the concept of pointers. If you have come to C by a different route and are uncertain about pointers then now's your chance to find out! Pointers are one of the most important features of C and as such contribute to the flexibility and power for which the language is known. The concept of pointers is crucial to a clear understanding of the way arrays work, and strings are simply arrays of type char. It is for this reason that we have not so far concerned ourselves very much with strings. However, by the time you have worked through this chapter, you should be proficient in the basic uses of pointers, be able to use one- and two-dimensional arrays and be at home with strings.

8.2 POINTERS

We begin our discussion of pointers by giving a simple definition:

> **A pointer is ...** *a symbolic representation of an address in the computer's memory*

As we saw in Chapter 3 all variables have an address at which the value of the variable is located or stored. We have already encountered the idea of an address when we used the scanf function. This function, you will remember, requires the address of the variable to be given as a parameter to the function rather than the name of the variable. The address operator (&) is used for this purpose. Thus if we have a variable called f i r s t, then &f i r s t is its address; &f i r s t is a pointer to the variable f i r s t and will have a numerical value within a function (or program) which will be constant. Thus &f i r s t is a pointer constant which cannot be changed by reassignment - just as 52 is a constant which cannot be assigned another value. So, although the value of f i r s t might change during the execution of a program, its address, &f i r s t, or the pointer to f i r s t will remain constant.

You might expect that, since we have pointer constants which are analogous to constants, there would also be pointer variables. If that is what you were thinking then you would be quite correct. A pointer variable can be assigned a value which will be the address of a variable. Thus

```
paddress = &first;
```

assigns to the pointer variable paddress the address of the variable f i r s t - paddress now 'points to' f i r s t. This variable can be assigned to the address of another variable, for example:

```
paddress = &second;
```

Any subsequent reference to paddress would be a reference to second rather than to f i r s t.

The indirection operator

Whilst it is useful, and necessary, to be able to use pointers to identify the address of a variable it is also necessary to be able to obtain access to the value stored at that address, i.e. the value at the address 'pointed to' by the pointer variable (or pointer constant). This is achieved by use of the **indirection** operator, or **dereferencing** operator (*). Thus if paddress is a pointer to the variable f i r s t, then the statement

```
second = *paddress;
```

will assign the current value of f i r s t to the variable second. A little thought will show that the pair of statements paddress = &first; and second = *paddress; put the same value in second as the single assignment statement second = first; as is illustrated in Figure 8.1. Thus the (unary) operator * together with the unary operator & allows us to indirectly achieve the same result as can be obtained by a single assignment statement - hence the term indirection operator.

Fig 8.1   *Using   a   pointer*

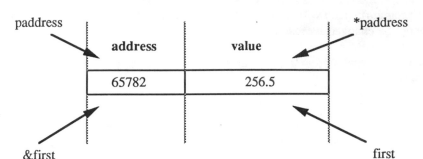

Notice that the indirection operator provides another example of an operator whose function is dependent upon the context in which it is used. In this case it is a **unary** operator, whose operand is the identifier on its right. The other use of * is as the binary multiplication operator which requires two operands.

Pointer declarations

Although we have illustrated the use of pointers we have still to show how a pointer variable is declared. A pointer variable must be assigned a data type just as do ordinary variables. Pointer variables do not simply point to an address; they point to the address of a particular variable and the variable has a pre-defined data type. So, in the example we used above, paddress will point to an int if the variable first is declared as an integer; it will point to a float if first is of type float. A pointer declaration must therefore have an indication of the data type to which it will be pointing as well as some means of identifying it as a pointer. The standard data types can be used for the former and the indirection operator can be used for the latter. Thus the declaration

```
int *paddress;
```

will declare a pointer variable paddress which may be used to point to a variable of type int. Other examples are:

```
char *cptr;      /* pointer to a char variable */
float *px;       /* pointer to a float variable */
double *dble;    /* pointer to a variable of type double */
```

Since each pointer is associated with a particular data type it is not permissible to use a pointer of one type to point to a variable of a different type. Thus, assuming we have the above pointer declarations, and z is of type double, then

```
px = &z;
```

would cause a compilation warning (or error) since an attempt is being made to use a pointer to float (px) to address a variable of type double.

8.3 POINTERS AND FUNCTIONS – CALL BY REFERENCE

In Chapter 6 we noted that the method of 'call by value' is used to pass information to and from a function via the argument list. This means that although in the function maximum() which we developed we are able to pass the current value of the global variable max into the function we have no means of modifying it within the function. Now that we have explored some elementary concepts regarding pointers we are in a position to take this problem up again and find another solution. This method simulates a means of argument passing known as 'call by reference' in which the argument is a reference to (or the address of) a variable. This method therefore allows the value of the variable to be modified from within the function.

Call by reference is achieved by

- Using the address of an external variable as an argument to the function.

- Declaring this function parameter as a pointer.

- Using, in the body of the function, the indirection operator whenever the parameter is being referenced.

These points are all illustrated in the complete solution to the maximum program and function which is given below.

Program 8.1

```
/* maximum program - solution 2 */
/* using indirect addressing    */

#define MAXNINT -32768

main()
{
    int i, num, max;
```

```
        printf("Please enter 10 integers \n");
        printf(" ...use spaces to separate the integers\n");
        printf(" and end the list with a return. \n");
        max = MAXNINT;
        for (i = 0; i < 10; i++){
                scanf("%d ", &num);
                maximum(num, &max);    /* address of max given */
        }
        printf("\n The maximum number entered was: %d \n", max);
}


/* maximum function - ver 2.0 */
void maximum(int n, int *cmax)
{                               /* cmax is now a pointer          */
        if (n > *cmax)          /* *cmax is the value required    */
                *cmax = n;      /* - that of the second argument  */

}
```

Discussion

The function maximum(int n, int *cmax) bears a superficial resemblance to the original function which we wrote in Chapter 6. However there are important differences which are central to the correct operation of the function. First of all note that cmax is now a pointer to an int variable; it represents the address of the second argument. Thus when called from the main program, the address of max is passed to the function. Since cmax is a pointer to an int then *cmax is a variable of type int. The test within the function uses the value of max (represented by *cmax in the function) and if the integer n passed to the function is greater than the value of max then this is updated accordingly.

If we look at the test program which calls the function we see that there is only one change from the previous version, which is that the address of max is passed as an argument to the function instead of the value. This is necessary since the function is expecting an address (cmax is a pointer).

Exchanging values

One further example of the use of pointers will help to consolidate your understanding of their operation. We will do this by taking as an illustration the basis of many sort routines, that of a function which will reorder two values if the first value is greater than the second. The pseudocode for such a function might be:

        exchange(a,b)
        declaration

```
            integer temp
    if a > b then
            set temp to a
            set a to b
            set b to temp
    end_if
```

Now although in pseudocode this function appears to be correct we know from the previous example that if we coded this in C, the function would not work as we had intended. To recap, the reason is that a and b are given temporary addresses (i.e. local addresses) within the function and it is these values which would be modified, not the values in the main program. Pointers will need to be introduced to produce a correctly working function. Thus a and b need to be the addresses of the variables which are to be tested rather than the actual values. So we need the declaration int *a, *b; in the function parameter list. All references to a and b within the function must then be of the form *a and *b since we need to access the values pointed to by the respective pointers (i.e. we require the 'dereferenced values' of a and b). The function thus becomes:

Program 8.2

```
/* function exchange (a, b)                   */
/* This is used to swap a and b if a is       */
/*  greater than b. This should be called     */
/*  using a statement of the form:            */
/*             exchange(&x, &y);              */

int exchange(int *a, int *b)
{
        int temp;

        if( *a > *b ) {
                temp = *a;      /* the contents of a */
                *a = *b;        /* the contents of b are placed in
                                the variable a */
                *b = temp;      /* the previous contents of a are
                                placed at the address pointed to
                                by b */
        }
}
```

Note that the variable temp does not need to be a pointer variable since it is accessing the contents of an address pointed to by a.

Functions and pointers – a summary

• A pointer is a symbolic representation of an address.

• The address of a variable is accessed by using the unary operator & - so &x is the address of the variable x.

• A pointer is assigned the address of a variable by means of an assignment statement like

```
ptr = &x;
```

• The contents of the address pointed to by a pointer variable can be accessed by means of the indirection (or dereferencing) operator *. For example:

```
contents_of_x = *ptr;
```

• Pointers are declared with the combination of a data type and the * operator, e.g.

```
int *ptr;
float *fptr;
```

• Information can be conveyed to a function in two ways:

(i) by value, e.g. sum(a, b), in which case the values of the variables a and b will not be changed.

(ii) by reference, e.g. exchange(&a, &b), which passes the addresses of a and b, thus allowing the contents of these locations in memory to be changed.

8.4 ARRAYS

In programming we often need to process a set of data all the items of which have the same data type. For example, we might wish to compute some simple statistics from a set of data on examination results. Each student's result will be of the same type (say a percentage mark). We could allocate a variable for each of the student marks. However this becomes very unwieldly once the numbers get to more than ten. In addition we will need to rewrite our program and/or function if the number of students changes. A much better solution is to use an array in which to store these marks. We mentioned briefly in Chapter 6 that an array is generally implemented as a block of storage in which the same data type is stored in consecutive locations. In C an array is a derived type which can be thought of as a variable which is indexed so as to refer to successive elements.

An array is declared by using square brackets which may be empty or which may enclose a constant (symbolic or numeric) defining the size of the array, i.e. the number of elements in the array. Thus

```
int marks[25];
```

declares an integer array called `marks` which has 25 elements. The first array element is defined as element 0, and thus the last element is element `SIZE-1`, where `SIZE` is the size of the array. So the last element of the array `marks` is `marks[24]`.

Fig 8.2   *Array   representation*

	a[0]		a[1]		a[2]	
address	64592	64593	64594	64595	64596	64597

an int array (each int occupies 2 bytes)

Values can be assigned to the individual elements of an array in the usual way, thus

```
marks[3] = 78;
```

will assign the value 78 to the contents of the fourth element of the array `marks` (remember to count from `marks[0]`). Similarly

```
marks[i] = 0;
```

will assign 0 to the `i+1`th element of the array. Note that `i` must be an integer and be within the range 0 to 24.

Storage class

Closely connected with assignment is initialisation, but whilst any array can have a value assigned to any of its elements only certain arrays can be initialised. Arrays possess a storage class either by default or explicitly on declaration. However arrays can only be of storage class **automatic, external** or **static** - they cannot be register. The storage class of an array can affect the values to which an array is initialised. Static and external arrays can have values specifically assigned to their elements in the following ways:

(i)   ```
        /* initialisation of an external array */
        int a[] = {10, 5, 20, 25}; /* declared outside main() */
        ```

will assign to a[0] the value 10, a[1] the value 5 etc. and also implicitly set the size of a to 4.

(ii)    ```
        extern int c[] = {4, 12, -23};
                                    /* declared inside main()*/
        ```

will assign to c[0] the value 4, c[1] the value 12 etc.

(iii)   ```
        /* initialisation of a static array */
        static int b[] = {5, 10, 15, 20, 25};
        ```

will assign to b[0] the value 5, b[1] the value 10 etc.

Note that in these examples the size of the arrays is not specified. The size is determined by the number of items enclosed by the braces. Thus a will have four elements a[0] to a[3] whilst b will contain five elements b[0] to b[4]. What happens if the size is specified and the number of items does not match? The answer is 'It depends'! Let's look at each possibility in turn. First we will consider the case when the number of values to be assigned is greater than the size of the array, e.g. a declaration of the form:

```
static int a[3] = {10, 5, 20, 25};      /* wrong */
```

in which the array size is set explicitly to 3, but four values are enclosed in the initialising braces. This is the simplest case and the end result is that a compilation error will occur.

The second case occurs when the number of initialising values is less than the specified array size. The first so many elements will be set as specified. The remaining elements will be initialised to zero in both static and external arrays. Note, however, that automatic arrays cannot be initialised and the elements of such arrays will contain 'garbage' until values are assigned to them.

Accessing array elements

In the examples above we used an integer constant (i.e. 3) and an integer variable (i.e. i) to access the individual array elements. However, more generally, we can use b[*integer_expression*] to access an element of the array b. An array element is accessed so long as the *integer_expression* evaluates to an integer greater than or equal to zero and less than the size of the array. An
```

attempt to access an array element outside these bounds may cause a run-time error to occur, the exact nature of which is system-dependent. In C there may be no automatic checking to see if an array index is outside the bounds of the array. It is therefore well worth checking all array indices, especially when they consist of a complex integer expression, to ensure that the index is within the array bounds.

Remember that if an array is declared as

```
int array_name[SIZE];
```

then the following relationships hold:

```
lower_bound = 0
upper_bound = SIZE - 1
SIZE = upper_bound + 1
```

A common mistake is to take the upper_bound equal to SIZE, so beware!

8.5 ARRAYS AND POINTERS

In this section we will be examining the relationship between pointers and arrays. There are some similarities between these two concepts, as well as some subtle differences. It is no exaggeration to say that, if you can understand clearly the relationship between pointers and arrays, and the use of pointer arithmetic with arrays, then you will be well on the way to mastering C. So this section is one of the most important sections in the book!

We saw earlier that a pointer is a symbolic representation of an address - a pointer is a variable which takes addresses as values. An array name is also a symbolic address; it is a pointer with a value which remains constant. The array address is the address of the first element of the array (i.e. a[0]) and the remaining elements are stored in consecutive addresses in the machine's memory.

Assigning a pointer to an array can be carried out in a variety of ways. Consider the following program fragment:

```
static int a[] = {2, 4, 6, 8};
int *aptr;
```

The assignment

```
aptr = &a[0];
```

will make the pointer variable aptr point to the initial element of a (that is to a[0]) – aptr thus contains the address of a [0]. Since the array name a stands for the address of the array, which is also the address of the initial element of a, then the assignment

```
aptr = a;
```

produces the same result as the previous assignment.

Once a pointer is assigned to an element of an array it can be used to index the array. The array name itself cannot be indexed even though it is a pointer – but it is a pointer constant and thus always points to the address of the first element of the array. Figure 8.3 illustrates how pointers can be used to access elements of an array. When the pointer p is incremented, it points to the next element in the array. Thus the code:

```
p = a;
p++;
num = *p;
```

is equivalent to:

```
num = a[1];
```

Fig 8.3 *Using a pointer to index an array*

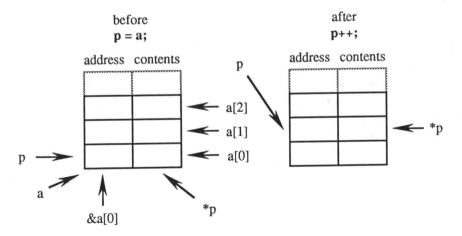

Example

Consider an array a of type int of size 5 and let a have values of 28, -63, 5, 192, 10. The following program illustrates both pointer and array indexing of arrays.

Program 8.3

```
/* illustrating pointers and arrays */

#include <stdio.h>

main ()
{
               /*      a[0] a[1] a[2] a[3] a[4]   */
       static int a[] = {28, -63,   5, 192,   10};
       int i, *p;       /* p declared as pointer to int */

       printf("\n Normal indexing \n");
       for( i = 0; i <= 4; i++)
              printf("element %d : contents = %d\n", i, a[i]);
       p = a;                     /* p now points to a[0] */
       printf("\n Pointer indexing \n");
       printf("\n The address of a[0] is %u \n", a);
       printf("\n The address of p is %u \n", p);
       for( p = a; i < &a[4]; p++)
              printf("address %u : contents = %d\n", p, *p);
}
```

The output I obtained from this program is given below. Run the program for yourself and compare your results with those shown here. The addresses of the pointers will be different. Notice that I have used the %u conversion string to print the addresses. This is because an address cannot be negative and it may be larger than a normal int value allows.

Output from Program 8.3

```
 Normal indexing
element 0 : contents = 28
element 1 : contents = -63
element 2 : contents = 5
element 3 : contents = 192
element 4 : contents = 10

 Pointer indexing
```

```
The address of a[0] is 404

 The address pointed to by p is 404
address 404 : contents = 28
address 406 : contents = -63
address 408 : contents = 5
address 410 : contents = 192
address 412 : contents = 10
```

The important point concerning these results is that once p is assigned the address of the array we can access successive elements by using pointer arithmetic. By adding 1 to the pointer we can point to the next element in the array. In this example we simply incremented p to step through the array. However we can also access a specific element. So, for example, following the assignment of p to a [0] we might access the contents of a [3] with the expression * (p+3).

Arrays using other data types

So far we have restricted our attention to int arrays. However, as you would expect, arrays of the other data types can also be used. They are declared in an obvious way. Some examples are:

```
float weight[50];   /* floating point array - 50 elements */
double x[1000];     /* double array - elements 0 to 999    */
char text[80];      /* character array - or string         */
```

and they are used in an equally obvious manner:

```
for( i = 0; i <= 50; i++)
        scanf("%f", weight[i]);

j = 0;
total = 0;
while( j < 1000 ) {
        total += x[j];
        j++;
}

printf("Message: %s \n", text);    /* prints all of text */
printf("Character : %c", text[4]); /* prints the 5th     */
                                   /*character from text */
```

The above points are fairly straightforward, but how do pointers work with arrays of data types other than int? Provided that the correct pointer is used with its corresponding data type, indexing an array using a pointer will still access the correct elements. Incrementing a pointer adds one to the pointer itself but the result is that the pointer now points to the next item of that particular data type. In order to prove that this is the case we can modify the above program to use a `float` array and a `float` pointer. With these modifications, and appropriate changes to the `printf` statements, I obtained the following output:

Output from Program 8.3 modified to use a float array

```
Normal indexing
element 0 : contents = 28.000000
element 1 : contents = -63.000000
element 2 : contents = 5.000000
element 3 : contents = 192.000000
element 4 : contents = 10.000000


Pointer indexing

The address of a[0] is 404

The address pointed to by p is 404
address 404 : contents = 28.000000
address 408 : contents = -63.000000
address 412 : contents = 5.000000
address 416 : contents = 192.000000
address 420 : contents = 10.000000
```

Again on your system the results may differ slightly, but the important point to note is the difference between the addresses of successive array elements. In this `float` example the difference in address between successive elements is 4 bytes (the size of a `float` variable on my system) whereas in the earlier `int` example the difference was 2 bytes (the size of an `int`). Thus pointers know the size of each data type, pointer arithmetic works in units of `sizeof(type)`.

8.6 ARRAYS AND FUNCTIONS

The programming style which we have adopted in this book is one of modularity and one consequence of this is that arrays will frequently be required for use with functions. We will begin our investigation of the use of arrays with functions by summarising the relationship between array addresses, array elements, array contents and pointers. Table 8.1 illustrates these relationships.

Table 8.1   *The relationship between array addresses, array elements, array contents and pointers*

```
data_type a[SIZE], *p;
/* data_type represents any valid data type */
```

array indexing		pointer equivalent	other
p = a;	a is the base address of array a	p	
	&a[0] the address of element a[0]	p	a
	&a[1] the address of element a[1]	++p	a+1
p = a;	a[0] the contents of element a[0]	*p	*a
	a[1] the contents of element a[1]	*(++p)	*(a+1)

Table 8.1 makes it clear that an array address is also a pointer and so if we wish to pass to a function the address of an array we can just use the array name as an argument in the function call. What form must the function definition take if a parameter is an array name? One method is to declare the parameter as an array of the appropriate type but with no size specified. Thus a function used to compute the arithmetic mean of data stored in an array might have the following structure:

```
float mean(int a[], int n)
{
        .......
        .......
}
```

Because of the equivalence between a pointer and an array address, which we noted above, a completely equivalent form would be:

```
float mean(int *a, int n)
{
        .......
        .......
}
```

Both of these functions would be called by a statement of the form:

```
mean(b, num);
/* Where b is an int array declared as int b[SIZE] */
```

As well as the address of an array we could also need to pass the address of a particular element of an array into a function. This is achieved by a call of the form:

```
function_name(&b[3]);
```

which passes the address of the fourth element of array b into the function. The function declaration of the function parameter would again have to be in one of the two forms just introduced, i.e. int a[], or int *a. Notice that an array element can also be passed as if it was a simple variable (i.e. as function_name(b[3]), with a declaration within the function parameter list of int a), but in this case the array element could not be modified from within the function.

Example – simple statistics

In order to illustrate the use of arrays within functions we will develop a program which enables some simple statistics to be computed on a set of data entered from the keyboard. The statistics we are going to compute are the arithmetic mean, maximum, minimum and standard deviation. The arithmetic mean is given by

$$\text{mean} = \frac{1}{n} \Sigma x_i$$

where Σ represents summation over the set of values (1..... n). The standard deviation is given by

$$\text{standard\_deviation} = \sqrt{(\Sigma(x_i - \text{mean})^2/n)}$$

The program can be broken down into the following modules:

> input the data
> compute the mean
> compute the maximum
> compute the minimum
> compute the standard deviation
> output the results

Each of these can be written as a function which can be called, in the order given above, by the main program. Apart from the above calls what else does the main program consist of? Obviously we will need to declare an array to hold the data which is to entered from the keyboard. This can be done in two ways, but in each case we need to specify the size of the array as well as determine its type. We will use double for the type as this should allow us to use the program for a wide range of data. The simplest way to declare the array is by including the size explicitly in the declaration of the array, e.g.

```
double data[100];
```

An alternative is to use a symbolic constant for the array size, in which case we would have

```
#define SIZE 100
double data[SIZE];
```

This second alternative is to be preferred since we can change the #define instruction if the size of the array requires altering. In addition the symbolic constant SIZE may be useful in checking if we are exceeding the upper bound of the array at any time during the calculations. One important point to note about the size of arrays is that they must be constant; their size cannot be treated as a variable which can be entered at runtime.

Now what about the functions? We need to decide for each function what information needs to be passed to the function and what information is to be passed from the function to the program, and how this is to be achieved. We will look at each in turn.

1. input_data()

This function needs the address of the array data to be passed to it so that the entries can be stored in the array. We can use the fact that a function can return a value back to the program to return the number of elements read. We can use -1 to flag if too many were entered. The function header will thus be of the form

```
int input_data(double a[])
```

Notice that, although the data we are analysing is to be stored in an array of type double, this does not alter the fact that the function itself (input_data()) is of type int. We wish to return the number of values entered and so int is the correct choice for this function.

2. mean()

Once again we will need to pass the address of the array to the function, but in addition we require the number of values read in, which is obtained from the input_data function. The value we wish to return is the mean of the data, which must be of type double, so if we use return to pass back the result then the function will also have to be of type `double`. The skeleton of this function therefore looks like

```
double mean(double a[], int n)
{
        .......
        .......
        return(average);
}
```

3. maximum()

You are already familiar with this function, all that is required is a modification to enable the function to accept an array as an argument rather than a single variable. Based on an earlier version of the `maximum()` function we might have the following code:

```
void maximum(double a[], int n, double *max)
{
        int i;

        for( i = 0; i < n; i++)
                if( a[i] > *max)
                        *max = a[i];
}
```

In this case we do not need to return a value so the function can be declared as type `void`. The address of the current value of the maxium is passed via the argument `*max`. This value must be initialised to the largest negative number before it is used anywhere else in the program.

4. minimum()

This function is very similar to the previous function and is left as an exercise for the reader to write.

5. st_deviation() (standard deviation)

This function requires three parameters:

the address of the array containing the data to be analysed,
the mean (from a previous calculation), and
the number of data values.

The function can now be written down as:

```
/* function st_deviation()                                */
/* this computes, and returns, the standard deviation     */
/* of a set (n) of data of type double.                   */
/* ensure that the header file                            */
/* <math.h> is included in the program                    */

double st_deviation(double a[], double mean, int n)
{
    int i;
    double sum = 0, st_dev;

    for( i = 0; i < n; i++)
        sum += (a[i] - mean)*(a[i] - mean);
    st_dev = sqrt(sum/n);          /* library function sqrt() */
    return(st_dev);
}
```

Since this function requires the square root function (sqrt ()) the maths header file must be included in the program header (i.e. #include <math.h>).

6. output_result ()

This is a simple function which need not return a value and so will be of type void. It requires as parameters the values of the mean, maximum, minimum and standard deviation. It would also be useful to pass into the function the number of data values upon which the statistics are based. As an exercise try writing this function for yourself before reading on.

The final program

The complete program to compute simple statistics is given below.

Program 8.4

```
/*    Simple Statistics      */
/*  This program uses functions to compute the following :
            arithmetic mean
            minimum
            maximum
            standard deviation
        of up to 100 real (floating point) numbers.
        More numbers can be analysed by change the value of SIZE
*/

#include <stdio.h>
#include <math.h>
#define SIZE 100
```

```
#define MAXDBLE 1.0e37 /* approx. largest positive number */
#define MINDBLE -1.0e38 /* approx. largest negative number */

main()
{
    void  maximum(double a[], int n, double *max),
          minimum(double a[], int n, double *min),
          output_result(double av, double max, double min,
                                   double std, int n);
    double mean(double a[], int n),
           st_deviation(double a[], double mean, int n);
    int input_data(double a[]);

    double data[SIZE], max = MINDBLE, min = MAXDBLE, av, std;
    int n;

    printf("\n This program computes simple statistics for ");
    printf("up to 100 real numbers \n");
    printf("\n Please enter the data separated by commas. \n");
    printf("Use an * followed by a newline to terminate \n");
    n = input_data(data);
    if( n > 0) {
        av = mean(data, n);
        maximum(data, n, &max);
        minimum(data, n, &min);
        std = st_deviation(data, av, n);
        output_result(av, max, min, std, n);
    } else
        printf("\n\n **** Error in data entry **** \n");
}

/* function to input data
      this returns the number of data items read
      or -1 if no valid data has been input
      or if the upper array bound has been exceeded
*/
int input_data(double a[])
{
    int i = -1;
    double x;

    while(scanf("%lf,", &x) == 1){     /* entry checking */
        i++;
        if( i >= SIZE ) {
            printf("\n *** too many numbers entered ***");
            return(-1);
        } else
            a[i] = x;
```

```
        return(++i);       /* return the no. of values entered
}

/* function mean - to compute the arithmetic mean */

double mean(double a[], int n)
{
     int i;
     double total = 0;

     for( i = 0; i < n; i++)
          total += a[i];
     return(total/n);
}

/* maximum function */

void maximum(double a[], int n, double *max)
{
     int i;

     for( i = 0; i < n; i++)
          if( a[i] > *max)
               *max = a[i];
}

/* minimum function */

void minimum(double a[], int n, double *min)
{
     int i;

     for( i = 0; i < n; i++)
          if( a[i] < *min)
               *min = a[i];
}
/* standard deviation function */
/*   as above   */

/* function : output_result */

void output_result(double av, double max, double min,
                                  double std, int n)
{
     printf("\n The statistics are as follows:\n\n");
     printf("\t\t There were %d data values\n",n);
     printf("\t\t Average: \t\t %lf\n", av);
     printf("\t\t Maximum: \t\t %lf\n", max);
```

```
printf("\t\t Minimum: \t\t %lf\n", min);
printf("\t\t Standard Deviation: \t %lf\n", std);
}
```

Exercise

Enter the complete program and test it. Use simple data to begin with so that you can hand test the results. To check the (limited) error trapping change SIZE to 10 and enter more than ten numbers.

8.7 STRINGS

A string in C simply consists of a consecutive collection of characters stored one character to a byte and terminated with the NULL character ('\0'). A string is thus a one-dimensional array of type char and is declared in a similar way to an array of any other data type. For example:

```
char name[20];
```

declares a char name of maximum length 19 characters (elements 0 to 18, element 19 stores the null character).

```
char prompta[] = "Press any key to continue \n";
char long_word[] =
        "pneumonoultramicroscopicsilicovolcanoconiosis";
```

declares and initialises string constants. (The second of which takes over as the longest word in the English language (*Oxford English Dictionary*, 2nd edn.)!) These must therefore be static arrays which are either declared outside the program definition (i.e. before main()) or preceded by the keyword static.

At first sight, a string consisting of a single character might be thought to be identical to a char variable. However this is not the case. The two representations are given below (Figure 8.4).

Fig 8.4 *Comparison of a single character stored in an array (*char) and stored as a char*

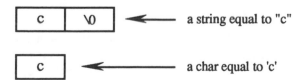

We have seen already that there is a close relationship between pointers and arrays and so it will come as no surprise that a string can be defined using pointers, i.e. by means of the de-referencing operator `*`. Thus the `prompta` string used above could also be written as

```
char *promptp = "Press any key to continue \n";
```

However, whilst in most cases the two representations can be thought of as equivalent there are one or two important differences. Let us look at the similarities and the differences, taking the similarities first. Both of these representations indicate that the names `prompta` and `promptp` point to the string "Press any key to continue \n" and that the amount of memory taken up by the string is determined by the length of the string itself, which in this case amounts to 29 characters (plus the NULL character). The string is also stored in `static` storage. So far so good, but now we come to the differences.

In the array version the name `prompta` stands for the address of the first element of the `char` array (i.e. the address of the first character 'P') and cannot be altered. Just as you cannot change the address of a memory location so too you cannot alter the address of an array name. However in the pointer version `promptp` is a variable which points to the first character in the string "Press any key to continue \n" and since it is a variable an extra location in memory has to be set aside to store the contents of `promptp` - i.e. the address to which the pointer `promptp` is pointing. So that is the first difference. The second difference you may have already spotted and this concerns the fact that `promptp` is a variable whilst `prompta` is a constant. This means that the value of `promptp` can be modified: it can be made to 'point to' another string. Thus, if we had a second string,

```
eprompt = "Press E to EXIT \n";
```

and this statement was followed by the statement

```
promptp = eprompt;
```

then `promptp` would now be pointing to the string

```
"Press E to EXIT \n"
```

Once this latter assignment has been made we have lost access to the original string "Press any key to continue \n" which was pointed to by `promptp`. However, provided that the array `prompta[]` is declared in our program, we can still obtain access to that string via the assignment statement

```
promptp = prompta;
```

Note, though, that the statement `prompta = promptp;` is illegal since `prompta` is a string constant.

Example - coded messages

One simple type of code involves the substitution of one letter for another. If for example the letter A is replaced by P once, in the coded message it will always be replaced by P. In order to generate the code the alphabet is randomised and placed under the normal alphabet, e.g.

ABCDEFGHIJKLMNOPQRSTUVWXYZ

BSKYETOVPRQDAZLCJHNMIGFXWU

The task of encoding a message then becomes simply that of replacing each letter in the message from line one with its substitute in line two.

We will illustrate the use of strings by coding functions to generate the code (i.e. line two), code the message, get the message and print it.

The code generation function is reasonably straightforward. We need to select a random number between 1 and 26 and then use this to place a letter in an array. However we need to be a little careful since we cannot allow duplicate letters - otherwise the code might become impossible! We can get over this problem by starting with an array filled with the alphabet and step through it exchanging each element of the array in turn with another element chosen at random. We can use the library function `rand()` to produce a pseudo random number and ensure that it is in the correct range by using the modulo operator. This function simply needs the address of the array which is to hold the code. One possible version is given below (Program 8.5).

Program 8.5

```
/* set_code function
     this generates a simple substitution code
     (upper_case letters only are used )
     The code is returned in the array code
*/

void set_code(char *code)    /* could also use code[] */
{
     int i, rnum;
     char c;

     for( i = 0; i < 26; i++)
```

```
            code[i] = 'A' + i;      /* set up initial alphabet */
                                    /*    now randomise it      */
       for( i = 0; i < 26; i++) {
            rnum = rand() % 26;
            c = code[i];            /* letter in position i     */
            code[i] = code[rnum];   /* put randomly selected    */
                              /.*    letter in its place  */
            code[rnum] = c;   /* put c in the random element    */
       }
       code[26] = NULL;             /* ensure character array has a */
                                    /*                  terminator  */

}
```

This function should be easy for you to understand, given the description above. Look over it to make sure that you understand how it works.

Before we start coding the message we need to have a message to code. So let's write the get_message() function. All this entails is reading characters from the keyboard into a character array. We can do it in a couple of ways. The way I have chosen to implement it uses pointer arithmetic. Try writing the code for yourself using normal array indexing.

Program 8.6

```
/* get_message() function
       This functions reads a message from the keyboard
            and stores it in a char array
*/

void get_message(char *mess)
{
       printf("\n Enter your message (max 80 characters) :\n");
       while((*mess = getchar()) != '\n')
            mess++;      /* increment pointer */
       }
       *mess = NULL;     /* NULL will be defined as '\0' */
}
```

The function to code the message is also quite straightforward. Assume that the array which holds the randomised alphabet is called code[]. Then element 0 of this array will contain the new letter for the letter A, element 1 the new letter for B and so on. If the coded message is to be placed in the array c_mess[] this can be achieved with a statement of the form:

```
       c_mess[i] = code[mess[i] - 'A'];
```

Or, as an alternative we can use:

```
*c_mess = code[*mess - 'A'];
```

We will use the second option. There are a couple of other points which we need to look at before we write the function. Firstly what are we to do about upper- and lower-case letters? We could make the cases correspond in both the original and the coded message, but that would be to give valuable information to any unauthorised person reading the coded message! So we will code all letters as upper-case. This means the function will need to convert lower-case letters to upper-case ones. (This can be achieved with a standard function (toupper()), but we will write our own code to illustrate the method.)

The next point involves characters other than letters. The simplest option is to ignore them and we will adopt this approach. However it might be useful to code the full stop - this could be done by replacing it with the word STOP, suitably encoded of course. We leave this as an exercise for the reader.

We can now write the code_message() function.

Program 8.7

```
/* code_message() function
        This takes as parameters the addresses of the arrays:
                mess - the original message
                code - the code being used
                c_mess - the final coded message
        Punctuation is ignored (including spaces)
        lower-case are converted to upper-case
*/
void code_message( char *mess, char *code, char *c_mess)
{
        int ucase_offset = 'A' - 'a';
        while( *mess != NULL ) {
                if( *mess >= 'a' && *mess <= 'z' )
                        *mess += ucase_offset;
                if( *mess >= 'A' && *mess <= 'Z' ) {
                        *c_mess = code[*mess - 'A'];
                        c_mess++;
                }
                mess++;
        }
        *c_mess = NULL;
}
```

The final function we require is to print out the message. This uses the library function putchar() to print one character at a time to the screen. Since there will be no spaces in the coded message we can add a space every five characters.

The function then takes the form given below.

Program 8.8

```
/* The print_message() function
      This takes the message supplied and prints it out
      adding a space every five characters
*/

void print_message(char *mess)
{
      int i = 0;

      putchar('\n');
      while( *mess != NULL ) {
            putchar(*mess);
            mess++;
            i++;
            if( i == 5 ) {   /* add a space every 5 characters */
                  putchar(' ');
                  i = 0;
            }
      }
      putchar('\n');
}
```

Now that we have the necessary functions it is a simple matter to write a program to use them. One possible program is given as Program 8.9 below. Work through all the functions given above and the program itself and check that you understand how they work. Finally try the program out for yourself.

Program 8.9

```
/* coded message example
      this uses simple substitution to generate a code
*/

#include <stdio.h>

void set_code(char *code), print_message(char *messout),
      get_message(char *mess),
      code_message(char *messin, char *code, char *messout);

main()
{
      char a[27], mess[80], coded_mess[80];

      printf("\n The code is: \n");      /* print code for
```

```
checking purposes */
      print_message(a);              /*    normal alphabet   */
      set_code(a);                   /*    generate code      */
      print_message(a);             /* randomised alphabet */
      get_message(mess);
      code_message(mess, a, coded_mess);
      printf("\n The coded message is : \n");
      print_message(coded_mess);
}


/* enter the functions here:
      program 8.5
      program 8.6
      program 8.7
      program 8.8
/*
```

8.8 STRING LIBRARY FUNCTIONS

Most versions of C currently available will contain a library of functions which can be used for handling strings. In this section we will list the most common of these functions, describe briefly how they work and look at a couple of examples which use them.

String handling functions

These functions which are contained in the header file string.h, fall into two broad categories, those which carry out tests on a string and return an int, and those which perform string manipulations (e.g. copy from one string to another). This latter group do not check that the destination string is large enough to hold the incoming string and thus array overflow may occur. It is therefore up to the programmer to make sure that possible overflows are trapped. We will see in one of the examples this process being implemented.

Test functions

strlen(s)

This function returns a count of the number of characters pointed to by s up to the \0 character, i.e. the length of the string.

```
int slen;
static char long_word[] =
            "pneumonoultramicroscopicsilicovolcanoconiosis";
{

      slen = strlen(long_word);
```

```
        printf("\n The length of the longest word ");
        printf("in the O.E.D. is %d \n", slen);
}
```

strcmp(s1, s2)

The strcmp() function compares string s1 with s2, where s1 and s2 are pointers to char. If s1 is lexicographically less than s2 (in dictionary order comes before s2) then the function returns a negative number, if s1 and s2 are equal it returns zero, and if s1 is lexicographically greater than s2 a positive integer is returned. Both s1 and s2 must be terminated with a NULL ('\0').

strncmp(s1, s2, n)

This function is similar to strcmp() but the maximum number of characters compared is n.

String manipulating functions

strcat(s1, s2)

s1 and s2 are pointers to char. The string s2, together with its null terminator is appended to the end of string s1, the first character of s2 replacing the null character in s1. The value of s1 is returned.

strncat(s1, s2, n)

This function is the same as the previous one but at most n characters are appended.

strcpy(s1, s2)

The strcpy() function copies the string s2 to string s1, including the '\0'. The function returns s1.

strncpy(s1, s2, n)

This function behaves as for strcpy but at most n characters are copied. s1 is padded out with '\0' s if s2 has less than n characters.

Example

The program given below illustrates a use of the strcpy() function and also illustrates an important point concerning strings. We noted earlier that many C compilers do not keep a check on array bounds and so the programmer needs to do this for him or herself. This is particularly important where strings are concerned as it is very easy to write over the end of an array using strings without realising it. We will first list the program and then present some typical output. We will then go on to discuss some points of interest involving strings.

Program 8.10

```
/* a program illustrating the importance
   of keeping track of string lengths
*/
#include <stdio.h>
#define SIZE 15

main()
{
        static char s1[SIZE], s2[SIZE];
        static char s3[] = "this program shows why ";
        static char s4[] = "you need to watch strings";
        /* neither of these arrays is long enough to hold their
                                                         strings */

        printf("\nafter copying s3 to s1 and s4 to s2\n\n");
        strcpy(s1, s3);
        strcat(s2, s4);
        printf("                 : .........|.........|.........|...\n");
        printf("s3 (%5u) : %-40s  len: %u\n", s3, s3, strlen(s3));
        printf("s4 (%5u) : %-40s  len: %u\n", s4, s4, strlen(s4));
        printf("s1 (%5u) : %-40s  len: %u\n", s4, s4, strlen(s1));
        printf("s2 (%5u) : %-40s  len: %u\n", s4, s4, strlen(s2));
}
```

The output produced by this program will be of the form:

```
After copying s3 to s1 and s4 to s2

               : .........|.........|.........|...
s3 (   404) : This program shows why                  len: 23
s4 (   428) : you need to watch strings               len: 25
s1 (  1716) : This program shyou need to watch strings len: 40
s2 (  1731) : you need to watch strings               len: 25
```

Discussion

First of all note that the value of SIZE is too small for the strings involved. Ideally it should be at least 26 to allow for the NULL character at the end of s4. Notice also the addresses of the strings. The addresses given in brackets are the starting location for the respective strings. These addresses are a key to understanding the output and the problem. In particular note the addresses of s1 and s2. They are separated by 15 bytes. This means that if s1 contains a string which is longer than 15 bytes it will overlap into the beginning of s2. Now look at the contents of s1 and s2. The idea was to copy 'This program shows why' into s1 and 'you need to watch strings' into s2. The output reveals that s1 contains part of the required string. However, because the string is longer than 15 bytes it overlaps into s2 so that when the string is copied to s2 it overwrites the end of s1. If you try this program out for yourself then beware! You may get runtime errors occurring. The moral is: make sure that the size of char arrays is big enough to hold the required strings. Also use strlen() to check the length of strings and prevent problems such as the above.

8.9 ARRAYS OF STRINGS

An array of strings is just an array, the elements of which are themselves arrays of characters. As such they can be considered as two-dimensional (rectangular) arrays or as ragged arrays. What is a ragged array? Consider the following character array declaration.

```
static char some_strings[][20] = {"This ",
                                   "is ",
                                   "an odd assortment ",
                                   "of strings "};
```

The declaration static char some_strings[][20] sets up four consecutive arrays each of length 20, as in Figure 8.5. In this case the strings are occupying the first elements in each array with the remaining elements padded out with nulls.

Now consider the alternative declaration:

```
static char *string_pointers[4] = {"This ",
                                    "is ",
                                    "an odd assortment ",
                                    "of strings "};
```

This is an array of four 'pointers to strings', or pointers to char arrays, and would be stored as an array with each string only occupying as much space in memory as it requires, that is the string length plus one for the NULL terminator. Arrays of this type are often called **ragged arrays** because of the uneven length of each string. This second method of constructing arrays of strings is more compact than the first one especially if there is a large variation in string length. So when storage space is at a premium or strings are likely to vary considerably in length, it is always worth considering this second approach.

Fig 8.5 *Arrays of strings*

static char some_strings[ ][20]

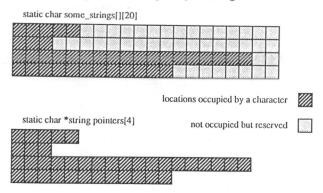

locations occupied by a character

not occupied but reserved

static char *string pointers[4]

8.10 TWO-DIMENSIONAL ARRAYS

The last section introduced two-dimensional arrays in the context of arrays of strings or arrays of type *char, or arrays of arrays of type char. In this section we will be looking at two-dimensional arrays of other types and in section 8.11 we will take a brief look some of the complexities involving pointers and two-dimensional arrays.

One situation where two-dimensional arrays are useful is in calculations involving matrix operations. The function m_mult(a, b, c) computes the product of two vectors (i.e. 1-dimensional arrays) a and b and places the result in the matrix c (i.e. 2-dimensional array). In general the matrix product is defined as:

$$c_{ij} = \sum_{k} a_{ik} b_{kj}$$

where the matrix a has *m* rows and *n* columns, and b has *n* rows and *p* columns. The matrix c therefore has dimensions of *m* rows by *p* columns. Notice that the number of columns of a must equal the number of rows of b.

Confining ourselves to vectors for a and b, the matrix multiplication reduces to

$$c_{ij} = a_{i1} b_{1j}$$

where b is now treated as a row vector ($b_{1j} = (b_{j1})^T$).

Since a and b are 1-dimensional arrays they can be declared in the function parameter list as a[ ], b[ ]. However c is a 2-dimensional array and we must therefore specify the number of columns (i.e. the second dimension of the array). The reason for this is due to the way in which C allocates memory to a multi-dimensional array. Suppose we have a 2-dimensional array a[4][3], then the elements of this array will be stored in memory in successive locations in the sequence:

```
a[0][0], a[0][1], a[0][2], a[1][0], ...... a[3][2]
```

Thus the second dimension is required in order to allocate memory as well as to compute the position of a particular element. Let the address of a[0][0] be n, then a[0][1] will be stored at location n + 1, a[0][j] will be stored at location n + j, and the general element a[i][j] will be stored at location n + 3 * i + j. The 3 in this expression originates from the size of the second dimension of the array. Without knowing the size of the second dimension there would be no means of locating an element.

Program 8.11

```
/* matrix multiplication function
        This function takes as arguments two vectors (a and b)
        of size 3 and places the vector product in the matrix c
*/
void m_mult(float a[], float b[], float c[][3])
{
        int i, j;

        for (i = 0; i < 3; i++)
                for (j = 0; j < 3; j++)
                        c[i][j] = a[i] * b[j];
}
```

Notice that, although the function modifies the contents of the array c, we have not used the dereferencing operator (*). The reason for this is that c represents the address of the first element of the 2-dimensional array, which is precisely what we want to pass to the function.

8.11 MORE ON POINTERS

We saw in sections 8.4 and 8.5 how pointers were related to one-dimensional arrays. How are they related to two-dimensional arrays? Consider the declaration:

```
int array a[3][5];
```

The variable a is the name of an array and as such it is also a pointer. This declaration can be thought of as an array of arrays of integers, that is three arrays each consisting of an array of 5 integers. The first element of the two-dimensional array is a[0][0], which is also the first element of the sub-array a[0]. So we would expect that the address pointed to by a[0][0] would be identical to the address pointed to by a[0]. Let's write a short program to try this out.

Program 8.12

```
/* pointer.c
        A program to find out how pointers and 2-D arrays work
*/

#define TEXT "\n The address pointed to by "

main()
{
     int a[3][5];

     printf("\n Pointers and two-dimensional arrays \n");
     printf("%s a \t \t = %u ", TEXT, a);            /* A */
     printf("%s a[0] \t = %u ", TEXT, a[0]);         /* B */
     printf("%s a[0][0] \t - %u ", TEXT, &a[0][0]); /* C */
}
```

There are a few points worth making about the program before we look at the output from it. Firstly, since we are using the same piece of text a number of times we have used a #define statement to make life easier! Secondly we have used tabs so that the output will be lined up. Notice also the difference in the printf() statements between line /* C */ and the other two. In order to get the address of a[0][0] we need to use the expression &a[0][0], the reason being that a[0][0] refers to the contents at that address, whereas a and a[0] are pointers. The output I obtained from this program was:

```
The address pointed to by a           = 65462
The address pointed to by a[0]        = 65462
The address pointed to by a[0][0]     = 65462
```

These results show the numerical equivalence of a, a[0] and &a[0][0]. However there are still differences between them. Remember that a pointer points to a particular data type so that when we increment a pointer (or add one to an array name) the address pointed to will depend upon what object was pointed to originally. Thus, since in this example a[0] points to the first element of an array containing five integers, then expression a[0] + 1 will point to the next int (i.e. a[0][1]). However a points to an array of five integers and so a + 1 points to the next sub-array, i.e. to the start of the sub-array a[1].

How do we use pointers with two dimensional arrays? One way forward is suggested by the discussion in the last paragraph. We can set up a pointer which points to an array. So using the example above we need a pointer pointing to an array of type int. On first sight the declaration

```
int *p[];    /* array of pointers to int */
```

would seem to be correct. However this is in fact an 'array of pointers to int', the reason being that the square brackets have higher precedence than the indirection operator. In order to obtain a 'pointer to an array of ints' we need to use parentheses to override the normal rules of precedence. The correct form is therefore:

```
int (*p)[];  /* pointer to an array of ints */
             /* or pointer to a pointer to an int */
```

If we now assign p to a (i.e. p = a;) then the address pointed to by p will be the address pointed to by a and by incrementing p we point to the next sub-array. Thus

p++   and   a + 1   refer to the same thing.

So much for the addresses. How do we obtain the value of an array element of a two-dimensional array using pointers? In the case of a simple pointer variable pfloat the value of the float is *pfloat. In the present case it should be obvious that *p will not work, as this is just another pointer (to a one- dimensional array). However we do in fact require the contents of the int pointed to by this second pointer. So we might try **p. This is indeed the solution. So if p = a then

**p   and   a[0][0]   refer to the same thing.

Then after p++, **p will equal a[1][0]. Now we have access to the first element of the subarray a[i] but it might also be useful if we could gain access to the other array elements as well. To achieve this using pointers we need to declare another pointer, this time of type int, to point to an individual integer in array a. So a declaration of the form

```
int *ip;
```

followed by the assignment

```
ip = p[1];
```

will enable ip to point to the int value in a[1][0]. Then all we need to do to access the contents of a[1][1] is to increment the int pointer ip (i.e. ++ip or ip++). Finally to obtain the actual value of the int stored in this element of the array we simply use *ip.

8.12 USING ARRAYS – THE BRIDGE TUTOR

This chapter has provided us with many of the necessary data structures to begin programming the Bridge Tutor program in earnest. We can use an array to simulate a deck of cards. For the moment we need not worry about the exact correspondence between array elements and a particular card. All we need to know is that such a correspondence is possible.

Shuffling

The first process which we require is one to shuffle the cards. This reduces to the problem of randomising array elements. There are a number of ways of simulating this task, but haven't we come across a similar problem already? The code program (Program 8.5) involved something almost identical. There we effectively shuffled a pack consisting of 26 cards with each one corresponding to a letter of the alphabet. So all we need do is modify the program to cater for 52 cards instead of 26 letters! Turn back to program 8.5 and see if you can work out the necessary changes. (We can simply fill the array with integers from 1 to 52 to represent the 52 cards.)

Dealing

The function to deal the cards simply involves distributing the 52 randomly distributed integers (cards) between four hands. In bridge the four hands (or players) are given the names North, East, South and West. We could distribute the cards between these four hands by giving the first 13 cards to South, the next thirteen to West and so on. However we may as well try and be as realistic as possible. This means that we deal cards in turn to South, West, North and East until all 52 cards are dealt. Assuming that we have an array called deck[52] and that each players cards are stored in arrays south[13], west[13], north[13] and east[13] then we can simulate a deal with a function of the form shown in Program 8.13.

Program 8.13

```
/* function void deal(void)
     This simulates the dealing of a pack of
     cards to four players: south, west, north and east.
     These should be declared outside of main()
     in order for them to be treated as external arrays.
     The pack of cards is represented by the int array deck,
     which should also be external.
*/
void deal(void)
{
```

```
    int i, j;

    for (j = 0, i = 0; j <52; j += 4, i++) {
         south[i] = deck[j];
         west[i] = deck[j+1];
         north[i] = deck[j+2];
         east[i] = deck[j+3];
    }
}
```

Sorting

Another function which is required is one to sort the cards within each hand, since we want to be able to display them in a sensible order, within each suit in ascending or descending order. We will assume that we have an array of n integers and we wish to sort these into order. There are many sort routines available but as we are not dealing with large arrays we will use a bubble sort, which is one of the simplest sort routines. A bubble sort works by comparing adjacent items and exchanging them if they are out of order. Thus items 'bubble' through the array. By using nested loops we can guarantee that all the items will be sorted when we exit the final loop. A possible algorithm is given below.

> **while** array not sorted **do**
>   set i equal to 1
>   **while** i is less than array_size **do**
>   **if** element[i-1] > element[1] **then** exchange()
>   set i equal to i plus 1
> **end_while**

We still need to expand on a couple of aspects of this algorithm. First of all, how do we know when the array is sorted? Consider the inner `while` loop. If this is traversed without any exchanges taking place, then the array must be sorted. So we can use a flag to test this condition and exit from the outer loop once the condition becomes TRUE. Secondly how does the function exchange work? Well, the answer to this question is very straightforward. We have already written just such a function (Program 8.2). Armed with this information we can write our sort function, i.e.:

Program 8.14

```
/* a simple bubble sort function
     This sorts into descending order
     elements in the array a.
     n is the number of elements in a
*/
```

```
void bubble(int a[], int n)
{
     int i, sorted = FALSE; /* sorted is a flag to indicate */
                            /* when the array has been sorted */
     while( !sorted){
          sorted = TRUE;
          for( i = 1; i < n; i++ )
               exchange(&a[i-1], &a[i], &sorted);
     }
}
```

This function uses a modified version of the exchange function which we wrote earlier. The new version is:

Program 8.15

```
/* function exchange()
   This function swaps two ints if the
   first parameter is less than the second.
   *sorted is set to FALSE if a swap took place

void exchange(int *p, int *q, int *sorted)
{
     int temp;

     if (*p < *q) {
          temp = *p;
          *p = *q;
          *q = temp;
          *sorted = FALSE;        /* not in order */
     }
}
```

Note the way in which the array elements are passed to the function exchange(). Since we may need to alter the contents of these elements we must pass the address of each element to the function. (Think of a[i] as a simple variable.) These functions are a beginning to the bridge tutor program; we will be extending them later on.

SUMMARY

In this chapter we:

> • saw that a pointer is defined as a symbolic
>   representation of an address.

> • were introduced to the indirection (or dereferencing)

operator * which is used to inform the compiler that the variable following the operator is a pointer variable.

- noted that pointer variables have data types associated with them.

- saw how pointer variables can be used within a function to change the value of parameters passed to the function.

- extended our understanding of arrays and noted that they can have storage classes of static, extern and auto.

- saw how pointers and arrays are linked, and in particular the equivalence of:
  pointer variables and array names, and
  *pointer_name and *array_name (to access the contents of array_name).

- investigated the use of arrays of pointers to access two-dimensional arrays.

- investigated the way arrays are used in functions.

- used arrays of characters to construct strings and noted the difference between **rectangular** arrays and **ragged** arrays.

EXERCISES

1. Write a function called replace(c) which takes as a parameter a character and, if it is in upper-case, replaces it with its lower-case equivalent. Write a program to test it.

2. Write a program to read in up to twenty lines of text and display the longest line.

3. Write a program to read in up to a hundred words and to keep track of the first and last word in alphabetical order, as well as the longest word. The program should display all three words.

4. Write a function to compute the area of a triangle, given the three sides. The function should return the area which should be of type float. (Use the

formula area = $\sqrt{s(s-a)(s-b)(s-c)}$ where $s = (a + b + c)/2$.)

5. Modify the function above to return -1.0 if the sides do not form a triangle.

6. Write a program to test the matrix multiplication function (Program 8.11). Produce two versions of your program, one using static arrays for the two vectors a and b, and one requesting the user to enter values for the two vectors concerned.

7. Modify function m_mult () (Program 8.11)to deal with the multiplication of matrices (2-dimensional arrays) rather than vectors.
a.   Assume that all the matrices are square matrices.
b.   Allow for rectangular matrices; you will need to specify the number of rows in matrix a   (and hence the number of columns in b).

8. Enter the program pointer.c (Program 8.12) and check your output with that given. Modify the program by giving values to the array a and by adding a pointer declaration of the form   (*p) [];. Add pointer indexing and print statements to find the addresses and contents of pointers as discussed in section 8.11. To check your results you will also need to print out the address of each arrray element.

9. Enter the bridge functions and the test program and test it.

10. Write a program which will generate 1000 random numbers and then carry out some simple statistics on them. Use the program developed earlier (statistical calculator) as a basis for computing the statistics.

11. Write a function char read_command(int *pn1, int *pn2, int *valid) for the line editor program, where *pn1 and *pn2 are the line numbers for editing and *valid is TRUE if the command line has valid syntax. The function should read the complete command line, which may be of the form n1,n2x, where n1 and n2 are the line numbers and x is the command. The correct values for *pn1 and *pn2 should be set within this function. For example, if % is entered, *pn1 should be set to 0 and *pn2 to the next available line (see the discussion on pp. 16 – 21). Before exiting the function check the bounds for *pn1 and *pn2 and if necessary make sensible adjustments to their values (e.g. neither should be negative or greater than next).

9 Input and output – more thoughts

"...How can I know what I think till I see what I say?"   Graham Wallas

9.1 INTRODUCTION

Throughout this book a number of functions have been used to enable information to be input to a program and information to be output from a program. In this chapter we will summarise and compare these functions and in the process introduce other standard input/ouput (i/o) functions which we have not encountered so far. In the second part of the chapter we will extend our knowledge of i/o to the reading and writing of data to and from files rather than the standard i/o with which we have been concerned so far. Finally we will use these functions to extend the programs we have been developing and to write one or two other useful programs.

9.2 INPUT AND OUTPUT – THE STORY SO FAR

Table 9.1 gives a comprehensive list of the functions available for input and output to the standard i/o devices – normally the keyboard for input and the screen for output. The functions fall into two main categories, those allowing for formatted input and output and those permitting unformatted input and output.

A note about printf()

In most of the programs so far we have used `printf()` whenever we have needed to output information to the screen. This function provides great flexibility; it can be used to output simple messages as well as to display the results of calculations in a variety of formats, for example,

```
printf("Welcome to the world of C\n");
```

and

Table 9.1 *Standard input/output functions*

Action	**Arguments**	**Returned value**	**Example**
Character i/o			
`getchar()` get a character from standard input (default keyboard)	none	the character read	`c= getchar();`
`putchar(c)` write a character to standard output (default screen)	character (c) for output	character written, EOF on error	`putchar('a');`
Line i/o			
`gets(*s)` get a string terminated by a '\n'. The '\n' is replaced with a '\0'	`char *s` - pointer to an array s	s or NULL if EOF occurs or error while getting the string	`ln = gets(s);`
`puts(*s)` write a string to the standard output plus a '\n'	`char *s` - pointer to an array s	EOF if an error occurs, else non-negative	`puts("bye!");`
Formatted i/o			
`scanf(control_string, ....)`		reads formatted input from the standard input file (keyboard)	
`printf(control_string, ....)`		writes formatted output to the standard output file (screen)	

```
printf("\n\t double \t %d", sizeof(double));
```

For small programs, and in the examples which we have been using to illustrate the constructs of C, using `printf()` has presented us with no problems. However because of the very flexibility of the function it takes up a significant amount of memory and because of its complexity takes longer to execute than other, simpler functions. Often the use of simpler alternatives can provide more precise control and improve the speed. In many instances we have used `printf()` to display a simple message, e.g. 'Data read in – starting processing'. In such cases there is no need to invoke the full capability of this function with all the overheads in additional memory which it entails. A simpler solution is to use the put string function `puts()` to display the desired string on the screen. Remember, though, that this function always appends a '\n' to the end of a string and so, if it is essential that the cursor remains at the end of the string, an alternative must be found.

9.3 MORE ON FORMATTING USING *PRINTF()*

The flexibility of `printf()` has already been mentioned and we have seen that the argument list in the function call can be of arbitrary length. We have used control strings of varying degrees of complexity employing most of the conversion characters listed in Table 3.5 (i.e. %c, %d, %e, %f, %g, %s). In this section we are going to look at the remaining conversion characters and then see how we can modify these conversion specifications to improve the layout of text.

Some other conversion characters

The three remaining conversion characters (which should be found in all versions of C) are o, x and u (which we have already used from time to time). These characters are used to print integers in octal and hexadecimal and unsigned integers respectively. Thus Program 9.1 will produce the output:

```
25 as an octal integer is 31
25 as a hexadecimal integer is f9
25 as an unsigned integer is 25
```

Program 9.1

```c
/* printing octal, hexadecimal and unsigned integers */
#include <stdio.h>

main()
{
    int num;

    num = 25;
    printf("\n %d as an octal integer is %o ",num, num);
    printf("\n %d as a hexadecimal integer is %x ",num, num);
    printf("\n %d as an unsigned integer is %u ",num, num);
}
```

Conversion specification modifiers

The output for `printf()` can be modified by use of explicit formatting information in a conversion specification. So, for example, a `float` can be output with 2 decimal place precision by using the conversion specification `%.2f` and an integer right justified in a field of width 8 characters with the specification `%8d`. Some examples involving integers are given in Table 9.2. (See also Table 9.4.)

Table 9.2   *printf() conversion_string examples: char and int*

```
int n = 23; char c = 'd'; long k = 4567821;
```

conversion string	variables	display
		`12345678901234567890`
`%c,`	c	`d,`
`%3c,`	c	`  d,`
`%10c,`	c	`         d,`
`%-10c,`	c	`d          ,`
`%d,`	n	`23,`
`%6d,`	n	`    23,`
`%-12d,`	n	`23          ,`
`%06d,`	n	`000023,`
`%012d,`	-n	` 00000000023,`
`%4Ld,`	k	`4567821,`
`%o,`	n	`27,`
`%8o,`	n	`      27,`
`%08o,`	n	`00000027,`
`%-8x,`	n	`f7      ,`

In Table 9.2 a comma is used to mark the right edge of the field width (see below). The allowable characters between the % sign and the conversion character are summarised in Table 9.3. Note that they must appear in the order given, although not all (or any) need be present.

The main purpose of the format characters is to position the converted argument in its own **field width**. The number after conversion will be printed in a field at least this many characters wide but wider if necessary. Padding will occur to the left if right justified (default) or to the right if left justified (this obviously depends on the flag).

Table 9.3   `printf()` *conversion characters*

ANSI C	explanation
• a flag	
-	left justification
+	number always printed with a sign
space	prefix with a space unless first character is a sign
0	in numeric conversion leading zeros used to pad out
#	alternate output form:
	o - first digit always zero
	x or X - 0x or 0X will prefix a non-zero result
	e, E, f, g, G - output will always contain a decimal point;
	for g & G trailing zeros not removed
• a number	specifying the minimum **field width**
• a full stop	separating the field width from the precision
• a number	specifying the **precision**, behaving as follows, for a:
string	maximum number of characters to be printed
float or double	
f, e, E	number of digits printed to the right of the decimal point
g, G	number of significant digits
d	minimum number of digits
• a length modifier	
l	long or unsigned long
L	long double
h	short or unsigned short

Note: The width or the precision, or both, can be replaced by *, in which case the * is replaced by the next argument in the list (which must be an int).

Obviously care must be taken to ensure that the argument list matches the conversion specification otherwise unpredictable results may occur.

Table 9.4 shows some examples using conversion_strings with float numbers. Again we use a comma to mark the right edge of the field width.

A careful study of this table will reveal how these conversion strings operate. Notice the way in which a number is rounded up: for example, the default display prints pi as 3.141593, and with the %4.2 conversion we obtain 3.14. Notice also the use of - to left justify a number in its field.

Table 9.4 ***printf()* *conversion_string examples: float***

```
f = 'f';
pi = 3.141592654;
c = 2.99793e8;            /* speed, of light (ms^-1) */
me0 = 9.1083e-31;         /* rest mass of the electron (kg) */
```

conversion string	variable	display
		`12345678901234567890`
`%f,`	`pi`	`3.141593,`
`%4.2f,`	`pi`	`3.14,`
`%10.4f,`	`pi`	`    3.1416,`
`%16.1f,`	`c,`	`     299793000.0,`
`%-16.1f,`	`c,`	`299793000.0     ,`
`%e,`	`c,`	`2.997930e+08,`
`%16.1e,`	`c,`	`         3.0e+08,`
`%-16.8e,`	`me0,`	`9.1083000e-31   ,`
`%f,`	`me0,`	`0.000000,`

The final set of format conversions involves strings and some examples are given in Table 9.5.

Table 9.5 ***printf()* *conversion_string examples: strings***

```
s1 = " a short string";
```

conversion string	variable	display
		`123456789012345678901234567890`
`%s,`	`s1`	` a short string,`
`%4s,`	`s1`	` a short string,`
`%-20s,`	`s1`	` a short string     ,`
`%25s,`	`s1`	`           a short string,`
`%-20.8s,`	`s1`	` a short            ,`
`%20.8s,`	`s1`	`             a short,`

9.4 INPUT FORMATTING USING *SCANF()*

We have already used some format specifications with `scanf()` and in this section we are going to summarise the various possibilities. This function has the form

```
scanf( control_string,  argument_list );
```

As with the `printf()` function which we have just been considering, this function requires a control_string which should match the arguments in its argument list. The control_string can consist of ordinary white spaces, conversion specifications and ordinary non-white characters (not %), in which case the next character in the input stream must match these characters.

The conversion_specification is made up of:

%   followed, if required, by:
*   to suppress assignment (i.e. skip until a white space is encountered)
an integer   specifying the maximum field width
l, L or h   as for `printf ()`
conversion character (see Table 9.6).

Table 9.6 *scanf()   conversions (main set)*

ANSI C	explanation
d	decimal integer expected
i	integer (decimal, octal - leading 0, or hexadecimal - leading 0x or 0X)
o	octal integer
u	unsigned decimal integer
x	hexadecimal integer
c	characters - next characters are placed in the array indicated, up to the number given by the field width (default 1). No '\0' is added. Normal skip over white space is suppressed
s	string of non-white characters
e, f, g	floating point number

An asterisk in the conversion specification informs `scanf()` to skip the input field and no assignment is made. The field width if present specifies the number of non-white space characters to be read from the input field before input is terminated. (Where an input field is defined as a stream of non-white space characters - i.e. not a space, tab, newline, return, formfeed or vertical tab.) If the appropriate argument is read before reaching the end of the field width then `scanf()` continues to process entries, if not, processing terminates. The l, L and h indicate to `scanf` that a long float, a long int, or a short int is to be expected.

As we noted earlier `scanf()` returns an integer which is either EOF if end of file or an error occurs before any conversion, or a positive integer representing the number of conversions made and assigned. Notice also that, using `scanf()`, a string may not contain any embedded spaces on input.

9.5 FILE I/O

The input and output functions mentioned in the previous section are special cases of more general i/o functions which can be used with any file. (A file can be a normal file as stored on a floppy or hard disk, a peripheral device (such as a printer), the keyboard or the screen.) The keyboard and screen are normally identified by the variables `stdin` and `stdout` respectively (meaning standard input and standard output). Thus, providing that these variables are not redirected, to refer to another file, the statement

```
fprintf(stdout, "Output to the screen\n");
```

is exactly equivalent in its operation to the more common one

```
printf("Output to the screen\n");
```

Similarly

```
fscanf(stdin, "%d, %d", &i, &j);
```

will perform the operation of reading in from the keyboard two integers separated by a comma, as will

```
scanf("%d, %d", &i, &j);
```

Opening files

The first parameter in the file versions of these functions is a file pointer which identifies the required input or output device. Two things are necessary before file operations can be performed. Firstly a file pointer must be defined using the special type name `FILE`. This is a derived type name which is defined in `stdio.h` and is a structure which, once a file is opened, contains information about the file pointed to. (We will be looking in detail at structures in the next chapter.) Thus the declaration

```
FILE *fp;
```

declares a pointer of type `FILE` which may subsequently be used with file i/o functions.

The second requirement is that the file must be open for access. This is achieved by the statement

```
fp = fopen(file_name, mode);
```

where `file_name` is the name of the file to which access is required, and `mode` is a character string indicating the method of access. Possible values for the mode parameter are given in Table 9.7.

Table 9.7   *Input/output   mode   parameters*

mode	file is opened for:
"r"	reading only
"w"	writing only (create new file)
"a"	appending (i.e. writing to the end of an existing file)
"r+"	reading and writing
"w+"	reading and writing (create new file)
"a+"	appending(write at end, read anywhere)

a "b" may be appended to any of the above to indicate that data transfer is in binary mode.

Binary mode is used with MS-DOS to provide another form of text file and should not be confused with the more common meaning (e.g. an executable binary file).

Examples of file declaration and opening include:

```
/* open the file addresses for reading */
FILE *fp;
fp = fopen("addresses","r");

/* open the file summary for appending*/
/* i.e. read access allowed,           */
/* write only at the end of the file   */
FILE *fout;
fout = fopen("summary","a+");

/* open the file dfile for writing in binary mode */
/* i.e. create a new file - write in binary mode */
FILE *data;
data = fopen("dfile","wb");
```

What happens if the file cannot be opened? For example, the file 'addresses' might not exist. With your familiarity of functions in C you will not be surprised to find that `fopen()` returns a value (integer) which is used to indicate whether or not the function call was successful. If the attempt to open a file is unsuccessful, then `fopen()` returns the value NULL (in fact 0) which is defined in `stdio.h`. With this additional knowledge we can rewrite the above examples to ensure that a file has been opened successfully before any attempt is made to access it. Thus the first example can also be written as:

```
FILE *fp;

if(( fp = fopen("address", "r")) == NULL){
        puts("Unable to open the file");
        exit(0);
}

/* rest of the program */
```

This version uses the library function `exit()` which terminates the program when it is called. Conventionally a 0 value for the argument indicates that normal termination occurred, whereas a non-zero value (typically 1) is used to indicate that abnormal program termination occurred.

Closing files

Normally when a C program terminates all open files are automatically closed. However it may be the case that a file is only used for a short time in an isolated part of the program and can be closed once it is no longer required. This means that the file will be available for other users, or even the same program later on. The function which is used to achieve this task is called, as you might guess, `fclose()` and it has the form

```
fclose(file_pointer);
```

Thus `fclose(fp);` would close the file opened with the statement

```
fp = fopen(file_name, mode);
```

stderr

There is one further file pointer which we need to mention; this is the file pointer `stderr`. This is used for writing error messages. The default file is the screen but output can be directed to another file for later perusal. The file pointers `stdin` and `stdout`, although normally identified with the keyboard and screen, can be reassigned to other files (under unix and MS-DOS this can be achieved by redirection and piping: see the operating system manual for your computer). Thus the message printed using the `puts()` function call above may be redirected to a disk file rather than to the screen. In order to ensure that this does not occur we can replace the `puts()` call with an `fputs()` call using the `stderr` file pointer. So

```
fputs(stderr, "Unable to open the file");
```

will ensure that the user gets the message!

Table 9.8 below gives a list of the file i/o functions, their equivalent forms for stdio, and a brief explanation of their use.

Table 9.8   *File i/o functions and their* **stdio** *equivalents*

function	stdio equivalent	explanation
fprintf(fp, cs, as) fprintf(stdout, cs, as)	printf(cs, as)	formatted output
fscanf(fp, cs, &as) fscanf(stdin, cs, &as)	scanf(cs, &as)	formatted input
getc(fp) (fgetc(fp))	getc(stdin) (fgetc(stdin)) getchar(ch)	get the next character from the file pointed to by fp
ungetc(ch, fp)	ungetc(ch, stdin)	push back the last character read from the file. This can be re-read by using ch = getc (fp);
putc(ch, fp) (fputc(ch, fp))	putc(ch, stdout) (fputc(ch, stdout)) putchar(ch)	adds the character ch to the output file pointed to by fp. The int value of ch is returned
fgets(s, n, fp)	gets(s)	Get a string s from the file pointed to by fp until a '\n' or n-1 characters are read
fputs(s, fp)	puts(s)	fputs(s, fp) copies the string s to the file pointed to by fp

Note: In this table cs represents a control string, as an argument string and &as an argument string of addresses.

9.6 DOING SOME FILE I/O

In this final section we are going to illustrate the use of some of the functions which we have just introduced by working on a couple of examples. We will be concerned with the formatted print options (fprintf() and fscanf()) and the character output function putc().

Formatted file i/o

As an example of how fscanf() and fprintf() work we are going to set up a simple database which contains the names (first name only) and telephone number of our friends and acquaintances. We will allow the user to create a file from within the program, read an existing file and display its contents, and add new entries to the existing file (append). Other functions can be added, such as search and edit, but these will be left as exercises for the reader. These three options will suffice to illustrate how the functions work and how they can be used in practice.

Let us begin by assuming that the user will initially be prompted to enter one of the characters 'w', 'r', or 'a', representing write, read and append, respectively. Any other entry is invalid. Once the option has been selected the next process is to open the file in the appropriate mode. At this stage there are many options regarding error trapping. For instance the file might not exist when the read option has been selected, or it may already exist when the write option has been selected, and so on. A limited amount of trapping can be achieved by noting the value of the file_pointer which is used to access the file. If this identifier returns a NULL when an attempt is made to open it in **read** mode, then the file does not exist. So a first step, even before opening for writing, might be to attempt to open the file for reading and note whether the file_pointer returned is a NULL. If it is not NULL then the file already exists and read or append can be carried out. If on the other hand the write option had been selected then a prompt to check if the file is to be overwritten would be sensible. The basic structure of the program has the form

```
declarations
initialise variables
check file status
display menu
get choice
use file_status to give futher prompt if necessary
        exit if error, or don't want to overwrite existing file
process choice
        read file and display, or
        get entries from keyboard and write, or
        get entries from keyboard and append
```

The last two entries in the pseudocode above are very similar. In fact, provided that the file is opened in the correct mode, the same process to display and write can be used for both options.

We now need to think a little about the data structure required for this program. A number of alternatives are open to us, using two-dimensional arrays, reading in data as single characters, reading them in as strings and so on. Since we have no need to store the entries in memory - we can always access them by reading the file - we can use simple string variables for the name and the telephone number. One point to note here is that neither of the two data items may have embedded spaces, as the %s conversion specification on reading considers a string to end on encountering a space. Thus the telephone numbers must be entered as 031-778-9965 and not as 031 778 9965. One way of writing the program is given below.

Program 9.2

```c
/* an example of formatted file i/o    */
/* a telephone database - phonedb.c    */

#include <stdio.h>

#define TRUE 1
#define FALSE 0

main()
{
    FILE *fp                    /* declare a file pointer */
    static char name[20], phone[15];
    int i, file_exist;
    char c, choice;

    /* enter choice */

    puts("\n\n\n\t\t **** The telephone list ****\n\n\n");
    puts("\t Options \t: r    read and display \n");
    puts("\t\t\t : w    create a new file \n");
    puts("\t\t\t : a    append to an existing file \n");
    puts("\t\t\t : q    quit\n");
    printf("\n Please enter your choice : ");
    /* only allow valid entries */
    while ((c = getchar()) != 'r' && c != 'w' &&
                            c != 'a' && c != 'q')
        printf("Invalid entry, try again : ");
    /* check if file exists already */
    if ((fp = fopen("phonelst.txt", "r")) == NULL)
        file_exist = FALSE;    /* file does not exist */
    else
        file_exist = TRUE;
    if (c == 'r' && !file_exist) {
        puts("File does not exist");
        printf(" do you want to create one (y/n)? ");
        while ((choice = getchar()) != 'y' && choice != 'n')
```

```
            printf(" y or n : ");
        if (choice == 'n')
            exit(0);    /* terminate program */
        else
            c = 'w';    /* create and open for writing    */
    }
    if ( c == 'a' && !file_exist)    /* file does not exist */
        c = 'w';                      /* open for writing    */
    switch( c) {
    case 'r' :
        fp = fopen("phonelst.txt", "r");
        printf("           NAME                    PHONE\n");
        printf("=======================================\n");
        while (fscanf(fp, "%s %s", name, phone) = 2){ /* A */
            printf(" %20s  :  %15s \n", name, phone);
            i++;
        }
        printf("\n Number of records read : %d \n", i);
        close(fp);
        exit(0);
    case 'w' :
        fp = fopen("phonelst.txt", "w");
        printf("\n **** Creating a new file ****\n");
        break;
    case 'a' :
        fp = fopen("phonelst.txt", "a");
        printf("\n **** Appending to existing file ****\n");
    }
    /* reading data from keyboard */
    puts("Enter a name followed by the telephone number");
    puts("  as prompted, end by entering an asterisk");
    puts("  as the first character of the name");
    do {
        printf("\n N :   ");
        scanf("%s", name);           /* B */
        if( name[0] != '*' ) {
            printf(" T : ");
            scanf("%s", phone);      /* C */
            fprintf(fp, "%s %s\n", name, phone);
            i++;
        }
    } while( name[0] != '*');
    printf("\n Number of records written : %d\n", i);
    fclose(fp);
}
```

We have used the `fclose()` function here before exiting from the file although it is not strictly necessary, as on normal exit from a C program all open files are closed. However it is good practice to close files as soon as they are no longer required in a program as, for one thing, they are then available for other programs to use.

Character input and output - *putc ()* and *getc ()*

As an example to illustrate the unformatted input and output we are going to modify the previous program. One of the problems we found in that program was that the names could not contain any spaces due to the way the scanf () function interprets strings. Using the putc () function we can write a function which allows a string containing spaces to be read from a file. We need some method other than the presence of a space to indicate the end of a string. A simple option is to use a newline character. Thus we can now have names of the form 'Ludwig Wittgenstein' or 'C P E Bach'. Data of this type can be read into a string, from the keyboard, simply by using the getchar () function and testing for a newline character. The following function achieves this task.

Program 9.3a

```
/* get_str() function
       This reads characters from the keyboard
       into a string. The string is complete
       once a newline character is read.
       The last character read is returned.
*/

int get_str(char *s)
{
       char c;

       while(( c = getchar() ) != '\n')
              *s++ = c;           /* increment string pointer */
       *s = '\0';                 /* terminate string with a NULL */
       return(c);
}
```

Next we need to find a means of writing this string to a file. This can be done just by using the fprintf () function we used previously. This is possible since strings which include spaces can be written.

The function to read characters from the file is just the above function (Program 9.3a) with getchar () replaced by getc (). For example:

```
       c = getc(fp)
```

However remembering that we can read from the keyboard by using stdin we can utilise the same function for both reading from the keyboard and reading from a file. We will need to pass the relevant file pointer via the function parameter list. Thus the modified function becomes:

Program 9.3b

```
/* get_str() function
      This reads characters from a file
      into a string. The string is complete
      once a newline character is read.
      The last character read is returned.
*/

int get_str(FILE *file, char *s)
{
      char c;

      while(( c = getc(fp)) != '\n' && c != EOF)
            *s++ = c;               /* increment string pointer */
      *s = '\0';                    /* terminate string with a NULL */
      return(c);
}
```

This function then replaces the `scanf()` calls with a statement of the form:

```
      get_str(stdin, name);
```

The changes which need making to Program 9.2 are listed below.

Add:
```
            int get_str(FILE *file, char *string);
```

to the declarations in `main()`.

Replace line `/* A */` with:

```
      while(get_str(fp, name) != EOF) {
            if(get_str(fp, phone) == EOF)
                  break;
```

Replace line `/* B */` with:

```
      get_str(stdin, name);
```

and line `/* C */` with:
```
      get_str(stdin, phone);
```

Add the `get_str()` function (Program 9.3b) to the end of the main program.

Choosing the file being accessed

There are a number of ways of choosing the file we are reading from or writing to. So far we have simply used a string constant to specify the file. One obvious alternative is to use a string variable the value of which can be entered by the user. Thus with a declaration of the form

```
char *fname;
```

and an assignment using `scanf`

```
scanf("%s", fname);
```

we can determine the name of the file we wish to open at run time.

Another method is to use command-line arguments. These are arguments which follow the program name when it is typed in for execution, i.e. the command-line. So `sort in.txt out.txt` might be a command-line which executes the program `sort` and uses file `in.txt` as the input file and `out.txt` as the output file. Of course the command-line arguments need not be file names. A further common use of command line arguments is to add switches to implement different program options at run time. This saves the bother of typing in responses within the program. (You will have noticed such switches in your C compiler, and you will be familiar with them in the context of your operating system commands.) However here we are only concerned with the use of command-line arguments to pass a filename to the program. When the function `main` is called it is called with two arguments conventionally known as `argc` and `argv`. The first of these is an `int` variable which indicates the number of command-line arguments in this particular call. The argument `argv` is a pointer to an array of character strings each string of which contains one of the arguments. The first element of the array (`argv[0]`) points to the name of the program and subsequent ones point to successive command-line arguments, so `argc` will have a value of at least one. Thus to use the file `phonlst2.txt` when running `phonedb` (Program 9.2) we would type

```
phonedb phonlst.txt
```

The program would be modified as shown below.

```
main(int argc, char *argv[])
{
      . . . .
      . . . .
```

```
if( argc != 1) {
       printf("\n ** Incorrect number of arguments ** \n");
       exit(0);
}
....
....
```

In addition, all references to the original file 'phonelst.txt' should be replaced by argv[1]. So, for example, the code to check if the file already exists now becomes:

```
if ((fp = fopen(argv[1], "r")) == NULL)
       file_exist = FALSE;     /* file does not exist */
else
       file_exist = TRUE;
```

Other possibilities exist in the use of command-line arguments. It is left to the reader to explore these.

One final point worth mentioning before we leave file input and output concerns the standard input/output files stdin and stdout. We saw earlier that the keyboard is usually designated as stdin and the screen as stdout. On occasions it is useful to reassign one or other of these to some other device. The most common one is to change the standard output device temporarily to the printer so that all printf(), putchar() functions etc. output their data streams to the printer. This can be achieved by using the function freopen(). This function has the form

```
freopen(filename, mode, filepointer)
```

where filename is the new filename, mode is as shown in Table 9.7, and filepointer is normally one of stdin, stdout or stderr. Thus to change the standard output file from the monitor to the printer we could use the statement

```
freopen("prn", "w", stdout);
```

and later on in the program the destination device could be changed back to the screen with

```
freopen("con", "w", stdout);
```

These device designators apply to the MS-DOS operating system. They may be different if you are working in a different environment.

Example – return of the line editor

We have been looking at the line editor from time to time in this book. You should now have collected a number of functions and program fragments which can be used in the program. We haven't, until now, discussed in any detail the way in which the data are to be stored. However we have now covered enough material to allow us to look at this problem. In addition we are in a position to program the file input and output.

Text storage

There are a number of ways of storing the text in memory during editing. We could use arrays, lists or a combination of the two. We mention lists in Chapter 11 and you may like to try adapting this program using linear linked lists once you have worked through that material. However at this particular juncture the simplest option is to use a two-dimensional array of type char. We use a two-dimensional array so that one dimension addresses a line of text and the other a character within that line. We now need to think about the size of the array. Assuming we have a standard screen display, then 25 lines can be displayed at once. So we will limit the number of lines to 25. We suggested in Chapter 1.7 that a line length of up to 75 characters would be sufficient. (To take into account the display of line numbers on the screen, for example.) So we can declare an array for this task as:

```
char text[25][76];
```

The increase from 75 to 76 is to accommodate the newline character at the end of each line.

Let's now consider the function to read the text from a file (for the moment we will assume a fixed name for the file i.e. data.txt). Before we can read the file we need to open it and there is the possibility that it may not exist, so we need to check for this eventuality. The pseudocode can be written down straight away.

```
line editor read text function
if data.txt does not exist then
        print "file data.txt does not exist"
else
        read text from file
```

We now need to expand on the read text from file part of this algorithm. The data will be read into the array text[line][column] until the End of File (EOF) is reached. Whenever a newline character is read we must increment line and reset column to zero. In addition it might be worthwhile checking that column does not exceed 75, e.g. a newline may be missing from the file. If this is the case we will also want to increment line and set column to zero. Finally we should keep a check on the value of line to see that it does not exceed 24. (Remember that arrays are indexed from 0, so the line range is 0 to 24 and the column range is from 0 to 75, including a newline character.) With this information we can expand on our original algorithm.

```
line editor read text function - refinement 2
declarations
        external array text[][]
        external integer next
        character c
set col to 0
if data.txt does not exist then
        print "file data.txt does not exist"
else
        read text from file
        read c from data.txt
        while c not equal to EOF do
                if c is equal to '\n' or col is greater than MAXCOLS-1 then
                        set text[next++][col] to '\n'
                        set col to 0
                        if next is greater than MAXLINES then
                                next = MAXLINES
                                print "Line limit reached"
                                close data.txt
                                return
                        end_if
                end if else
                        set text[next][col++] to c
                end_if
                read c from data.txt
        end_while
end_if
```

The function can now be written from this pseudocode. However, before we do that, notice one or two points about the algorithm. We have used symbolic constants MAXLINES and MAXCOLS, rather than 25 and 75, as this makes future alterations to the function easier. We have also declared the array text and the integer next as external to the function. Since both of these variables will be used in most functions it is sensible to do this. However to make the program and functions clear we must explicitly note this in our function definitions by use of extern. Finally next holds the current line number of the next line available for appending (in the range 0 to 25) - this will normally be set to zero on entry to this function. The function to achieve the reading of text from a file is given in Program 9.4 below. Read through the code and see that you understand how it works. The exercises at the end of the chapter enable you to write other functions and a simple program to try them and this one out.

Program 9.4

```
/* function read_file()
**
** this function reads text from file data.txt
** next is set equal to the number of lines read + 1
** unless the line limit is exceeded in which case
** next is set equal to MAXLINES
*/
void read_file(void)
{
        extern char text[][];
        extern int next;

        FILE *fp;
        char c;
        int col = 0;

        next = 0;  /* ensure text is read into the array from 0 */
        if(( fp = fopen("data.txt","r")) == NULL {
                puts("\n *** New file: data.txt does not exist ***");
                return;
        } else while(( c = getc(fp)) != EOF) {
                if( c == NL || col >= MAXCOLS - 1 ) {
                        text[next++][col] = NL;
                        col = 0;
                        if( next > MAXLINES ) {
                                next = MAXLINES;
                                puts("\n *** Line limit exceeded ***"),
                                fclose(fp);
                                return;
                        }
                } else
                        text[next][col++] = c; /* normal text not EOL */
        }                                      /* or '\n, */
        if( col != 0 && c == EOF ) {
                text[next][col] = NL;
                next++;               /* update next if EOF and no '\n' */
        }
        fclose(fp);
}
```

SUMMARY

In this chapter we :

> • took a quick look at the standard input/output
> functions.

• examined the formatting capabilities of `printf()` in more detail and were introduced to the concept of field_width and precision.

• looked at the format_characters associated with `scanf()`.

• found out how to open files for reading and writing and looked at the basic file i/o functions.

• used the functions `fscanf()`, `fprintf()` and `putc()` for file reading and writing.

• saw how `argc` and `argv` are used to pass information from a command_line and noted how `freopen()` can be used to redirect data to files and devices other than `stdin` and `stdout`.

EXERCISES

1. Write a function called `prompt(s)` which writes the string s to the standard output file but does not append a newline. Once you have written it, write a suitable test program, then compile and run it. This will be much simpler than `printf()` and will not have the disadvantage (which in this case `puts()` has) of appending a newline.

2. Enter the telephone database program and test it with some real data. Modify it so that other files than phonelst.txt can be used. Try the various methods discussed above.

3. Write a function to write the text from array `test[][]` to the file data.txt.

4. Write a program to test the `read_file()` and `write_file()` functions (Program 9.4 and Exercise 3 above.) You will also need to write a function to display on the screen the text that has been read, as well as one to read text from the keyboard into the array `text[][]`.

5. Modify your program and functions in 4 to use a variable file name for the data - using command line arguments (`argc` and `argv`).

6. Modify the telephone database program to allow for the editing of existing entries and for the deletion of entries.

10 Typedef, structures and unions

"In short, the notion of structure is comprised of three key ideas: the idea of wholeness, the idea of transformation and the idea of self-regulation."

Jean Piaget

10.1 INTRODUCTION

In this chapter we will be examining ways of extending the data types which we have covered in earlier chapters. The three keywords `struct`, `union` and `typedef` enable a great variety of data structures to be created. The ability to create structures to represent complex arrangements of data is a very important part of program design. Often half the battle in solving a problem is getting the data representation correct. Before you work through this chapter you should make sure that you are familiar with the material covered in the earlier chapters. Many of the ideas we will be discussing require a good understanding of the earlier material. In particular you should be happy with arrays of various types and pointers.

10.2 *TYPEDEF*

The keyword `typedef` provides a means of creating new names for data types. It can be useful for improving the readability of a program by providing better self-documentation. Thus we can create new data type names for frequently occurring types. However its use need not be confined to simple data types such as `int`, `float` or `char`. We can use a `typedef` declaration to associate a name with a more complex combination of data types such as might be represented by structures. We will look at this aspect in Section 10.4. Finally `typedef` is often used to guard against problems arising through porting: that is when a program written for one system is used in another environment. In such cases the exact representation of the basic data types may differ. If this is the case and if the size of a particular data type is crucial to the correct operation of the program, then `typedef` can be employed to associate a new name with this data type. When the program is moved to another system only the `typedef` declaration will need to be altered.

A typedef declaration has the form

```
typedef data_type variable_name;
```

It works in a similar manner to the preprocessor instruction #define but with two important differences

- the typedef declaration can only be used with data types

- the processes implied by the typedef declaration are carried out by the compiler rather than by the preprocessor.

Some examples of typedef are:

```
typedef float Pounds;

typedef char *String;

typedef float Real, Imaginary;

typedef int Matrix[3][3], Vector[3];
```

Each of these declarations can be thought of as adding another data type name to the existing list. Using typedef does not replace the existing data type by the newly declared one. It simply adds another name to the list of available types.

It is very easy, especially when first introduced to typedef, to become confused as to the order of the declaration. Remember that the declaration has a similar form to that of a normal declaration. The variable name is replaced by the newly defined data type name and the keyword typedef added to the front of the declaration.

Having defined String as a data type pointer to char we can then declare variables directly using the new name String (rather than using the common form char *). For example:

```
String p_reply, p_error_message[50];

int strcpy(String s1, String s2)
{
      .....
}
```

The new type definition can therefore be used anywhere a declaration is needed -

provided of course that the use of the new name follows the typedef declaration itself.

Notice that in the above definitions we have used an upper-case letter for the initial character of the new data type names. This is not obligatory but if it is adhered to it does help in making it clear which names are variables, which symbolic constants and which are names created by typedef.

Example – matrix multiplication

In Chapter 8 we used matrix arithmetic as an example of the use of two-dimensional arrays. The typdef declaration can be used to simplify the writing of matrix functions and thus make it easier to program applications using matrices. First of all we will begin by declaring a new data type with the statements

```
#define N 3                        /* matrix dimensions */
typedef float Matrix[N][N];        /* notice the order */
```

We may also be using one-dimensional arrays, which correspond to vectors, so it would be sensible to declare Vector as a data type associated with a one-dimensional array of floats. We therefore have an additional typedef declaration, i.e.

```
typedef float Vector[N];
```

The new version of our matrix multiplication function now becomes:

Program 10.1

```
/* Matrix multiplication function - using the data types
            Matrix[N][N] and Vector[N]
      This function takes as arguments two vectors (a and b)
      of size 3 and places the vector product in the Matrix c
*/
void m_mult1(Vector a[], Vector b[], Matrix c)
{
      int i, j;

      for (i = 0; i < 3; i++)
            for (j = 0; j < 3; j++)
                  c[i][j] = a[i] * b[j];
}
```

Finally we can generalise the function even more by replacing the vectors by square matrices (m1 and m2). However we need to modify the structure of the inner `for` loop by adding yet another loop since now a matrix element of the product is the sum of the products of elements in m1 and m2. Thus we obtain:

Program 10.2

```
/* Matrix multiplication function - using the
            data type Matrix
      This function takes as arguments two square
      matrices (m1 and m2) of size N and
      places the vector product in the matrix c
*/

void m_mult3 (Matrix m1, Matrix m2, Matrix c)
{
      int i, j, k;

      for (i = 0; i < N; i++)
            for (j = 0; j < N; j++)
                  for (k = 0, c[i][j] = 0.0; k < N ; k++)
                        c[i][j] += m1[i] * m2[j];
}
```

Notice that in the innermost `for` loop the element `c[i][j]` is initialised to zero.

One other useful matrix function is the determinant. For a 2 x 2 matrix (a) the determinant (a scalar) is defined by

$$D = a_{11} a_{22} - a_{12} a_{21}$$

which in terms of array elements is

```
determ = a[0][0]*a[1][1] - a[0][1]*a[1][0]
```

For a 3 x 3 matrix the determinant becomes

$$D = a_{11}(a_{22} a_{33} - a_{32} a_{23}) + a_{21}(a_{32} a_{13} - a_{12} a_{33}) + a_{32}(a_{12} a_{23} - a_{22} a_{13}).$$

We can use this definition to write a determinant function (`float det(a)`) which returns the determinat of a 3 x 3 matrix.

Program 10.3

```
/* Determinant function det(a) for a 3 x 3 Matrix.
      Individual terms are calculated separately
      to aid clarity.
```

```
*/
float det(Matrix a)
{
     float t1, t2, t3;

     t1 = a[0][0]*(a[1][1]*a[2][2] - a[2][1]*a[1][2]);
     t2 = a[1][0]*(a[2][1]*a[0][2] - a[0][2]*a[0][1]);
     t3 = a[2][1]*(a[0][1]*a[1][2] - a[1][1]*a[0][2]);
     return(t1 + t2 + t3);
}
```

10.3 STRUCTURES

So far we have been dealing with data of specific data types. Arrays were introduced to allow data of the same type to be accessed by means of a single variable (i.e. the array name). What happens if we want to set up data such that each item consists of a number of different types of data? A common example where this might occur is in the creation of a record in a database consisting of various fields which hold the name, address and telephone number of various individuals or establishments. One solution to this problem is to set up a series of arrays of type char, one for each item (or field). So, for example, we might have:

```
char name[100][20], address[100][60], phone[100][12];
```

This statement declares three arrays, each consisting of 100 elements, each of which is a one-dimensional array of type char. In order to access any of the details of a particular entry we simply use array indexing, or pointers. Thus the program fragment

```
printf("Name: \t %s\n", *name[5]);
printf("Address: \t %s\n", *address[5]);
printf("Phone: \t %s\n", *phone[5]);
```

will print out the name, address and telephone number on successive lines. However this, as it stands, is not very satisfactory as the address may well be up to 100 characters long, and that will certainly make a mess of our display! So a better solution might be to split the address array up into four further arrays (e.g. address1, address2, town, postcode). We might also want to break the name into its constituent parts (e.g. initials and surname). If we continue on in this manner it won't be long before we forget what arrays hold what and programming becomes a slog rather than a joy! What we need is some means of simulating the field structure found in databases where a single record is associated with a particular collection of fields. Structures enable just such a collection of variables to be grouped together and identified by a single variable.

We will begin by extending the definition we had above but restricting ourselves to a single entry – not too useful but we will soon see how to extend our definition by using arrays of structures. A structure definition for our new address book might take the form:

```
struct personal_data {
        char surname[20];
        char initials[4];
        char address1[20];
        char address2[20];
        char town[20];
        char post_code[8];
        char phone[12];
};
```

We have now declared a data type `personal_data` consisting of seven `char` arrays which contain all the information we require. The structure definition, or structure template, contains a number of elements:

`struct`	– this is a structure (a keyword of C).
`personal_data`	– a structure identifier which can be used subsequently as a derived data type to declare variables.
`{`	– an opening brace indicating the start of a block.
`char surname[20];` ..... `char phone[12];`	– a number of declarations indicating the elements which go to make up the structure. (These are known as *members*.)
`};`	– a right brace indicating the end of the structure declaration.

Note the semi-colon following the right brace. This is one of the few places when it is legal, and essential, to follow a brace with a semi-colon.

This new structure definition can now be used to declare a variable, e.g.

```
struct personal_data n1;
```

which will declare a variable n1 of type `struct personal_data` and will set aside storage for all the elements included in the structure template. In this particular example it will be useful to declare an array for this variable so that we can store more than one of our friends' details.

```
struct personal_data address_book[10];

/* we are limiting our list to only our closest friends! */
```

Having defined a structure the next problem is how to enter information into it. One method is similar to the initialisation of arrays, with the same proviso that only external or static **variables** can be initialised. Thus, in the following program fragment, the variable `best_friend` must be preceded by the key word `static` to allow it to be initialised.

Program 10.4

```
/* illustrating structure initialisation */
      /* structure definition */
      struct personal_data {
            char surname[20];
            char initials[4];
            char address1[20];
            char address2[20];
            char town[20];
            char post_code[8];
            char phone[12];
      };

main()
{            /* structure initialisation */
      static struct personal_data best_friend = {
            "Campbell",
            "N.D.",
            "Shangrila"
            "2 North Road",
            "Treebridge",
            "TD9 12XT"},
            "0567 2237"
      };
```

Another method of assigning values to structures is by means of the structure member operator (.). So if we wish to assign the name `"Jones"` to the `surname` member of `n1` we could achieve this by using the statement:

```
      n1.surname = "Jones";
```

or, in the case of the array address_book,

```
      address_book[0].surname = "Jones";
```

This last example illustrates an important point concerning the use of the member operator with arrays. The name `address_book[0]` is the structure variable name and is in fact a pointer to the first element of the array `address_book` and it is the member within this variable which we wish to access. Suppose that we wish to search through our address book and locate all our friends whose telephone number begins with "041"; then we could use an expression of the form:

```
for( i = 0; i < 10; i++)
        if (strncmp("041", address_book[i].phone, 3) == 0)
            /* found */
```

Two further examples of statements which access members of structures, using the above definitions and assignments, are:

```
char friend[5], s1[10], s2[] = "Dear ";

strcpy(friend, n1.initials);    /* friend assigned "A.J." */
strcpy(s1, s2);
strcat(s1, best_friend.initials);    /* s1 = "Dear N.D." */
```

Including declarations with the template definition

Until now we have declared variables of type st ruct struct_name by first setting up a structure template, including with it an identifier (sometimes referred to as a tagname) and then using the form

```
struct    struct_name    variable_list;
```

to declare the variables. Another method is available which combines the template definition with the variable declarations. Consider the statement

Program 10.5

```
/* structure for classical discs */
    struct class_disc {
            char composer[20];
            char initials[5];
            char composition[40];
            char *other;
            char conductor[20];
            char orchestra[30]
            float price;
    } disc1, disc2, disc3;
```

This has a form very similar to our earlier structure definitions but in addition a number of variable names are added between the closing brace and the final semi-colon. This is useful in that it combines two processes into a single process. Provided that the structure definition is outside ma in (), the variables disc1, disc2 and disc3 will be automatically external variables and can therefore be initialised within the program. Note that this can be condensed still further by removing the tagname (i.e. `class_disc`) to give:

```
struct {
        char composer[20];
        char initials[5];
        char composition[40];
        char *other;
        char conductor[20];
        char orchestra[30]
        float price;
} disc1, disc2, disc3;
```

Although this form is quite neat, it has the big disadvantage that, if this structure is to be used to declare other variables, for example in another function, then we have no means of doing this other than by typing out the complete template yet again. Consequently this form should only be used when the variables are required to be external , or are only needed in one function.

One final point is that a structure variable can be initialised, declared and the structure template set up all in one go. So, for example, if we wish to set up a structure like the above and initialise `disc1` we might have:

```
struct class_disc {
        char composer[20];
        char initials[5];
        char composition[40];
        char *other;
        char conductor[20];
        char orchestra[30]
        float price;
}   disc1= {
        "Shostakovitch",
        "D",
        "Symph. #7 in C maj. - The Leningrad",
        "Kabalevsky - Cello Concerto #2",
        "Svetlanov",
        "USSR Symphony",
        10.95
};
```

10.4 STRUCTURES AND *TYPEDEF*

The structures we have looked at so far have used a tagname, preceding the structure template definition, to enable variables to be declared as structures. Unless the variables are declared and the structure template is set up at the same time,we need to use both the keyword `struct` and the tagname when declaring new variables. The `typedef` keyword can be used to shorten this process, as is shown in the next example.

```
typedef struct {
        float real;     /* real  part */
        float imag;     /* imaginary part */
}Complex;
```

This definition sets up a structure called Complex and defines it as a new data type (made up of two members real and imag which represent float variables). We can now use Complex to declare variables with this structure elsewhere in the program. So

```
Complex x, y, z;
```

will declare three variables each consisting of a real and an imag part.

We can now use this definition in a program which will add together two complex numbers.

Program 10.6

```
/* program to illustrate structures and complex numbers */

#include <stdio.h>

typedef struct {
            float real;     /* real  part */
            float imag;     /* imaginary part */
        } Complex;

main()
{
    Complex x, y, z;

    puts("Enter the first complex number (r, i)\n");
    while(scanf("%f, %f", &x.real, &x.imag) != 2)
            puts("\n invalid entry - try again\n");
    puts("... and now the next number \n");
    while(scanf("%f, %f", &y.real, &y.imag) != 2)
            puts("\n invalid entry - try again\n");

    printf("\n the sum is ( %5.1f, %5.1fi ) \n",
                    x.real + y.real, x.imag + y.imag);
}
```

It is a simple matter to write a function to carry out the complex addition. There are three main approaches to this problem: pass the individual elements, pass a complete structure or pass a pointer to a structure. Perhaps the most intuitive is to pass the complete structure. Since structures are analogous to simple data types all we are doing is extending the use of functions to this new situation. (Although this is intuitively correct the old standard did not allow this. However the new ANSI standard does.) So using this approach we can declare a function c_add(a, b) of type `Complex` as follows.

Program 10.7

```
/* Complex addition function
       - version 1 using a function
       of type struct.
*/
Complex c_add(Complex a, Complex b)
{
        Complex z;

        z.real = x.real + y.real ;
        z.imag = x.imag + y.imag ;
        return(z);
}
```

It is left as an exercise to the reader to modify Program 10.6 to test this function. In this example we passed complete structures into a function. The way in which individual members are passed to a function has already been illustrated in our use of the `printf()` and `scant()` functions, each member is treated as a simple variable. Thus, supposing we have a `float` function called add(x, y) which returns the sum of the variables x and y, the above single call of the complex function c_add() could be replaced by two calls of add().

```
z.r = add(x.r, y.r); /* a longer alternative to */
z.i = add(x.i, y.i); /*     z = c_add(x, y);    */
```

We will look at a third way of using structures with functions in section 10.6. For the moment we turn to the topic of structures containing structures.

10.5 STRUCTURES WITHIN STRUCTURES

A structure can not only contain the standard data types as members but it can also contain other structures. Let's take another look at our address book example, which we explored in Section 10.3. This structure template personal_data was made up of seven members, the first two of which relate to an individual's name. With the ability to use structures nested within structures we can go back to our original attempt which used just three members (name, address and phone). So we begin by setting up the main

`Address_entry` template; this has the form

```
/* structure definition of Address_entry */
typedef struct {
        Name            person;         /* structure */
        Address         address;        /* structure */
        char            phone[12];      /* simple data type */
} Address_entry ;
```

Next we can set up the `Name` template containing the surname and initials of an individual.

```
/* structure definition for Name */
typedef struct {
        char surname[20];
        char initials[4];
} Name;
```

Finally we can set up an `Address` template containing the members relating to the address of an individual, i.e. (`address1`, `address2`, `town` and `post_code`).

```
/*structure definition for Address */
typedef struct {
        char address1[20];
        char address2[20];
        char town[20];
        char post_code[8];
} Address ;
```

Notice that we have used `typedef` here to simplify the naming of variables, and we have also capitalised the initial letter of the various structure definitions to make it clear that these are derived types and not simple variables.

The new version which we have arrived at emphasises the form of the data structure more clearly than the earlier version, which did not use nested structures. (You could think of this type of data structure as being generated by a form of stepwise refinement. First of all the main data categories are decided upon (e.g. Name, Address, phone) and then they are refined to greater detail (e.g. surname, initials)). One important point to notice about this particular template is that the same name is used for both a `typedef` (`Address`) and for a structure member (`address`). This is permissible in C since this language is case sensitive, so that although on the surface the two are the same, because the initial letter of the `struct` name is capitalised they are treated as different identifiers.

Now that we have this fancy structure how do we access its members? Assume we want to initialise the first two entries in our address book. We can use the following definition

```
Address_entry address_book[2] = {
      {
              {"Jones", "A.J"},
              {"45 Stoneybank","","Treebridge","TD9 5XT"},
              "0567 2451"
      },
      {

              {"Smith", "P.S"}
              {"Hollybush","Devon Road","Treebridge","TD95XR"},
              "0567 3476"

      }
};          /* assuming this is an external definition */
            /* otherwise we would need to prefix the    */
            /* definition with static.                  */
```

There are a few important points to note about the form of this definition.

- There is no need to use the keyword struct since `Address_entry` includes the `struct` keyword in its definition through the use of `typedef`.

- The initialisation of sub-structures (`Name` and `Address`) is included within braces as for a simple structure.

- Blank entries are included by entering a null string (i.e. `""`).

Now that we have something to work on, the next step is to access individual members of our new structure. We can get AJ's telephone number in the usual manner:

```
      phone = address_book[0].phone;
```

Logic dictates that we would access a member of a structure which is itself a member of another structure in a recursive manner, i.e. by using an expression of the form *struct1.struct2.member*. Since by now you will be appreciating the logic of C you will not be surprised to learn that this is indeed the case. So to find AJ's post code we simply use

```
      p_code = address_book[0].address.post_code;
```

and to verify that this is indeed the correct entry we can use

```
      int i;
```

```
Name individual;

i = 0;
individual = address_book[i].person;
printf("\n The entry for %d is for %5s %-12s \n", i,
       individual.initials, individual.surname);
```

10.6 POINTERS AND STRUCTURES

Before leaving the topic of structures we must take a look at the way pointers can be used with them. We shall explore very briefly pointers to structures and accessing members using pointers. There are a number of reasons for raising this topic. Firstly, just as it is easier in many applications to manipulate pointers to arrays rather than the arrays themselves so are pointers to structures easier to manipulate than the structures themselves. Secondly, in the old standard and therefore in some of the earlier implementations of C it was not permissible to pass structures to functions; however a pointer to a structure could be passed.

The function c_add() which we wrote earlier can be rewritten using pointers in the following way.

Program 10.8

```
/* using pointers with structures
      to place the sum of two
      complex numbers in a third.
*/
void c_add2(Complex *x, Complex *y, Complex *sum)
{                    /* pointers to structures (Complex)*/

      (*sum).real = (*x).real + (*y).real;
      (*sum).imag = (*x).imag + (*y).imag;
}
```

Notice the use of brackets around the dereferencing operator (*) and structure variables x, y and sum. This is necessary because the member operator (.) has higher precedence than the dereferencing operator and thus without the brackets the expression *sum.real, for example, would be interpreted by the compiler as *(sum.real).

In order illustrate the use of pointers with structures we can return to the previous address book example. We declare a pointer of type Address_entry, i.e.

```
Address_entry *aptr;
```

The pointer at present points nowhere, so we need to assign a value to it. Let's make it point to the first entry in our address book.

```
aptr = &address_book[0];
```

Now what happens when `aptr` is incremented? Since it is a pointer to a structure we would expect that it would point to the next element in the structure array address_book, i.e. to `address_book[1]`. Let's try it and see. The program to test this out is:

Program 10.9

```
/* structures and pointers
     The address book example
*/

#include <stdio.h>

typedef struct {
            char surname[20];
            char initials[4];
        } Name;

typedef struct {
            char address1[20];
            char address2[20];
            char town[20];
            char post_code[8];
        } Address ;

typedef struct {
            Name          person;
            Address       address;
            char          phone[12];
        } Address_entry;

Address_entry address_book[] = {
    {
        {"Jones", "A.J"},
        {"45 Stoneybank","","Treebridge","TD9 5XT"},
        "0567 2451"
    },
    {
        {"Smith", "P.S"}
        {"Hollybush","Devon Road","Treebridge","TD95XR"},
        "0567 3476"
    }
};
```

```
main()
{
     int i;
     Address_entry *aptr; /* pointer to structure */

     aptr = &address_book[0];
     printf("The address of address_book[0] is : %u\n",
     &address_book[0]);
     printf("The address of address_book[1] is : %u\n",
     &address_book[1]);
     printf("The address of aptr is : %u \n", aptr);
     printf("The address of ++aptr is : %u \n", ++aptr);
     aptr = &address_book[0];  /* reinitialize aptr */
     for( i = 0; i < 2; i++) {
             printf("%s's phone no. is : %s\n",
                     ((*aptr).person).initials, (*aptr).phone);
             ++aptr; /* move to next entry */
     }
}
```

and the output when I ran this program was:

```
The address of address_book[0] is : 404
The address of address_book[1] is : 512
The address of aptr is : 404
The address of ++aptr is : 512
A.J's phone no. is : 0567 2451
P.S's phone no. is : 0567 3476
```

Voilà! it works as we expected. The last few lines of the program show how we can access a member using a pointer. We saw above one method which involved using the dereferencing operator and so in this example, to access the telephone number of A.J. Jones we can use the statements

```
aptr = &address_book[0];
phone_no = (*aptr).phone;
```

and in a similar way we can find his post code, i.e.

```
p_code = (*aptr).address.post_code;
```

Since it is often necessary to access a member of a structure indirectly by means of a pointer, a special notation for this task is employed. This new operator is the structure pointer operator and consists of a minus sign followed by a greater than symbol, to produce an arrow head (->). This operator is a binary operator with the left operand a variable of type *pointer_to_structure* and the right operand being a structure member. Although the left operand is a pointer the complete expression is a variable with a data type the same as that of the member of the structure pointed to. The above two examples can now be rewritten as

```
phone_no = aptr -> phone;

p_code = aptr -> address.post_code;
```

respectively. We will be using forms like these in the next chapter when we examine lists and list processing.

Notice in the output to Program 10.8 that the sum of all the bytes used by the `Address_entry` structure is 108, and 404 plus 108 is 512, i.e. the address of the second entry in the `address_book` array. Two points are worth stressing, one rather obvious, the second not so obvious. The first point is that the addresses will obviously be machine-dependent and so if you run this program it will be extremely unlikely for you to obtain the same addresses. The second point to note concerns the size of the structures. In this particular example the size of the structure is the sum of the size of its members. (The size of `Name` is 28, the size of `Address` is 68 and the size of `phone` is 12.) However this need not be the case, owing to the way in which different objects are stored. The correct way to obtain the size of a structure is to use the `sizeof()` operator. Thus

```
printf("\n No. of bytes in Address_entry = %u\n",
        sizeof(Address_entry));
```

This ends our look at structures; we will be using them again in the next chapter when we investigate their use with lists.

10.7 UNIONS

Unions closely resemble structures in that they are a derived type. Their syntax is the same and the method of accessing a member of a union is the same. The difference is that the union members share storage and consequently they can be used when storage is at a premium. Another use for unions is when mutually exclusive options of different data types are used for a single variable. Storage allocation is such that enough memory is set aside to take the largest of the union members (there can be more than two). For example a month can be expressed either as an integer or as a string. The program below sets up such a union and performs simple input and output using it.

Program 10.10

```
/* simple union example
```

```
                 - storing month as int or string
*/

union month {
        int     number;
        char    string[10];
};               /* definition same form as that for a struct */

main()
{
        union month m;

        m.number = 6;
        printf("\n The month number is : %d \n", m.number);
        m.string = "August";
        puts(" \n With a new assignment to m.string ");
        printf("\n The month string is : %s \n", m.string);
}
```

The output on my system is:

```
The month number is : 6
With a new assignment to m.string
The month string is : August
```

An important point to note about using unions is that it is up to the programmer to keep track of what was last stored in the union structure. Don't think of a union as magically transforming a month string into its equivalent month number, but simply as allowing one or the other to be stored in the same variable. So, if we tried to access the month which was last assigned as an integer as a string, garbage would result, and vice versa.

Suppose we have another structure which holds the date in the form

```
        day_of_month, month, year
```

where the two forms 21 January 1989 and 21 /1 / 89 are equally permissible. We can add an extra member to the structure to indicate in which form the month was last stored. So we could have a structure definition like this:

```
typedef struct {
        int     day,
        union   month   mm,
        int     yr,
        char    short_long      /* S for short form ( 21 /1 / 89 ),
}Date;                          L for long ( 21 January 1989 ) */
```

This definition and the one for month might be used in a program to allow either format to be input.

Program 10.11

```
/* Illustrating a use of unions.
     A date can be stored in two formats -
     short: day/month_number/year, or
     long: day/month_name/year.
     date_flag is used to indicate which form was last used.
     S for short, L for short.
*/

#include <stdio.h>

/*     union month .... and
       typdef struct .... Date
       definitions in here */

main()
{
     int isin(char c, char str[]);
     char date_flag;

     puts("Which date format? short: 21 / 1 / 89 ");
     puts("           or  long : 21 January 1989 ?");
     puts(" Enter S for short L for long ");
     while(!isin((date_flag = getchar()), "SL"))
           puts("You must enter a 0 or a 1 !);
     if (date_flag = 'L') {
           puts("You have selected the long form");
           puts(" please enter the date e.g. 16 March 1972");
           while(scanf("%d %s %d", &date.day, date.mm.string,
                                        &date.yr) != 3)
           puts(" Try again please ...");
     } else {
           puts("You have selected the short form");
           puts(" please enter the date e.g. 16 3 72");
           while(scanf("%d %d %d", &date.day, &date.mm.number,
                                        &date.yr) != 3)
                 puts(" Try again please ...");
     }
     date.short_long = date_flag;

/* now output the date */
     if (date.short_long == 'L') {
           printf(" The date was : %d %s %d\n", date.day,
           date.mm.string, date.yr);
```

```
        } else {
                printf(" The date was : %d %d %d\n", date.day,
                date.mm.number, date.yr);
        }
}


/* function isin(ch, str) returns
        TRUE if ch is found in str
        FALSE otherwise
*/
int isin(char c, char str[])
{
        while( *str != '\0' ) {
                if( c == *str )
                        return(1);  /* found */
                str++;
        }
        return(0);                  /* not found */
}
```

Enter this program and try it out.

SUMMARY

In this chapter we:

- saw how `typedef` can be used to define new names for existing data types.

- were introduced to structures as another of the derived data types of C.

- noted how `typedef` can be used with structures to define new data types.

- saw how structures can be nested to make up complex data types.

- examined the use of pointers with structures.

- took a brief look at unions.

EXERCISES

1. Write a program to test the matrix multiplication and determinant functions (Programs 10.2 and 10.3.)

2. Using the `typedef` statements and the matrix functions already written write the following functions:

a. `m_sum(a, b)` to add together the matrices a and b, placing the result in b.

b. `float dot_product(v1, v2)` which forms the dot product of v1 and v2 and returns the answer.

c. `transpose(a, b)` which performs the matrix operation of transposing (i.e. `b[i][j] = a[j][i]`).

d. `s_mult(s, a)` which multiplies the matrix a by a scalar s.

e. `unit(a)` which returns the matrix a as a unit matrix (i.e. `a[i][i] = 1.0`, all other elements = 0.0).

3. The readability of the above functions can be improved by using `typedef` for the scalar variables. How would you do this? Modify the functions and function definitions accordingly.

4. What is wrong with this template?

```
structure struct {
        char    c;
        float   fnum,
        int     aint[10];
        }
```

5. Construct a structure template to hold the time of day using hours, minutes, seconds and "am" or "pm" for a twelve-hour clock.

6. Write a program, using structures, to output the day number within the year of a date entered from the keyboard. Allow dates to be entered only in the form 25-Jan-1978. Restrict this program to non-leap years only.

7. The following definition of a leap year comes from *The Encyclopaedia Britannica* (1898) vol. *IV*, p. 667.

> "*According to the Gregorian rule of intercalation, therefore, every year of which the number is divisible by four is a leap year, excepting the centurial years, which are only leap years when divisible by four after omitting the two ciphers. Thus 1600 was a leap year, but 1700, 1800, and 1900 are common years; 2000 will be a leap year, and so on.*"

By interpreting this definition modify the program above to work for leap years as well.

8. Implement the address book example using nested structures and check that you understand fully how it works.

9. Modify the structure class_disc (Program 10.5) to use nested structures. Use a separate structure for the composers's name and initials, and one to include the conductor and orchestra members. Construct a new structure in place of composition with members' title, popular_title and opus_no. Make this and the *other member in the original definition a further structure called contents.

a. How would you access the opus_no?
b. Write down an expression to access the conductor.

10. Modify the Complex function c_add2 () (Program 10.8) so that it uses structure pointer operators. Test the function with your existing program.

11. A structure defining some bicycle characteristics has the form:

```
struct cycle {
        int     rear;   /* number of teeth on the rear sprocket */
        int     chain;  /* number of teeth on the chain wheel   */
        float   diam;   /* diameter of the wheels (inches)       */
        float   dist;   /* distance travelled for one revolution*/
};                      /*    of the pedals                     */
```

Write and implement a function which takes a pointer to the cycle structure and computes the value of dist from the structure members rear, chain and diam and puts the result (in metres) in the dist member (cf. Chapter 3, exercise 9).

12. The following programming fragment uses structures to hold biographical information about philosophers.

```
typedef struct {
      char   surname[20];
      char   first_name[20];
} Name ;

struct life {
      char   place[20];
      int    born;
      int    died;
};
```

```
struct sage {
      Name   philosopher;
      struct      life  biog;
      char  interests[50];
};

struct sage phil = {
      {"Wittgenstein", "Ludwig"},
      {1889, 1951, "Vienna"},
      "logic, epistemology, language"
};

struct sage *sptr;

sptr = &phil;
```

a. Write a function which takes the address of a sage as an argument and prints out the contents of the structure in the form:

Ludwig Wittgenstein was born in 1889 in Vienna and died in 1951. His main philosophical interests included logic, epistemology and language.

b. What would the following print?

```
printf("%d", p1.biog,birth);
printf("%s", (*sptr) interests);
printf("%s", sptr -> biog.place);
printf("%s", sptr -> philosopher.surname + 4);
```

13. Design a structure for a stock control program. The structure should contain a code number, the name of the stock the quantity and the units (as separate entries), the cost per item and the stock level at which to reorder. Use nested structures as necessary.

Lists and list processing

"In my beginning is my end." T.S.Eliot

11.1 INTRODUCTION

In this chapter we will be extending our knowledge of C to include the important topics of lists and list processing. In an earlier chapter we looked at arrays and how they could be used to store data, and we noted some of the restrictions inherent in these data structures: for example, the need to declare an array large enough to hold all the data likely to be needed in any one run of the program. Lists are a general data structure which allow such restrictions to be overcome and which leave the storage allocation details to the software. This chapter can only serve as an introduction to these topics but after working through it you should have a firm grasp of the concepts involved as well as having your understanding of pointers reinforced. Much of this chapter will be centred on functions related to list processing and discussions on their operation. It is important that you read through each one, spend time analysing its operation and test it out on your own system. For this reason exercises are interspersed with the text, rather than appearing at the end of the chapter.

11.2 BASIC CONCEPTS

The idea of a list follows on from structures which we dealt with in the last chapter. A list is made up of elements which contain data and a pointer to the next element in the list. A list element is often represented diagrammatically as in Figure 11.1.

The contents of a list element can consist of any data types dealt with so far, including structures and unions and even lists. However in this chapter we will be confining our discussion to an element consisting of a single character and a pointer, so that we can concentrate on the central aspects of lists and list processing and not get bogged down in the details of the data held in the list element.

Figure 11.1 *A list element*

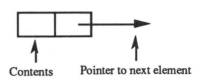

Contents   Pointer to next element

Since the pointer in a list element is a pointer to the next element it will have a data type given by the data type of the element. Thus each element in a list is a self-referential structure. The basic list element can therefore be defined as follows:

Program 11.1

```
typedef char Contents;          /* can be changed to other  */
                                /* data types as necessary  */
struct list {
     Contents c;                /* where the data is held    */
     struct list *pn;           /* pointer to next element   */
};                              /*    in the list            */

typedef struct list L_member;   /* we can now use typedef    */
                                /*    L_member to declare    */
                                /*    additional variables   */
                                /*       of this type        */
```

The declarations above are sufficient to describe the general element of a list. However before we can proceed with using lists we need to consider two important questions concerning the structure of a list. Firstly where does a list start, and secondly where does it end? A list begins with a pointer to the first element in the list (Figure 11.2).

Figure 11.2 *Addressing the first element of a list*

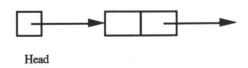

Head

This first pointer is often referred to as the head (the end of the list being the tail!) and is simply the address of the first element in the list. A single variable of type `L_member` can be declared in the usual way, for example:

```
L_member        element;
```

and an array can be declared as

```
L_member        group[20];
```

which declares an array `group` consisting of 20 elements of type `L_member`, i.e. of type `struct list`.

What about the end of a list? How do we know when and where the list ends? Conventionally a NULL pointer is used as the last pointer in a list. It is usual to #define NULL at the start of the program, or in a list header file. Thus

```
#define NULL 0
```

will set up the desired symbolic constant so that assigning a list element to NULL can be achieved in the usual way. For example,

```
element -> *pn = NULL;
```

will assign NULL to the pointer field of the variable element.

Our final diagrammatic representation of a list is shown in Figure 11.3.

Figure 11.3   A simple list

In a structure of this form all that is available, and in fact need be available, to the programmer is a pointer to the first element in the list (i.e. to the head of the list). Having this, together with a few functions, enables us to set up a system for generating and processing linear linked lists. A linear linked list is a list in which each element points to, at most, one other element – if it points to no element (i.e. to NULL) then this is the end of the list.

Generating a list from a string

Before we move on to an exploration of the more general list functions needed in list processing we will examine how to generate a simple list from a string of characters. This is an obvious application since in general we will not know in advance how long a string is likely to be (how long is a piece of string?). In order to make this function as general and as flexible as possible, we want it to return a pointer to the head of the list. Since, as we have just noted, we do not know how many members will be in the list, storage will need to be allocated as the list is generated. This is achieved by use of the standard library function `malloc()`. This function allows for the dynamic allocation of storage and thus makes list generation possible. It allocates storage in multiples of bytes and returns a pointer to the first byte allocated. This, together with the operator `sizeof()` enables the correct amount of memory to be set aside for a list element. Thus

```
p = (L_member *) malloc( sizeof( L_member));
```

will allocate sufficient storage for a single element of the list, as defined above, and will assign p to the first byte of allocated memory space. Notice that we have had to cast `malloc()` to a pointer to `L_member`. This is because the function normally returns a pointer to `char` and using the appropriate cast prevents the type mismatch.

The pointer type `L_member` * occurs frequently in list processing and so it is often given a data type all to itself, e.g.

```
typedef L_member *Link;
```

which declares `Link` to be of type pointer to `L_member`. Other pointers of this type can then be declared in the usual way, e.g.

```
Link temp, p1, next();
```

where `temp` and `p1` are both simple variables whilst `next()` is a function which returns a pointer of type `L_member`.

Let us now return to the function to generate a simple list. We require as an argument to this function a string, which is to be converted to a list. The function should return a pointer to the first element in the list that it generates. Within the function the following processes need to be carried out:

allocate storage for a character
set list data element **to** current character
move to next character

Since a string will be terminated by the `'\0'` character we can use this to check for the end of the string and return NULL. All other cases continue the process of allocation, assignment and moving to the next character. Processes of this type lend themselves to solutions involving recursion and the following pseudocode illustrates one such solution.

```
function string-to-list(string)
if end of string then
        return NULL
else
        allocate storage
        copy current character to the memory just allocated
        set pointer-to-next to string-to-list(string+1)
        return pointer-to-next
end_if
```

Before looking at the code for this function let us consider the basic operation using the string 'to' as a sample. This will help to explain how recursion works in this particular case and provide a further insight into the whole concept of recursion in general. (We met recursion in Chapter 7 when we developed the simple calculator.) Let us assume that the function is called in the following way

```
phead = string_to_list("to");
```

where phead is a pointer assigned to the head of the list which, if the process is successful, will contain 't' 'o' '\0'. The process can be set out as shown in Figure 11.4.

Fig 11.4 *Converting a two-character string to a list using recursion*

operation	local variable	call number
string_to_list("to")		1
allocate storage	ptce1	
copy 't' to this memory location		
pointer_to_next = string_to_list("o")	ptne1	2
string_to_list("o")		
allocate storage	ptce2	
copy 'o' to this memory location		
pointer_to_next = string_to_list("")	ptne2	3
string_to_list("")		
return(NULL)	ptne2 = '\0'	
	/* end of string */	end of 3
return(ptce2)	ptne1 = ptce2(o)	end of 2
return(ptce1)	phead = ptce1(t)	end of 1

ptce = pointer_to_current_element,   ptne = pointer_to_next_element

On the first call to `string_to_list()` storage is allocated and 't' is placed in this location. A second call to the function is made with the string pointer moved to the next character (i.e. 'o'). Storage is again allocated and an assignment made. On the third call the character in the string is the NULL character. Thus the function returns a NULL and this is assigned to the pointer-to-next from the third call (i.e. ptne2). This means that a return from the second call can be made, returning the address of the second element (i.e. 'o'). Finally return from the first call is achieved and the address of the first element assigned to phead, i.e. the element now holding 't'.

The functions required to carry out the above processes are:

Program 11.2

```
/* function generate() to convert a string to a list.
     The argument can be an array, a pointer to a string,
     or a string constant.
*/

Link generate(char *s)
{
        Link         p;

        if( *s == '\0')
                return(NULL);     /* end of string reached       */
        else {                    /* allocate storage and assign */
                p = assign(s);    /* character to new member     */
                p -> pn = generate(s + 1);
                                  /* recursive call assigning next */
                                  /* character to next member in   */
                return(p);        /*              the list         */
        }
}


/* assign() returns a pointer to the next member in the list
     at which the first element in q is to be found
*/

Link assign(Contents *q)
{
        Link         p;

        p = allocate();   /* allocate storage for a new member   */
        if( p == NULL ) {
                puts("\n *** Unable to allocate storage ***");
                exit(0);   /* error trap, exit from program if   */
                           /*  not able to allocate storage       */
        } else {
```

```
        p -> c = *q;      /* Contents of member p now equals*/
        p -> pn = NULL;   /*    *q (the first member of q)   */
        return(p);
    }
}


/* function to allocate storage */
Link allocate(void)
{
        return((Link) malloc(sizeof(L_member)));
}
```

Discussion

The first function (generate()) follows the algorithm quite closely; however it uses another function (assign()) to allocate storage and assign the current character to the newly created member. This function calls another function (allocate()) which simply allocates storage. The code is written in this way because both of the latter operations are frequently needed in list processing and therefore it is sensible to turn them into functions.

Notice in assign() that we have included an error trap to check that there is room to store the new element. Although in this particular problem such an error is very unlikely to occur it is sensible always to check that storage allocation has been successful before continuing. One other point to note is that, after assigning the first character of the string to the contents of the new element, the pointer to the next element is set to NULL. This ensures that a well-formed list is generated. This is again a sensible precaution since, if the pointer is not set outside the function, its contents will be unknown and therefore data will be written to memory which has not been made available.

We require one further function before we can write the complete string_to_list program. This is a function which will print a complete list. One possible version is:

Program 11.3

```
void list_print(Link p)
{
        if( p == NULL)
                printf("NULL : %c (%6u) \n", p -> c, p);
        else {
                printf(" %c (%6u) --> ", p -> c, p);
                list_print( next(p));
        }
}
```

```
Link next(Link p)
{
      return( p -> pn );
}
```

Again this function employs another list-processing function (next ()). This function simply returns a pointer to the next element in the list and is used once again because such a process is frequently needed, and next (p) is rather easier to spot in a program, and understand at a glance, than p = p -> pn.

The list_print () function is also a recursive function. It prints the value of the member and its address and then moves to the next member of the list and so on until a NULL member is reached, at which point it terminates. This function is slightly more complex than is strictly necessary, as it prints both the Contents of each member and its address. To begin with, however, it will help you to understand how a list is set up and how list processing works.

Now that we have written the functions, all that we require is a program to use them and some suitable data. The program below (Program 11.4) is one such example.

Program 11.4

```
/* simple list program */
/* demonstrating the list_print() function */

#include <stdio.h>

#define NULL 0

/* insert the structure definitions in here - Program 11.1   */

typedef L_member *Link;
main()
{
      void          list_print(Link p);
      Link          generate(char *s), assign(Contents *q),
                    allocate(void), next(Link p);
                         /* prototyping for functions */
      Link          list1, list2;

      list1 = generate("Welcome to ");
      list2 = generate("lists in C\n");
      list_print(list1);
      list_print(list2);
}
```

```
/* insert functions
      generate():        Program 11.2
      assign():          Program 11.2
      allocate():        Program 11.2
      list_print():      Program 11.3
      next()  :          Program 11.3
 in here.
*/
```

Exercise

Enter the above program, together with all the functions, and try it out.

11.3 SIMPLE LISTS

The program above is only of limited value. However we can extend it without too much trouble and in the process develop some other useful list processing functions. These functions, although written for the simple list example, can be easily adapted for use with more complex structures. In such cases all that is required is to replace char in the Contents type definition by another data type or structure. Then whenever reference is made to the value stored in a member you must ensure that the correct operations are carried out. Consider a list which holds a string and an integer. The type definition of Contents would be

```
typedef struct {
      char  name[10];
      int   number;
} Contents;
```

The statements to copy the contents of a single element to the list (e.g. in assign() above, Program 11.2) would be

```
strcpy(p -> name, q -> name);
p -> number = q -> number;
```

instead of

```
p -> c = q -> c;
```

as at present. You may like to investigate the use of this structure with lists once you have worked through this chapter.

So far we have functions to generate, and print lists. We also require some means of entering a list from the keyboard. In our present example this simply means reading a string of characters and then using generate to convert them into a list. However if we wish to include spaces in our list a simple scanf ()

function call will not be sufficient as in scanf() a space terminates a string. One alternative is to use repeated calls of getchar() to input a string of characters. Let us assume that a string is terminated by a return character. We then have the following function.

Program 11.5

```
/* function to read characters from stdin and generate a list.
*/
Link get_list(void)
{
      char in[80];

      puts("\n Enter a string (< 80 characters)");
      get_string(in);
      return(generate(in));
}


/* get_string() reads a string from stdin possibly containing
      spaces.
*/
void get_string(char *s)
{
      char c;

      while(( c = getchar()) != '\n')
            *s++ = c;
      *s = '\0';
}
```

Once again we have used modularisation by writing a second function get_string() which does the bulk of the work. (We used a similar function in Chapter 9 for getting a string, possibly containing spaces, from a file.)

Exercise

Incorporate these two functions in the main program and try them out.

11.4 MORE LIST PROCESSING FUNCTIONS

Now that we have introduced the basic concepts of lists and some of the fundamental functions required for processing lists we can investigate what other functions might be required. Operations which need to be carried out on lists include: add a new element, insert one list into another, delete an element, find an element, count the number of elements and order a list. Others may arise in particular circumstances, depending upon the nature of the data stored in the list. Functions which carry out these operations can be generated by writing a number of generalised functions such as `insert()`, `delete()`, `find()`, `count()` and `order()`.

The `insert()` function can be used to add one list to another (i.e. concatenate two lists) as well as to insert one list into another. It can also be used to perform the same operation with a single element, since this is simply a special case of a list (i.e. a list consisting of only one element). Although the `delete()` function might more often be used to remove just one element from a list, it too can be generalised to enable a series of consecutive elements to be deleted (i.e. a sub-list) or to enable a complete list to be deleted.

All of these functions require that a list be traversed or stepped through, either partially or completely, to the end of the list. The simplest example is the function to count the number of elements in the list and so we will begin by writing this. All `count()` has to do is to move through the list one element at a time and keep a running total of the number of elements visited. This function can be written in two ways; recursively or iteratively. Both versions are given below (Program 11.6 and Program 11.7).

Program 11.6

```
/* recursive count */
int count(Link p)
{
      if( p == NULL )
            return(0);
      else  return((count(next(p))) + 1);
}
```

Program 11.7

```
/* iterative count */
int counti(Link p)
{
      int total = 0;
      while(p) {
            total++;
            p = next(p);
      }
      return(total);
}
```

Notice the base case in the recursive version. When a NULL is encountered the function returns 0 since we do not wish to count this element. Otherwise one is added to the return value. Since nothing is returned until the end of the list is reached this results in the number of elements being returned to the calling environment.

The iterative solution should be self-explanatory. However notice that since p will be non-zero (i.e. not NULL) except when the last element is reached, and since zero is FALSE we do not need to use the expression p != NULL as a test but we can just test p. How would you modify the recursive version to incorporate a similar idea?

The find() function can again be written in both recursive and iterative forms. We will write a recursive function and leave the iterative version as an exercise for the reader. This function requires some parameters: a pointer to the list to be searched and a value to compare, or a pointer to a value to compare. Which of these two options should we choose? Both have their advantages. The first option is the clearest for a simple list whose contents is just a single value (e.g. a char, int or string). However the latter option is required when a more complex structure is being processed, although it may be less clear when used with a simple list. Despite this slight disadvantage we will use the pointer version as then the function can be more readily modified for use with more complex structures.

The output for this function should be a pointer to the position in this list where the element lies or NULL if it does not occur in the list. We can use this latter value to check if the search has been successful. The pseudocode takes the form:

```
find (p, q)
if p is NULL then
        return NULL
if Contents of p = Contents of q then
        return p
else
        find(next(p), q)
```

which when translated into C code becomes:

Program 11.8

```
Link  find(Link p, Link q)
{
      if( !p )                      /* End of List p */
            return(NULL);
      if( p -> c == q -> c )
            return(p);             /* found */
      else
            find(next(p), q);
}
```

Insertion

The insert function requires a little more thought so that all possible cases are covered. Consider the list L shown below (Figure 11.5). Possible insertion points are indicated in the diagram.

Figure 11.5 *Inserting elements into a list*

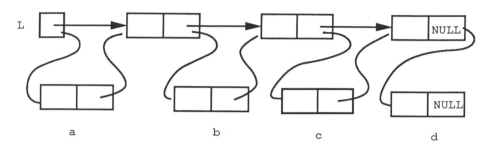

Insertion at b, c and d can be facilitated by an insert function which inserts after the current element. In case a, however, insertion is at the beginning of the list and the new element becomes the first element in the list. The solution must also take account of this special case. A problem now becomes apparent: if we use the address of the first element in the list to indicate that we wish to make the new element the head of the list, what address do we use to insert an element after the first in the list? One solution is to use a NULL pointer to indicate that insertion has to be at the head of the list.

Now let us look at the other cases. Insertion at b and c are identical in principle and are represented by the general case of insertion in the middle of a list. In such cases the link from the previous element has to be broken and redirected to point to the new element. The pointer of the new element (or list) must point to the next element in the original list. Figure 11.6 illustrates this process.

The link from Lx to Ly needs to be preserved in order to complete the insertion. This can be achieved by using a temporary variable to keep this address. The steps are:

> **set** temp_pn **to** Lx -> pn
> **set** Lx -> pn **to** N
> **set** last Link in N (e.g. N2 -> pn) **to** temp

The last step in this process involves traversing the list and returning a link to the last element. This is another of the list processes which is required quite frequently and so would be a useful function. The function `get_tail()` given in Program 11.9 is one such solution.

Figure 11.6   *Insertion in the middle of a list*

Before insertion

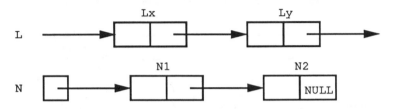

After insertion

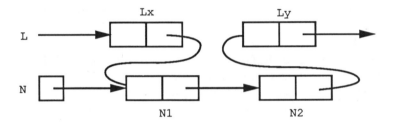

Program 11.9

```
/* function get_tail()
      move to the end of a list
      return a pointer to the last element
*/

Link get_tail(Link p)
{
      if( !next(p) )
            return(p);
      else
            get_tail(next(p));
}
```

Exercise

Check that this function works correctly by going through it on paper, then implement it in the existing program and test it.

   Inserting a new last element in a list is straighforward (we assume that the new list, to be inserted, terminates correctly). All that is necessary is for the Link from the last element of the old list to point to the head of the new list. The complete insert_list() function is given in Program 11.10.

Program 11.10

```
/* insert list b at a in list phead
      phead is a pointer to the head of the first list
      a is a pointer to the position immediately before the point
      of insertion, which is NULL if insertion is to be at the
      head of the list
      b is a pointer to the list to be inserted
*/

void insert_list(Link *phead, Link a, Link b)
{
      Link        temp, thead;


      if (a == NULL) {                      /* insert at beginning */
            thead = *phead;   /* temporary pointer to list head */
            *phead = b;       /*    assign new head to list b    */
            temp = get_tail(b);   /*   get last element of b    */
            temp -> pn = thead;   /* set Link to start of       */
                                  /*    first list              */
      } else if (a -> pn == NULL)  /* insert at end              */
            a -> pn = b;          /* Link to start of list b    */
      else {                      /* insert in middle of head   */
            thead = next(a);      /* pointer to rest of list    */
            a -> pn = b;          /* Link to start of list b    */
            temp = get_tail(b);
            temp -> pn = thead;   /* Link to rest of list       */
      }
}
```

Deletion

The next function which we need to consider is the delete function. This process can be represented diagrammatically as in Figure 11.7.

Deletion involves the modification of links and the releasing of storage back to the system. We deal with the changes in the links first of all. Recall that the find function returns a pointer to the element found. Thus if we search for 'D' in the above list the pointer returned will be L2. At first sight all that needs to be done is to free memory at this address and change L2 to L3. However, in order to do this we require the address of the previous element (i.e. L1) which is not available to us. One solution is to copy the next element (L3) into the one to be deleted and then free the storage previously allocated to the element pointed to by L3. Figure 11.8 provides a visual representation of these stages.

Figure 11.7   *Deleting an element from a list*

Before deletion

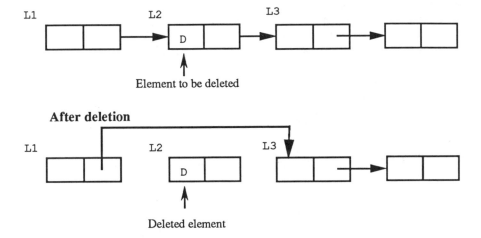

Element to be deleted

After deletion

Deleted element

Figure 11.8   *Deleting by copying the next element*

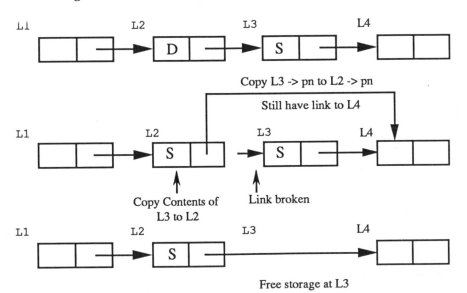

Copy L3 -> pn to L2 -> pn

Still have link to L4

Copy Contents of   Link broken
L3 to L2

Free storage at L3

Releasing storage previously allocated by `malloc()` is achieved with the function `free()`. Thus, if `p` points to an area to be released, `free(p)` will return that area to the system, making it available as storage for other variables

We are now in a position to sketch out the stages in the element deletion process. (Assume that p points to the element to be deleted.)

> **set** ptemp **to** p -> pn
> **copy** next element to p into p (both the Contents and the Link)
> **release** the storage pointed to by ptemp

This function has no special cases and so we can write down the code immediately.

Program 11.11

```
/* delete an element in a list. p points to the element
       to be deleted. Nothing is returned from this function. */
void delete(Link p)
{
      Link        ptemp;
      ptemp = next(p);
      el_copy(p, next(p));
      free(ptemp);
}

/* function el_copy(p,q) copies Contents and Link from q to p */
void el_copy(Link p, Link q)
{
      p -> pn = q -> pn;              /* copy link */
      p -> c = q -> c;               /* copy contents */
}
```

In this function we have used yet another simple function (el_copy()) which copies the element at q to p.

Exercise

1. Enter the insert, delete and associated functions and try them out in your list program. One problem with the present insert function is that the list being inserted can no longer be referenced as a separate list once it has been inserted into the new list (see Figure 11.6). This can be overcome by copying the list to be inserted into a temporary list before carrying out the insertion - write a copy_list function and incorporate this in the insert function.

2. Write a list_delete function which will delete a list from p to the end of the list (inclusive). Make sure that if the list to be deleted is a sub-list (i.e. the latter part of a list) then the former part of the list is terminated correctly.

Ordering

The final list processing function we are going to look at is one to order a list. We will assume that we have a simple list consisting of characters and that we wish to arrange them in ASCII order. Once the function is written it can be modified to deal with other types of ordering and with more complex structures, using a key field for example.

Consider the list shown in Figure 11.9.

Figure 11.9   *A list requiring ordering*

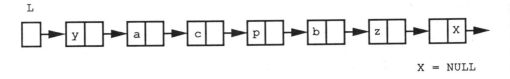

X = NULL

One way to achieve an ordering of the list is to traverse the original list and place each element in turn in the correct place in a second list. Thus we would have the end result shown in Figure 11.10.

Figure 11.10   *The ordered list*

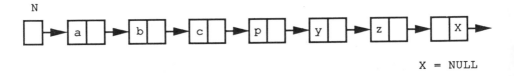

X = NULL

We begin with a pointer N, whose Contents and Link are set to NULL. This represents the initial set-up for the ordered list. The Contents of the first element of list L are then copied into this initial element. We can now use a recursive function to order the rest of the original list. The process involves comparing the current element of L with each element of N until the position for insertion is found. The element from L is then inserted into N and the process repeated until the end of list L is reached. At this point, the ordered list resides in N.

This process can usefully be broken into two sections. The first involves the main function which selects the element to insert, calls a function to find the position in the ordered list at which to insert the element, carries out the insertion and finally gets the next element. This function, which we will call order(), will require two parameters, the address of the start of the unordered list and a pointer to the start of the ordered list.

The function position() which finds the correct place in which to insert the new element is of type Link since it is required to return a pointer to the element after which the new element is to be inserted. As before, with insert(), we will use NULL to indicate insertion at the head of the list.

These two functions are given below.

Program 11.12

```
/* put list in ASCII order
        p is source list
        q is address of ordered list
*/

void order(Link  p,  Link  q)
{
        Link        q1, temp;

        if (p == NULL)                    /* end of list p reached    */
               return;
        else {
               temp = assign(&(p -> c));
               q1 = position(temp, q);    /* find place to insert */
               printf("\n q1 = %6u\n", q1);
               insert_list(q, q1, temp, TRUE);
               p_list(*q);
               order(next(p), q);                 /* order rest of p      */
        }
}

/* find position to insert an element in order
        p is a pointer to the required element
        q is a pointer to current element in the ordered list
        the function returns a pointer to the insertion position
        NULL is returned for insertion at the head of the list
*/

Link position(Link  p,  Link  *q)
{
        Contents prevc, nextc, cc;

        if (*q == NULL)                       /* first element    */
               return(NULL);
        cc = p -> c;
        prevc = (*q) -> c;
```

```
        nextc = (*q) -> pn -> c;
        if (prevc >= cc)                    /* insert at start   */
                return(NULL);
        else if (nextc == NULL)             /* insert at end     */
                return(*q);
        else if (cc <= nextc)               /* insert inside     */
                return(*q);
        else                /* place not found - continue search */

                return(position(p, &((*q) -> pn)));

                        /* move to next element in q     */
}
```

Exercise

Enter the above functions and try them out.

SUMMARY

In this chapter we:

- saw that a list element is a self-referential structure in that the structure contains a pointer which points to the same structure type.

- saw that in the simplest list an element consists of a data item and a pointer to the next element.

- noted the use of malloc() and free() to manage list storage.

- developed basic list processing functions.

CONCLUSION

This concludes our tour of C. I hope you have found the book useful and that it has whetted your appetite for C programming. Programming can be fun, programming even should be fun. So go ahead and play. Good luck!

Dec	Char			Dec	Char	Dec	Char	Dec	Char
0	^@		NUL	32	SPACE	64	@	96	`
1	^A		SOH	33	!	65	A	97	a
2	^B		STX	34	"	66	B	98	b
3	^C	♥	ETX	35	#	67	C	99	c
4	^D	♦	EOT	36	$	68	D	100	d
5	^E	♣	ENQ	37	%	69	E	101	e
6	^F	♠	ACK	38	&	70	F	102	f
7	^G		BEL	39	'	71	G	103	g
8	^H		\b	40	(	72	H	104	h
9	^I		\t	41	)	73	I	105	i
10	^J		\r	42	*	74	J	106	j
11	^K		VT	43	+	75	K	107	k
12	^L		\f	44	,	76	L	108	l
13	^M		\n	45	-	77	M	109	m
14	^N		SO	46	.	78	N	110	n
15	^O		SI	47	/	79	O	111	o
16	^P		DLE	48	0	80	P	112	p
17	^Q		DC1	49	1	81	Q	113	q
18	^R		DC2	50	2	82	R	114	r
19	^S	!!	DC3	51	3	83	S	115	s
20	^T	¶	DC4	52	4	84	T	116	t
21	^U	§	NAK	53	5	85	U	117	u
22	^V		SYN	54	6	86	V	118	v
23	^W		ETB	55	7	87	W	119	w
24	^X		CAN	56	8	88	X	120	x
25	^Y		EM	57	9	89	Y	121	y
26	^Z		SUB	58	:	90	Z	122	z
27	^[		ESC	59	;	91	[	123	{
28	^\		FS	60	<	92	\	124		
29	^]		GS	61	=	93	]	125	}
30	^^		RS	62	>	94	^	126	~
31	^_		US	63	?	95	_	127	

Appendix B: the line editor

This appendix contains the complete line editor which we have looked at from time to time throughout the book. Some of the constructs will be familiar to you as we have used similar examples before, others will be less familiar. However you should be able to understand how each function works and how it interacts with the other functions and with the main program. The complete listing is given with comments interspersed between the functions explaining any interesting or unusual features.

Some of the exercises in the preceding chapters have asked you to write functions for the line editor. You will find solutions to these particular exercises at the appropriate points in the program listings. If you have attempted the exercises and have reached a different solution to that given here don't worry, there is more than one solution. If yours is markedly different read through the function given and make sure that you understand how it works.

There are a number of modifications which could usefully be made to this program such as: allow any file to be edited, use a linked list instead of an array to store the text, allow the editing of a line, implement a search and replace option. Once you have become conversant with the program as it exists you should experiment with some of these ideas in an attempt to improve the program and develop your understanding of C.

Program B.1 – The line editor program

```
/* the line editor
      This editor allows simple line editing.
      The options are : a - append,
                        d - delete,
                        h - help,
                        i - insert,
                        p - print (i.e. display),
                        q - quit,
                        r - read file,
                        s - save edited text.
```

The general syntax of the command line is n1,n2x where :

 n1 is the first line to be edited,
 n2 is the last line to be edited and
 x is the appropriate edit command.

If either n1 or n2 references a line past the current text it is
set to the current end of text. If either n1 or n2 is less than
zero it is set to zero.

Two further symbols are used to aid editing :

 % - edit all the text and
 $ - to refer to the current last line of text.

The allowable form of the command line is left flexible.
Possible valid command lines are :

 1,5p print lines 1 to 5 inclusive,
 ,5p   print from current line to line 5,
 2,p   print from line 1 to current line,
 3d   delete line 3,
 4,$d delete from line 4 to the end,
 $p   print last line,
 %p   print all lines,
 4i   insert before line 4.

The commands p and d can be used with the above command syntax.
The insert command should be either used alone or preceded by a
single line number, which may be $ (signifying insert before the
last line). The commands a, q, r and s should be used alone,
they require no line specifiers.

A limited amount of in-line editing is allowed (i.e. the use of
backspace).
*/

```
#include <stdio.h>
#define MAXLINES 25   /* number of lines of text allowed */
#define MAXCOLS 75    /* number of columns of text (i.e.
                         characters in a line ) */
#define FALSE 0
#define TRUE 1
#define SPACE ' '
#define NL '\n'
#define CR '\r'
#define BS '\b'        /* backspace */

/* function prototypes */
char getnextchar(void),
     read_command(int *pn1, int *pn2, int *valid);
int check_command(char cm, int n1, int n2), isadigit(char c),
     save_text(void);
void process_option(char com, int *n1, int *n2),
     helpscreen(void), insert(int line),
     delete(int n1, int *n2), print(int start, int end),
```

```
        movetext(int line), read_file(void), init_text(void);

/* external declarations */
int next = 0;    /* next available line for appending, i.e.
                    current last line + 1 */
char text[MAXLINES][MAXCOLS];    /* array to hold edited text */

main()
{
        char command = 'x';        /* a dummy value to start */
        int valid_com, n1 = 0, n2 = 0;  /* n1 and n2 are line
                                           numbers for editing */

        puts("\n\n");
        puts("                     T H E   C   E D I T O R");
        puts("                     ========================");
        puts(" a: append, d: delete, h: help, i: insert, p:
             display, q: quit, r: read, s: save");
        init_text();  /* ensure array is initialised with NULLS */
        read_file();     /* read data.txt, if it exists ... */
        if( next != 0 ) {      /* and display the text */
             n2 = next - 1; /* next -1 is the last line of text */
             print(0, n2);
        }
        while(command != 'q') {
             printf("\n :> ");                 /* command prompt */
             command = read_command(&n1, &n2, &valid_com);
             if(!valid_com)
                  puts("*** Incorrect syntax ***");
             else
                  process_option(command, &n1, &n2);
        }
}
```

The main program is quite short, it displays the opening screen, calls the file read function (`read_file()`) and then uses a `while` loop to process the editing commands. Notice the use of `#define` instructions to improve readability and aid future modification. Notice also that all functions are prototyped at the beginning of the program.

Functions

The functions appear in the following pages approximtely in the order in which they are used in the main program. Each function is numbered and named for easy reference. The first function (Program B.2) is the `read_command()` function which was given as an exercise in Chapter 8 (Exercise 11). This reads in and parses the command line.

Program B.2 – read_command()
(Exercise 8.11)

```
/* function read_command()
**
** this function parses the command and obtains the line numbers
** *pn1 is a pointer to the first line for editing
** *pn2 is a pointer to the last line for editing
** valid is a flag to indicate correct syntax
** on exit the editor command character is returned.
*/
char read_command(int *pn1, int *pn2, int *valid)
{
        extern int next;
        char c1;

        c1 = getnextchar();   /* skip leading spaces in command  */
        *valid = TRUE;   /* TRUE unless invalid line number n2 */
        switch(c1) {
        case '%' :         /* edit whole text */
             *pn1 = 0;
             *pn2 = next - 1;
             c1 = getnextchar();
             break;
        case '$' :              /* edit last line only */
             *pn1 = *pn2 = next -1 ;
             c1 = getnextchar();
             break;
        case '0' :              /* digit read */
        case '1' :
        case '2' :
        case '3' :
        case '4' :
        case '5' :
        case '6' :
        case '7' :
        case '8' :
        case '9' :
             *pn1 = get_int(c1) - 1; /* array index starts at 0*/
                               /* lines start from 1 */
             if( c1 == ',') { /* line possibly of form: n1,n2x */
                  c1 = getnextchar();
                  if( c1 == '$') {
                       *pn2 = next - 1;/* edit n1 to last line */
                       c1 = getnextchar();
                  } else if (isadigit(c1)) {
                       *pn2 = get_int(c1) - 1;
                       c1 = getnextchar();
```

```
                    }
                    break;
              } else
                    *pn2 = *pn1;            /* only one line to edit */
              break;
        case ',' :                          /* command of form ,n2x */
              cl = getnextchar();
              if( cl == '$') {
                    *pn1 = *pn2 = next - 1;/* edit nl to last line*/
                    cl = getnextchar();
              } else if(isadigit(cl)) {
                    *pn1 = *pn2;
                    *pn2 = get_int(cl) - 1;
                    cl = getnextchar();
              } else
                    *valid = FALSE; /* invalid second number */
              break;
        default :                           /* no numbers, just a command */
              *pn1 = *pn2;                   /* edit one line only */
              break;
        }
        fflush(stdin);  /* clear characters from input buffer */
        /* check line bounds */
        if( next == 0 )   *pn1 = *pn2 = 0;
        if( *pn1 < 0 )    *pn1 = 0;
        if( *pn2 < 0 )    *pn2 = 0;
        if( *pn1 > next ) *pn1 = next - 1;
        if( *pn2 > next ) *pn2 = next - 1;
        if( *pn1 > *pn2 ) *pn1 = *pn2;
        return(cl);
}
```

This function carries out all the necessary operations for reading and parsing the command line. It consists of a single `switch` statement with nested `if` statements to take care of the various valid command sequences. The table on page 18 (Table 1.1) should be used to verify the logic of this function.

The library function `fflush()` is used to flush the input buffer and thus remove any spurious characters. This means that the next character entered, after a newline, is read by the `read_command()` function. It also guarantees that unwanted characters are not inserted into the command line following an insert or append command. The majority of invalid line combinations are trapped and corrected by the series of `if` statements at the end of the function. These error traps make some assumptions about what are invalid combinations, e.g. that n1 should be less than n2. However they do not trap and correct commands consisting of a single comma and a command, e.g. ,d. This prevents the accidental deletion of a line of text.

The next few functions are some basic ones which are used by the above function (Program B.2). They are getnextchar(), isadigit() and get_int(). These were discussed in Chapter 6.5 (Programs 6.8, 6.9 and 6.10) and are included here (Program B.3) for completeness.

Program B.3 – getnextchar(), isadigit() and getint()

```
/* function getnextchar()
**
** this function skips spaces read from stdin
** it returns the first non-space character read
*/
char getnextchar()
{
    char c;

    while((c = getchar()) == SPACE)
         ;
    return(c);
}


/* function isadigit()
**
** this takes a character as an argument and returns
** TRUE if it is a digit and FALSE otherwise
*/
int isadigit(char c)
{
    if( c >= '0' && c <= '9' )
         return(TRUE);
    else
         return(FALSE);
}


/* function getint()
**
** this function reads charcaters while they are digits
** and converts them to a decimal integer.
** This integer is returned on exit.
*/
int getint(char c)
{
    int i = 0;                    /* initialise the number to 0 */

    while(isadigit(c)) {          /* execute while c is a digit */
         i = 10 * i + (c - '0');    /* decimal conversion */
         c = getchar();
    }
```

```
        ungetc(c, stdin);              /* put first non-didgit back in
                                       input buffer */

        return(i);
}
```

The only comment necessary concerning these functions relates to the last one (i.e. getint()). This function continues reading characters while they are digits. However once a non-digit is read, it is required by the read_command() function (Program B.2). The present function cannot return the character as it is already returning the converted integer (i) so another solution has to be found. The one we have used here is to employ the library function ungetc(). This places the character just read back into the input buffer – it can then be read by the next character read instruction. Another solution is to alter the function so that the value of parameter c is changed from within the function. You may like to try modifying get_int() and read_command() using this method.

The next function is the one to check that a valid command character has been entered. This was dealt with earlier, in Chapter 4 (Program 4.3), and so requires no further discussion.

Program B.4 – check_command()
(cf. Program 4.3)

```
/* function check command()
**
** this function simply checks for valid commands
** if command is insert then it also checks that n1 = n2
**
**      TRUE is returned if the command is valid, FALSE otherwise
*/
int check_command(char cm, int n1, int n2)
{
        int valid = FALSE;

        if(cm == 'i' && n2 == n1)
                valid = TRUE;
        else if( cm == 'a' || cm == 'd' || cm == 'h' || cm == 'p'
        || cm == 'q' || cm == 'r' || cm == 's')
                valid = TRUE;
        return(valid);
}
```

The next function (process_option()) is the heart of the program, it processes the commands once they are entered. Apart from adjusting the values of the line numbers (*pn1 and *pn2), when relevant, the main task of this function is to transfer control to the appropriate function to enable the required task to be performed. The structure consists of a switch statement, with a case statement for each valid option. (See Chapter 4, page 100 for the basic pseudocode.)

Program B.5 – `process_option()`

```c
/* function process_option()
**
** this function switches control to the appropriate function
** depending on the command entered
*/
void process_option(char com, int *pn1, int *pn2)
{
     extern char text[][];
     extern int next;

     switch(com) {
          case 'a' : /* append to end of existing text */
               *pn2 = next;
               insert(*pn2);
               break;
          case 'd' : /* delete line(s) */
               delete(*pn1, pn2);
               break;
          case 'h' : /* help */
               helpscreen();
               break;
          case 'i' : /* insert line(s) in middle of text */
               insert(*pn1);    /* insert before line n1 */
               break;
          case 'p' : /* display selected lines */
               if( next > -1 )
                    print(*pn1, *pn2);
               else
                    puts("\n *** Editor is empty ***");
               break;
          case 'q' : /* quit the editor */
               break;
          case ' r': /* read the file data.txt if it exists */
               *pn1 = *pn2 = next = 0;
               init_text();    /* fill array with NULLS */
               read_file();
               if( next != 0 ) {
                    *pn2 = next - 1;
                    print(0, *pn2); /* display text just read*/
               }
               break;
          case 's' : /* save all the text to file: data.txt */
               if(!save_text())
```

```
                                puts("\n *** Cannot save text ***");
                    else
                                puts("\n *** Text saved to data.txt ***");
                    break;
        }
}
```

The remaining functions are the actual processing functions themselves. It is these function which modify, print, read and save the text. The first of these is the delete() function. This simply moves lines within the array text [] [] by overwriting the deleted lines. The variables *pn2 and next are then updated. On exit n1 and n2 both point to the line number of the first deleted line.

Program B.6 – delete()

```
/* function delete()
**
** this function deletes lines n1 to n2 inclusive
** next and n2 are updated accordingly
*/
void delete(int n1, int *pn2)
{
        int line, col, diff;
        extern int next;
        extern char text[][];

        diff = *pn2 - n1 + 1; /* get number of lines to delete */
        for( line = n1, col = 0; line < next; col++) {
                text[line][col] = text[line + diff][col];
                if( text[line + diff][col] == NL) {
                                /* delete another line */
                        col = -1;
                        line++;
                }
        }
        if( next != 0 )            /* update next */
                next = next - diff;
        *pn2 = n1;                 /* update *pn2 */
}
```

The helpscreen() function which follows (Program B.7) should require no explanation! It simply displays on the screen some basic help information. (See Chapter 3, Exercise 7.)

Program B.7 - helpscreen()

```
/* function helpscreen()
**
```

```
** no explanatory comments needed!
*/
void helpscreen()
{
    puts(" H E L P   F O R   T H E   C   E D I T O R");
    puts(" =========================================");
    puts("The p command : displays lines of text.");
    puts("============= A range can be specified as - ");
    puts("e.g.            1,4p        lines 1 to 4");
    puts("                2p          line 2");
    puts("                %%p         all the lines");
    puts("                $p          the last line only");
    puts("                p           the current line ");
    puts("                            (i.e. the last line edited)");
    puts("The d command : deletes lines of text.");
    puts("============= The syntax is as for p");
    puts("e.g.            1,4d        deletes lines 1 to 4");
    puts("                etc.");
    puts("The i command : inserts lines of text.");
    puts("============= Insertion is before the line given ");
    puts("e.g.            2i          before line 2");
    puts("                $i          before the last line")·
    puts("                i           before the current li  ;");
    puts("The a command : appends to the end of present text");
    puts("============= an * at start of line stops insert");
    puts("The s command : saves the text to file data.txt");
    puts("=============");
    puts("The r command : reads file data.txt into memory");
    puts("=============");
}
```

The next function (Program B.8) displays the text on the screen. Once again it is reasonably straightforward. The only test is to see if any text is available for displaying. The simplest way to determine this is to test the value of next – this is set to zero if the array text [ ] [ ] is empty. (See Chapter 9, Exercise 4.)

Program B.8 – print()

```
/* function print()
**
** this displays on the screen the specified text
** between lines n1 and n2 inclusive
*/
void print(int n1, int n2)
{
    int line, col;
    extern char text[][];
    extern int next;
```

```
        if( next == 0) {
                puts(" *** Editor is empty ***");
                return;
        }
        line = n1;
        printf("%2d : ", line + 1);
        for( col = 0; line <= n2; col++) {
                putchar(text[line][col]);
                if(text[line][col] == NL ) {
                        line++;
                        col = -1;
                        if( line <= n2 )
                                printf("%2d : ", line + 1);
                }
        }
}
```

The insert function which follows (Program B.9) is the most complex of the functions in the line editor. This function reads in characters from the keyboard and stores them in the character array text [] []. A number of conditions have to be checked: for example, is the editor already full?, has a newline (or return) been entered? has the maximum number of columns been reached? The main structure of the function consists of two while loops. The inner one reads a line of text, i.e. until a return is entered or the maximum number of columns is reached. The outer one reads lines of text until a terminating character is entered at the beginning of a line (STOP) or the maximum number of lines is reached (MAXLINES).

Additional tasks involve the in-line editing capability and how to adjust data in the array when text is being inserted rather than appended. The first of these tasks is achieved by using the library function getch() instead of getchar(). The former function is an unbuffered read, which means that the character read is immediately available for use. On the other hand getchar() is a buffered read, which presents the problem that there is no easy way of telling when text has overlapped into the next line. Using getch() means that the echoing of the entered character has to be specifically programmed and also has the added complication that the ENTER or RETURN key is a carriage return ('\r') rather than a newline ('\n'). The in-line editing is achieved by noting that the backspace key ('\b') can be recognised. This fact can be used to enable on-screen editing to take place in the line being entered. However, we need to remember to update the array at the same time. Look carefully at the code for reading a line, including the use of backspace, and check that you understand how it works.

The problem of adjusting text already in the array when inserting rather than appending is solved by use of another function, movetext(). The code for this function is given below at Program B.10 – we will discuss it shortly.

Program B.9 – insert()

```
/* function insert()
**
** this function inserts line(s) of text before line ln
** unless ln equals next in which case the text is appended.
** unbuffered input is used to allow for
** limited in-line editing - e.g.  backspace can be used
** to delete characters entered on the current line
** entry is terminated by typing * at the start of a line -
** the symbol can be changed by altering the #define instruction
**
*/
void insert(int ln)
{
        #define STOP '*' /* use asterisk to terminate text entry */

        extern char text[][];
        extern int next;
        int col = 0, line;
        char ch;

        line = ln;
        if(next >= MAXLINES) {/* check array is not already full */
                puts("\n *** Editor is full ***");
                next = MAXLINES;
                return;
        }
        printf("%2d : ", line + 1");
        ch = getch();
        putchar(ch);
        if( ch == STOP )
                return;              /* decide not to insert after all! */
        col = 0;
        while( ch != STOP ) {
                if( next >= 0 && line < next)
                        movetext(line); /* adjust text already in array
                                        from line to the end */
                next++;     /* set next to next available line for
                                appending */
                text[line][col++] = ch;
                text[line][MAXCOLS-1] = NL; /* put \n in last col. */
                while(!( ch == CR || col == MAXCOLS - 1)) {
                        ch = getch();
                        while( ch == BS ) {/* limited in-line editing */
                                putchar(ch);
```

```
                        putchar(SPACE);/* rubout last character */
                        putchar(BS);/* position to insert next ch*/
                        col--;      /* adjust col. accordingly */
                        text[line][col] = SPACE;
                        while(( ch = getch()) == BS && col == 0)
                            ;       /* only allow deletion to
                                    beginning of the line */
                }
                if( ch == CR)
                        text[line][col++] = NL;
                                    /* replace CR with NL */
                else {
                        putchar(ch);
                        text[line][col++] = ch;
                }
        }       /* read a line of text */
        col = 0;                /* set variables for another line */
        if( next >= MAXLINES ) {
                next = MAXLINES;
                puts("\n *** Array is full ***");
                ch = STOP;
        } else {
                line++;
                printf("\n%2d : ", line + 1);
                ch = getch();
                putchar(ch);
        }
    }
    fflush(stdin);   /* clean any remaining characters from the
                     input buffer */
}
```

As was mentioned above the movetext() function moves text up the array to release room for the new line being inserted. It is only invoked if the first character of the new line is not the terminating character (i.e. STOP) and if there is room to add more lines (i.e. as long as line is less than next and next is less than or equal to MAXLINES). This function starts at the current last line of the text in the array and shifts the text up into a new line until the position where the line is to be inserted is reached. So this uses the decrement operator to count down from next to ln (i.e. line--).

Program B.10 – movetext()

```
/* function movetext()
**
** this function moves text up the array by one line
** it starts at the end of the array and works down to ln
*/
```

```
void movetext(int ln)
{
    extern int next;
    extern char text[][];
    int line col;

    for( line = next. col = 0; line >= ln; col++) {
        text[line + 1][col] = text[line][col];
        if( text[line][col] == NL || col == MAXCOLS - 1 ) {
            col = -1;
            line--;
        }
    }
}
```

The remaining functions concern file i/o and initialisation of the `char` array `text[][]`. The `read_file()` function (Program B.11) was discussed briefly in Chapter 9 and the reader should refer to the relevant section for further details (see pages 224–226 and Program 9.4).

Program B.11 – `read_file()`
(Program 9.4)

```
/* function read_file()
**
** this function reads text from file data.txt
** next is set equal to the number of lines read + 1
** unless the line limit is exceeded in which case
** next is set equal to MAXLINES
*/
void read_file(void)
{
    extern char text[][];
    extern int next;

    FILE *fp;
    char c;
    int col = 0;

    next = 0;   /* ensure text is read into the array from the
                beginning */
    if(( fp = fopen("data.txt","r")) == NULL {
        puts("\n *** New file: data.txt does not exist ***");
        return;
    } else while(( c = getc(fp)) != EOF) {
        if( c == NL || col >= MAXCOLS - 1 ) {
            text[next++][col] = NL;
            col = 0;
```

```
                    if( next > MAXLINES ) {
                        next = MAXLINES;
                        puts("\n *** Line limit exceeded ***");
                        fclose(fp);
                        return;
                    }
            } else                /* normal text, not EOL or '\n, */
                    text[next][col++] = c;
    }
    if( col != 0 && c == EOF ) {
        text[next][col] = NL;
        next++;              /* update next if EOF and no '\n' */
    }
    fclose(fp);
}
```

The save_text() function (Program B.12) is quite straightforward. It uses a couple of nested for loops to copy the data from the array text[][] to the file data.txt. No variables need to be modified by this function. However it returns FALSE if the file cannot be opened for any reason. With a little thought these two functions can be modified so that any file can be edited. You may like to try such a modification. You could use command line arguments (i.e. making use of argc and argv[]) or you could enter the file name from within the editor.

Program B.12   save_text()
(See Exercise 9.3)

```
/* function save_text()
**
** this function saves the text stored in the array text[][]
** to the file data.txt
** it returns TRUE if saved successfully, FALSE if not
*/
int save_text(void)
{
    extern char text[][];
    extern int next;

    int line, coll
    FILE *fp;

    if(( fp = fopen("data.txt","w")) == NULL) {
        puts("\n *** Unable to open file data.txt ***");
        return(FALSE);
    }
    for( line = 0; line < next; line++) {
        for( col = 0; col < MAXCOLS; col++) {
```

```
            putc(text[line][col], fp);
            if ( text[line][col] == NL )
                col = MAXCOLS;              /* save next line */
      }
   }
   fclose(fp);
   return(TRUE);
}
```

Notice the use of `fclose()` in both of the above functions. If `fopen()` is used to open an input or output stream then you should use `fclose()` to close the stream especially if the file is to be re-used within the program. Conversely if `open()` is used then `close()` should be used.

The final function (`init_text()`) is used to fill the array `text[][]` with NULLs. This is not essential but it does prevent spurious characters appearing in the array. Again it consists simply of two nested `for` loops.

Program B.13 – `init_text()`

```
/* function init_text()
**
** this functions fills the array with NULLS
*/
void init text(void)
{
      extern char text[][];

      int line, col;

      for( line = 0; line <= MAXLINES; line++ )
            for( col = 0; col <= MAXCOLS; col++)
                  text[line][col] = NULL;
}
```

This brings us to the end of our discussion of the Line Editor program. Read through each of the functions above and check that you understand how they work. Try typing them into your own machine and then test out the complete program. It is not guaranteed to be bug free, but it has been tested fairly rigorously. As already noted, there are a number of improvements which could be made and the logic could be tidied up in places. Use the program as a basis for experimenting and see what improvements you can make.

Appendix C: the bridge tutor

In this appendix we present some of the functions for the basic bridge tutor. These are limited to the easiest options of shuffling, dealing, displaying, sorting, counting points and bidding (opening bid only). Some of these functions have already appeared in various places throughout the book. They provide another example, along with the calculator and the line editor of a working program. Although in this case the options are limited you could modify the program to simulate a simpler card game or if you are familiar with bridge you could extend it to provide the points count and the opening bid for a specific hand instead of a random hand. Further extensions might be to continue the bidding and playing bridge – the computer against you and dummy! You should read through these functions and make sure that you understand how they operate and then incorporate them in the menu driven main program (Program 6.7 or, the slightly modified version, Program C.1). Many improvements and refinements can be made on them and it would be well worth you while trying to improve some of them.

As with the line editor program we will take each function, or group of functions, in turn and comment on the structure and any points of interest. The first piece of code is the main program. This is a slightly modified version of Program 6.7. The main changes include the prototyping of all the functions used in the latest version and an option to allow the main menu to only be displayed when requested. (This helps when checking the program operation.)

Program C.1

```
/* Bridge Tutor - bridge.c
** development version
**
** this uses a simple int array to hold the cards: i.e.
**   0 .... 12 (2 .... A) clubs
** 13 .... 25 (2 .... A) diamonds
** 26 .... 38 (2 .... A) hearts
** 39 .... 51 (2 .... A) spades
*/
```

```
#include <stdio.h>
#define FALSE 0
#define TRUE 1

int deck[52], north[13], east[13], south[13], west[13];

/* prototype functions */
void main_menu(void), deal(void), shuffle(void), display(void),
     bubble(int a[], int n), print(int a[], int size),
     exchange(int *p, int *q, int *sorted),
     o_bids(int points, int balanced);
char valid_c(void), * print_bal(int balanced),
     * bid_suit(int balanced, int min, int max, int cards[]);
int execute_option(char ch), count_points(int a[]),
     balanced(int a[], int *min, int *max, int cards[]);

main()
{
     char c = 'm';    /* display menu to begin with */

     do {
          if( c == 'm' )
               main_menu();  /* only display menu if needed */
          c = valid_c();
     } while(execute_option(c));
}
```

The functions main_menu(), valid_c() and execute_option()
(Program C.2) were introduced earlier (Programs 2.2, 6.5 and 6.6 respectively).
The functions presented here do not differ markedly from the earlier ones. The
main changes involve the inclusion of an extra option to display the menu – as
noted above. The execute_option() function has also been expanded to
include functions to perform some of the required tasks. The exception is the
'playing bridge' option. This function has some additional variables declared
which are used during the bidding section. Notice in particular the way in which
a function (bid_suit()) is used to return a string indicating which suit to
bid. The details of the logic underlying the bidding section are dealt with when
we examine the relevant functions later on in this appendix.

Program C.2 – main_menu(), valid_c(), execute_option()

```
/* function main_menu()
**
** This displays a menu on the screen.
*/
void main_menu(void)
{
     puts("\n\n");
```

```
        puts ("                    ******************************") ;
        puts ("                               BRIDGE TUTOR") ;
        puts ("                    ******************************\n") ;
        puts ("                         1. shuffle") ;
        puts ("                         2. deal") ;
        puts ("                         3. display the hands") ;
        puts ("                         4. count the points") ;
        puts ("                         5. bid") ;
        puts ("                         6. play") ;
        puts ("                         m. display this menu") ;
        puts ("                         Q. quit\n\n") ;
        puts ("Press a digit (1-6), m, or Q to Quit.") ;
}


/* function valid_c(void)
**
** This function checks for a valid command -
** only valid commands are accepted.
** To improve presentation unbuffered input is used
** with no echoing (i.e. getch()).
** On exit the function returns the (valid) character entered.
*/
char valid_c(void)
{
        char c;

        do {
                c = getch();
        } while( c != 'Q' && c != 'm' && (c < '1' || c > '6'));
        return(c);
}


/* function execute_option()
**
** This function switches control to the appropriate
** set of functions depending on the argument (c).
** FALSE is returned if c == 'Q' and TRUE otherwise.
*/
int execute_option(char c)
{
        int points, bal, max, min, cards[4];

        switch(c) {
        case '1' :
                printf("\n Executing shuffle ");
                shuffle();
                break;
        case '2' :
                printf("\n Dealing the hands ");
```

```
        deal();
        bubble(north, 13);      /* sort each hand into suit */
        bubble(east, 13);       /* & denomination order */
        bubble(south, 13);
        bubble(west, 13);
        break;
case '3' :
        printf("\n Displaying the hands ");
        display();
        break;
case '4' :
        puts("\n Counting the points ");
        puts("    The points are .... ");
        printf("\t NORTH : %d\n", count_points(north));
        printf("\t  EAST : %d\n", count_points(east));
        printf("\t SOUTH : %d\n", count_points(south));
        printf("\t  WEST : %d\n", count_points(west));
        break;
case '5' : /* only simple opening bids implemented */
        printf("\n Bidding ");
        bal = balanced(north, &min, &max, cards);
        printf("\n NORTH : %s ", print_bal(bal));
        points = count_points(north);
        o_bids(points, bal);
        if(((points == 13 || points == 14) && bal) || !bal)
            printf(" %s ", bid_suit(bal, min, max, cards));

        bal = balanced(east, &min, &max, cards);
        printf("\n  EAST : %s ", print_bal(bal));
        points = count_points(east);
        o_bids(points, bal);
        if(((points == 13 || points == 14) && bal) || !bal)
            printf(" %s ", bid_suit(bal, min, max, cards));

        bal = balanced(south, &min, &max, cards);
        printf("\n SOUTH : %s ", print_bal(bal));
        points = count_points(south);
        o_bids(points, bal);
        if(((points == 13 || points == 14) && bal) || !bal)
            printf(" %s ", bid_suit(bal, min, max, cards));

        bal = balanced(west, &min, &max, cards);
        printf("\n  WEST : %s ", print_bal(bal));
        points = count_points(west);
        o_bids(points, bal);
        if(((points == 13 || points == 14) && bal) || !bal)
            printf(" %s ", bid_suit(bal, min, max, cards));

        break;
```

```
      case '6' :
            printf("\n Playing bridge - maybe ! ");
            break;
      case 'm' :  /* display the menu */
            break;
      case 'Q' :
            return(FALSE);
      }
      return(TRUE);
}
```

The next set of functions (Program C.3) concern the shuffling and dealing of the cards. These were discussed in Chapter 8. The shuffle() function is a modification of the function to generate a random character and should be easy to follow. The deal() function simply distributes the cards between the four hands north, east, south and west and is identical to Program 8.13. Note that on each run of the program the first call of shuffle will produce a particular sequence of random numbers, the second call a different set, and so on. So that new hands can be obtained by repeating the shuffle a different number of times (i.e. select option 1 3, 7, 8 etc. times before selecting option 2 to deal).

Program C.3 – shuffle(), deal()

```
/* function shuffle()
**
** This function simulates the shuffling of a deck of cards. It
** uses the library function rand() to produce a pseudo-random
** number.
*/
void shuffle(void)
{
      extern int deck[];
      int i, rnum, temp;

      for(i = 0; i < 52; i++)
            deck[i] = i;       /* set up basic pack */
      /* now randomise it */
      for( i = 0; i < 52; i++) {
            rnum = rand % 52; /* get a random no. range 0 - 51 */
            temp = deck[i];          /* exchange cards */
            deck[i] = deck[rnum];
            deck[rnum] = temp;
      }
}


/* function deal()
**
** this function distributes the cards in deck to
```

```
** the four players north, east, south and west
*/
void deal(void)
{
        extern int deck[], north[], east[], south[], west[];
        int i, j;

        for( j = 0, i = 0; j < 52; j += 4, i++) {
                south[i] = deck[j];
                west[i]  = deck[j+1];
                north[i] = deck[j+2];
                east[i]  = deck[j+3];
        }
}
```

The next two functions (Program C.4) are used to display the cards on the screen. The first one is very simple. It just displays a prompt and then calls the print() function for each of the four hands of cards. The second function is worth discussing a little further. We will do so once you have read it over.

Program C.4 – display(), print()

```
/* function display()
**
** this function displays all four hands, it uses the
** function print() to improve the display
*/

void display()
{
        printf("\n North's hand : ");
        print(north, 13);
        printf("\n  East's hand : ");
        print(east, 13);
        printf("\n South's hand : ");
        print(south, 13);
        printf("\n  West's hand : ");
        print(west, 13);
}

/* function print()
**
** this function provides a simple screen display
** of a hand of cards. It uses the ASCII characters
** for each suit. These will be available in most
** implementations but may use different codes.
*/
void print(int a[], int n)
```

```
{
    int i, suit = 3;
    static int suit_symbol[] = {6, 3, 4, 5}; /* ♠ ♥ ♦ ♣ */
    static char *face_value[] =
    {"2","3","4","5","6","7","8","9","10","J","Q","K","A"};

    for( i = 0; i < n; i++) {
        if( suit != a[i]/13 && i != 0)
            printf("%c   ", suit_symbol[a[i]/13]);
        suit = a[i]/13;
        printf(" %s ", face_value[a[i]%13]);
        if( i == n - 1)
            putchar(suit_symbol[a[i]/13]);
    }
}
```

The first point to note about the `print()` function is the way in which the integer operators / and % are used on the integer array a[] to determine the suit and face value of the cards. The array will contain 13 integers in the range 0 to 51. Using integer division by 13 we can obtain another integer in the range 0 to 3. Assuming that the integers 0 - 12 represent clubs, 13 - 25 diamonds and so on, we can associate each of these digits with a particular suit.

In order to find the face value of a card we can use the modulo operator (%). The integer obtained will be in the range 0 to 12. This time we associate each integer with a card value. So 0 corresponds to a 2, and 12 to an Ace. These integers can therefore be used as indexes to the array `face_value[]`. The various conditional statements in the function govern when the suit symbol is printed. In this case the suit is printed after the cards it contains. You may like to try modifying the function to display the suit first. This last part requires that the array be in order before the function is invoked.

Finally we should point out the use of the ASCII code to obtain the symbols for each suit. Most implementations will provide a code for each of these symbols although their exact value may vary. If your implementation does not include these symbols in its character set then you can modify the function by replacing the symbols with the initial letters of the suits.

Program C.5 contains the code necessary to perform the sorting of the integer arrays just mentioned. The two functions `bubble()` and `exchange()` were discussed in Chapter 8 (Program 8.14 and Program 8.15) and should require no further explanation.

Program C.5 – `bubble()`,   `exchange()`

```
/* a simple bubble sort function
```

```
** This sorts into order elements in the array a.
**     n is the number of elements in a.
*/
void bubble(int a[], int n)
{
        int i, sorted = FALSE; /* sorted is a flag to indicate */
                               /* when the array has been sorted */
        while( !sorted){
                sorted = TRUE;
                for( i = 1; i < n; i++ )
                        exchange(&a[i-1], &a[i], &sorted);
        }
}


/* function exchange()
**  This function swaps two ints if the
**  first argument is less than the second.
**  *sorted is set to FALSE if a swap takes place.
*/
void exchange(int *p, int *q, int *sorted)
{
        int temp;

        if (*p < *q) {                    /* descending order */
                temp = *p;
                *p - *q;
                *q = temp;
                *sorted = FALSE;          /* not in order */
        }
}
```

The remaining functions used in the bridge program concern the evaluation of a hand, by counting the points, and the choosing of what bid to make.

The first function (Program C.6) provides one answer to exercise 6 in Chapter 4. Refer back to that exercise if you are not familiar with how the point count is arrived at.

Program C.6 – count_points()
(See Chapter 4, Exercise 6)

```
/* function count_points()
**
** this function uses the standard method of counting points
** in bridge. A, K, Q & J count 4, 3, 2 and 1 point
** respectively. Additional points are added for distribution.
** The function returns the total point count.
*/
```

```
int count_points(int a[])
{       /* assume hand is in descending order */
        int i, suit, cards, points = 0;

        /* distribution count */
        for( i = 0, suit = 3, cards = 0; i < 13; i++) {
            while( a[j]/13 < i ) {
                    suit--;
                    cards = 0;
            }
            if( a[i]/13 == suit) { /* count cards in each suit */
                    cards++;
                    if (cards>4)      /* add 1 point for 5th & 6th */
                            points++;
                    if (cards>6)      /* 2 points for 7th & above */
                            points++;
            }
        }
        for( i = 0; i < 13; i++ )
                if(a[i]%13 == 12)
                        points += 4;      /* Ace */
                else if( a[i]%13 == 11)
                        points += 3;      /* King */
                else if( a[i]%13 == 10)
                        points += 2;      /* Queen */
                else if( a[i]%13 == 9)
                        points++;         /* Jack */
        return(points);
}
```

The local variables used by this function (i, suit, cards and points) are all integers. i is used as an index to the array a[] holding the hand to be analysed and suit is an integer representing each of the suits in turn (from Spades down to Clubs). The variable cards is used to keep track of the number of cards in each suit and points is a variable holding the point count.

The first for loop adds up the points based on distribution. This uses a while loop and integer division to check when the suit changes. (Again the array must be in order before this function is invoked.) An if statement is not sufficient here since a suit may be missing altogether (i.e. void), in which case the conditional statement which computes the distributional count would not be executed.

The second for loop uses the modulo operation discussed above but this time to identify the face value of the cards. A series of if ... else statements are then used to add the appropriate number of points, if any, to the running total.

The function `balanced()` shown in Program C.7 determines whether or not a hand contained in the array `cards[]` is balanced. A balanced hand is one in which there is no suit with more than four cards and no suit with less than two cards. There is one exception and that is a 5-3-3-2 distribution where the five card suit is either Clubs or Diamonds (i.e. a minor suit). Given this information you should be able to follow the logic of the program even if you have no knowledge of bridge.

One other function is included in the following listing which is a function to print the words 'balanced' or 'unbalanced' depending on the value of its argument. Again this returns a string and so the function definition is of the form `char * print_bal()`.

Program C.7 – `balanced()`, `print_bal()`

```
/* function balanced()
**
** this returns TRUE if the hand is balanced
** i.e. 4-4-3-2, 4-3-3-3 or 5-3-3-2 with 5 in Clubs or Diamonds
*/
int balanced(int a[], int *min, int *max, int cards[])
{
        int i, j, minor = FALSE, three = FALSE;

        /* initialise max and min */
        *min = 13;   /* *min = minimum no. of cards in one suit */
        *max = 0;    /* *max = maximum no. of cards in one suit */
        j = 0;       /* clubs */
        for( j = 0; j < 4; j++)        /* cards[] holds no. of */
                cards[j] = 0;          /* cards in each suit */
        for( i = 0; i < 13; i++)
                cards[a[i]/13]++;
        for( j = 0; j < 4; j++) {
                if( cards[j] == 3 )
                        three = TRUE; /* at least one 3-card suit */
                if( cards[j] < *min )
                        *min = cards[j];
                if( cards[j] > *max ) {
                        *max = cards[j];
                        if( j == 0 || j == 1 )
                                minor = TRUE;     /* Club or Diamond */
                }
        }
        if(*max == 4)     /*distribution is 4-3-3-3 or 4-4-3-2 */
                if( *min == 2 || *min == 3 )
                        return(TRUE);
        if(*min == 2 && *max == 5 && minor && three) /* 5-3-3-2 */
```

```
            return(TRUE);
        return(FALSE);
}

/* function print_bal()
**
** this function just returns "balanced" or "unbalanced"
*/
char * print_bal(int balanced)      /* note function returns a */
{                                   /*    'pointer to char'    */
        if(balanced) return("balanced  ");
        else return("unbalanced");
}
```

The function o_bids() given in Program C.8 is one solution to exercise 7 of Chapter 4. This provides a simplified opening bid and together with balanced() and bid_suit() (Program C.9) produces reasonable bids for the majority of hands. Only opening bids up to a maximum of two are considered, but it could be adapted to provide other bids as required. (If you are very familiar with bridge you could try extending it to cover all the possible opening bids as listed in the Table in Exercise 7 of Chapter 4, or according to some other system.)

The logic of this function is quite straightforward and you should find no difficulty in understanding its operation.

Program C.8 – o_bids()

```
/* function o_bids()
**
** This function calculates an opening bid based on the points
** and the basic make-up of the hand (i.e. balanced/unbalanced).
** This does not take account of the number of playing tricks
** in the hand and it requires a minimum of 13 points for a bid
*/
void o_bids(int points, int bal)
{
        if( points < 13 ) {
                printf("No Bid ");
                return;
        }
        switch( points ) {
                case 13 :
                case 14 : printf("One in a suit ");
                        break;
                case 15 :
                case 16 :
                case 17 : if( bal )
```

```
                    printf("One No Trump ");
              else
                    printf("One in a suit ");
              break;
        case 18 :
        case 19 :
        case 20 : if( bal )
                    printf("Two No Trumps ");
              else
                    printf("One in a suit ");
              break;
        case 21 :
        case 22 : if( bal )
                    printf("Two No Trumps ");
              else
                    printf("Two Clubs ");
              break;
        default : if( bal)      /* 23 points and above */
                    printf("Two Clubs ");
              else
                    printf("Two in a suit ");
      }
}
```

The final function developed for the bridge program is given in Program C.9. This is used to determine which suit to bid, if any, based on some standard principles of bridge. In outline these are as follows. If a hand is unbalanced with more than six cards in one suit then you should bid the longest suit. If two suits each have six cards then bid the higher ranking of the two. (The suits are ranked in ascending order as Clubs, Diamonds, Hearts and Spades.) In a hand containing a maximum of five cards in a suit that suit should be bid. If two suits contain five cards each then, unless the suits are Clubs and Spades, the higher ranking of the two suits should be bid. In the case of Clubs and Spades each with five cards you should bid Clubs.

With balanced hands we only need to deal with a point count of 13 or 14. (Hence the conditional statement in the bidding option of the execute_option() function, e.g. if((((points == 13 || points == 14) && bal) || !bal).) In other cases the choice of bid is determined by the point count (see the Table on page 102). The suit to bid in the case of a balanced hand containing 13 or 14 points depends upon a variety of factors. If a five-card suit is present (which will be either Clubs or Diamonds) then that suit should be bid. With a 4-3-3-3 distribution bid Clubs. With a 4-4-3-2 distribution a number of possibilities arise. If Spades and Diamonds both have four cards then you should bid the suit 'below' the 2 card suit, i.e. Spades if Clubs has only two cards and Diamonds if Hearts has only two cards. If Clubs is one of the four-card suits and either Hearts or Spades is the other then bid Clubs. Finally we are left with the touching combinations, i.e. when Clubs and Diamonds, Diamonds and Hearts or Hearts and Spades both have four cards. In such cases the opening bid should be that of the higher ranking of the two suits.

The above notes should allow you to check the logic of the `bid_suit()` function. It relies on simple control structures, basically `for` loops and `if` statements. The return value is a pointer to a string holding the name of the suit to bid.

Program C.9 – `bid_suit()`

```
/* function bid_suit()
**
** This function returns a string indicating the suit to bid.
** It takes as parameters the minimum no. of cards in a suit,
** the maximum no. of cards in a suit,
** a flag indicating balance and an array holding the no.
** of cards in each suit for the hand concerned.
*/
int bid_suit(int bal, int min, int max, int cards[])
{
    int i, j;
    static char *suit[] =
        {" Clubs "," Diamonds "," Hearts "," Spades "};
    /* determine suit to bid in balanced hand - used for 13 */
    if( bal ) {                            /*   a 14 points */
        /* 4-4-3-2 distribution */
        /* check if touching - i.e. CD, DH or HS */
        for( i = 0; i < 3; i++)
            if( cards[i] == max && cards[i+1] == max )
                return(suit[i+1]);/* bid higher ranking */
        /* suits not touching */
        if(cards[0] == max && (cards[2] == max || cards[3] == max))
            return(suit[0]); /* two suits same length: 1 Club */
        /* Spades and Diamonds same length */
        if( cards[1] == max && cards[3] == max )
            if( cards[0] == min )
                return(suit[3]); /* spades */
            else
                return(suit[1]); /* diamonds */
        /* 4-3-3-3 distribution */
        if( max == 4 && min == 3 )
            return(suit[0]);        /* clubs */
        /* 5-3-3-2 distribution */
        for( i = 0; i < 4; i++ )
            if( cards[i] == max )
                return(suit[i]); /* 5-card suit */
                                  /* unbalanced */
    } else {
```